THIS IS PHILOSOPHY OF RELIGION

THIS IS PHILOSOPHY
Series editor: Steven D. Hales

Reading philosophy can be like trying to ride a bucking bronco—you hold on for dear life while "transcendental deduction" twists you to one side, "causa sui" throws you to the other, and a 300-word, 300-year-old sentence comes down on you like an iron-shod hoof the size of a dinner plate. *This Is Philosophy* is the riding academy that solves these problems. Each book in the series is written by an expert who knows how to gently guide students into the subject regardless of the reader's ability or previous level of knowledge. Their reader-friendly prose is designed to help students find their way into the fascinating, challenging ideas that compose philosophy without simply sticking the hapless novice on the back of the bronco, as so many texts do. All the books in the series provide ample pedagogical aids, including links to free online primary sources. When students are ready to take the next step in their philosophical education, *This Is Philosophy* is right there with them to help them along the way.

THIS IS
PHILOSOPHY OF
RELIGION
AN INTRODUCTION

NEIL A. MANSON

WILEY Blackwell

Registered Office
John Wiley & Sons, Inc., 111 River Street, Hoboken, NJ 07030, USA

Editorial Office
111 River Street, Hoboken, NJ 07030, USA

For details of our global editorial offices, customer services, and more information about Wiley products visit us at www.wiley.com.

Wiley also publishes its books in a variety of electronic formats and by print-on-demand. Some content that appears in standard print versions of this book may not be available in other formats.

Library of Congress Cataloging-in-Publication Data
Names: Manson, Neil A., 1967- author.
Title: This is philosophy of religion : an introduction / Neil Manson.
Description: Hoboken, NJ : John Wiley & Sons, [2021] | Series: This is
    metaphysics | Includes bibliographical references and index.
Identifiers: LCCN 2020043036 (print) | LCCN 2020043037 (ebook) |
    ISBN 9780470674284 | ISBN 9781119769903 (pdf) | ISBN 9781119769927 (epub)
Subjects: LCSH: Religion–Philosophy–Textbooks.
Classification: LCC BL51 .M324 2021 (print) | LCC BL51 (ebook) |
    DDC 210–dc23
LC record available at https://lccn.loc.gov/2020043036
LC ebook record available at https://lccn.loc.gov/2020043037

Cover design by Wiley

Set in 10/12pt Minion Pro by Integra Software Services, Pondicherry, India

SKY10025030_021821

CONTENTS

ACKNOWLEDGMENTS

This book is dedicated to the many philosophers over the years who have influenced my thinking in philosophy of religion. First and foremost, I want to acknowledge two giants of philosophy of religion, both at Syracuse University when I was there in the first half of the 1990s: Peter van Inwagen and William Alston. Van Inwagen directed my dissertation on the fine-tuning argument, and before that he let me sit in on his course on the design argument in the fall of 1993. My understanding of free will also benefited from taking his course on that topic in the fall of 1991. I took a course on the nature and attributes of God from Alston in the spring of 1992. I am deeply indebted to them both, as well as to my classmates in those courses. Another Syracuse professor meriting mention is Jonathan Bennett. Almost everything I know about the early modern philosophers from Descartes to Hume I learned from him. I also thank Jan Cover and Rudy Garns for their textbook *Theories of Knowledge and Reality* (1994). It provided an excellent model of how to write analytic philosophy for students. My discussion of atheism benefited tremendously from a lecture Timothy Kenyon gave to my "Philosophy of Religion" class at the University of Mississippi in the fall of 2003. I thank Graham Oppy and Routledge for permitting me to reprint (in substantially revised form) the bulk of the material from my paper "Naturalism and Religion," which appeared in *The Routledge Handbook of Contemporary Philosophy of Religion* (2015). That material appears in Chapter 7. I thank many graduate students in philosophy at the University of Mississippi for their help. Celine Geday and David Harmon reviewed the entire manuscript, while Kelly Adkins, Joseph Duda, and Makensey Sanders suggested some great examples that ended up in the book. I thank all of my colleagues in the Department of Philosophy and Religion at the University of Mississippi for conversations and comments that have improved this book. I thank the team at Wiley Blackwell for all their help, particularly Marissa Koors, Rachel Greenberg, Charlie Hamlyn, and Jacqueline Harvey. I also thank Jeff Dean, who was the commissioning editor for philosophy at Wiley Blackwell when I was asked to write this book. I thank Arthi Kangeyan and the team at Integra for all their work at the production phase. Finally, this book has been far too long in the making. I thank the *This Is Philosophy* series editor, Steven Hales, for both his guidance and his patience.

AN INTRODUCTION TO
THIS IS PHILOSOPHY OF RELIGION

This book was written with my University of Mississippi "Philosophy of Religion" students in mind. Many of them have no prior experience with philosophy. That is why Chapter 1 begins with a crash course in philosophy, with an emphasis on the basic concepts in logic, metaphysics, and epistemology. While not all students may need to cover that material, quite a few will. And, for the rest, a refresher never hurts. I am sure this applies to many "Philosophy of Religion" courses taught elsewhere. With that in mind, instructors are advised to begin with Chapter 1. The subsequent chapters have been arranged in sequence, with each chapter building on the prior ones. However, the chapters are not that tightly bound, so instructors could cover the chapters out of sequence without much disruption.

Key terms, which are explained in the Glossary at the end of the book, are underlined. Other terms have an endnote/hyperlink associated with them, and these appear in bold. Terms that have a glossary entry and an associated endnote/hyperlink appear in bold and are underlined. In general, the hyperlinks follow a pattern. First, key terms are often linked to entries in online academic encyclopedias: the *Stanford Encyclopedia of Philosophy*, the *Internet Encyclopedia of Philosophy*, or the *Encyclopedia Britannica*. (Students are recommended also to consult *The Encyclopedia of Philosophy*, ed. Paul Edwards [New York: Macmillan, 1967]; it is still an excellent resource and has entries corresponding to many key terms. Almost every university library has a copy.) Second, named individuals are sometimes linked to an encyclopedia entry. In both sorts of cases, the URL is provided in an endnote (in the print edition) or as a hyperlink (in the electronic edition). In some cases, a

This Is Philosophy of Religion: An Introduction, First Edition. Neil A. Manson.
© 2021 John Wiley & Sons, Inc. Published 2021 by John Wiley & Sons, Inc.

short description of the contents of the web page is provided in the endnote. Each chapter includes an annotated bibliography for more advanced material. Helpful material is also available on the website for this book. This material includes a sample syllabus (with recommended readings), study questions, and a test bank, among other features.

1

WHAT IS PHILOSOPHY? WHAT IS RELIGION?

If you are reading this book, you are almost certainly taking a philosophy class. There is a good chance you are coming into it not having read much philosophy. So you may have several questions at the start. What is philosophy? What is religion? And how is philosophy even relevant to religion? We will address those questions in this chapter.

1.1 What Philosophy Is

The word "philosophy" comes from the Greek roots *philo* (love) and *sophia* (wisdom). So one basic definition of philosophy is that it is the pursuit of wisdom, where wisdom is understood as some sort of deep insight into or understanding of the truth. Another definition says that philosophy addresses the "big questions" about the meaning of life, the nature of the universe, and whether we know anything for sure. The answers to these big questions are often presupposed in other areas of thought such as mathematics, physics, politics, history, and psychology. These big questions fall under more specific fields and subfields of philosophy. There are enough of those subfields of philosophy to fill up an encyclopedia, but we can focus on just a few main branches.

Metaphysics concerns the nature of reality – for example, whether everything that exists is a physical thing or whether there are nonphysical things too (things such as souls, God, and numbers). Epistemology concerns belief, justification, rationality, and knowledge – for example, what it takes for a belief to count as knowledge rather than just opinion. Ethics concerns moral right and wrong, as well as value judgments generally – for example, what the scope and extent of human rights is. Logic concerns the standards for proper reasoning – for example,

This Is Philosophy of Religion: An Introduction, First Edition. Neil A. Manson.
© 2021 John Wiley & Sons, Inc. Published 2021 by John Wiley & Sons, Inc.

what it takes for one set of propositions to guarantee the truth of a further proposition. These specific categories, in turn, have subcategories themselves, and many big questions fall under more than one category. For example, some people think morality is real or objective, while others think morality is just a social or cultural construction. The dispute between these two sorts of people concerns not only ethics, but also metaphysics, epistemology, and the nature of language.

Despite this diversity of philosophical categories, however, philosophy (or, at least, the analytic approach to philosophy taken in this book) involves a commitment to providing logical arguments for one's views. It also involves conceptual analysis. In the next section we will get an initial sense of what logic, arguments, and conceptual analysis are by using examples that are relevant to some of the material covered later in this book.

1.2 Basic Tools of Philosophy: Logic and Analysis

As we have already seen, logic is the study of reasoning. You probably have a good sense already that many people reason very poorly. They form generalizations much too quickly. They base their opinions on irrelevant factors such as emotion and popularity. They try to reject views they do not like by criticizing the character of the people with whom they disagree rather than their ideas. Indeed, poor reasoning is so common that there are innumerable books, lectures, websites, and podcasts about it. But if some people reason poorly there must be such a thing as reasoning well. Logicians are the philosophers who specialize in the study of logic. They attempt to identify and develop these good forms of reasoning. They do so with the help of a toolkit of basic ideas. Let us familiarize ourselves with these basic tools.

1.2.1 Propositions and Their Qualities

A proposition is something that can be either true or false. A proposition claims to represent some fact about the world, and either it does (in which case it is true) or it does not (in which case it is false). Typically, propositions are expressed by declarative sentences. From the logician's perspective, the same proposition – for example, "I love you" – can be expressed by a variety of declarative sentences, including sentences in different languages. Consider the following declarative sentences.

God exists. (English)
Est Deus. (Latin)
Gött existiert. (German)
Dios existe. (Spanish)

These sentences all convey the same information and have the same content; they all express the same proposition.

1.2.1.1 The Relationships Between Propositions

Logicians identify several important ways in which propositions can stand in relationship to one another. One proposition <u>entails</u> another if the truth of the first guarantees the truth of the second. For example "Andrea is over six feet tall" entails "Andrea is over five feet tall." Furthermore, a set of propositions is <u>consistent</u> if it is possible for them all to be true and is <u>inconsistent</u> if it is not possible for them all to be true. "Andrea is over six feet tall" and "Andrea has red hair" are consistent, whereas "Andrea is over six feet tall" and "Andrea is under five feet tall" are inconsistent. While those examples are clear, it is not always clear whether one proposition entails another, or whether a set of propositions is consistent. Indeed, questions about entailment and consistency are some of the most fundamental and intensely debated of all religious questions. Consider these four propositions: (i) God can do anything; (ii) God knows everything; (iii) God is perfectly good; and (iv) there is pain, suffering, and horrendous evil in the world. Are they consistent? That is, is it possible that all four of those propositions are true? Many articles and books have been written on that very question. It is called the problem of evil. We will encounter it later.

1.2.1.2 Modal Propositions

Most propositions are about the way things were, are, or will be. For example, "Germany won the Men's World Cup in 2014" is a true proposition about the way things were. But some propositions are about the way things could be, could not be, or must be. Logicians call these <u>modal propositions</u>. Consider the proposition "Germany could not have lost the Men's World Cup in 2014." It is quite different from the first proposition, and it seems to be false. (Germany only beat Argentina 1–0, and they did so in extra time.) Logicians define three modes a proposition can take: <u>necessity</u>, <u>impossibility</u>, and <u>contingency</u>. A necessary proposition has to be true; it is not possible that it be false. For example, "All triangles have three sides" is necessary (or necessarily true or a necessity). An impossible proposition has to be false; it is not possible that it be true. For example, "All squares have eleven sides" is impossible (or necessarily false or an impossibility). A contingent proposition is neither necessary nor impossible. A contingently true proposition might have been false, and a contingently false proposition might have been true. So, "Germany won the Men's World Cup in 2014" is contingently true and "Argentina won the Men's World Cup in 2014" is contingently false.

Many important religious questions concern the modal status of propositions. Consider this proposition about God and creation: "At the beginning of time, God created the universe." Many theists (people who believe that God exists) believe that this proposition is true. But does being a theist require that you think that this proposition is *necessarily* true? Perhaps not.

Some theists say it is not necessarily true. They say that God was free not to create the universe at all. God might have done no creating, in which case reality would have consisted of God but nothing else. Other theists say it is necessarily true. Given God's very nature as a good, loving being, God had to create a world with beings other than God – beings that are capable of loving and being loved by God. God would not be perfectly good if God did not create such a world and such beings.

Some theists say it is possible that God is responsible for the existence of the universe, but that the universe never came into existence at any particular point in time. Some say this because they think that it is possible that the universe is eternal and so is God: they are coeternal. Some say this because they think that time itself depends on the existence of the universe, so that it makes no sense to talk about times prior to or outside of the universe. Despite denying that the universe came into existence at a particular point in time, these theists also say that, if it were not for God, the universe would not exist. So, for them, "At the beginning of time, God created the universe" is not necessarily true, even though they do think that the universe is completely dependent on God.

Atheists (people who believe that God does not exist) of course think that "At the beginning of time, God created the universe" is false. They think that, somehow, the universe exists uncreated – either because it exists of its own nature or because it exists for no reason at all. But even some theists think it is possible that the universe exists for no reason at all. That is, they admit that it is possible that the universe exists without existing *for* any reason or *because of* any prior cause. They think that "At the beginning of time, God created the universe" is true, not because it is necessarily true, but merely because it is the best overall explanation of what science tells us about the universe.

We will return to many of these questions about God and creation later in this book. For now, just remember that questions about modality – questions concerning whether a proposition is necessary, is impossible, or is neither – are some of the most important questions in philosophy and in religion.

1.2.1.3 A Priori and A Posteriori Propositions

Another important distinction among propositions concerns the ways we are capable of coming to know them. What philosophers call *a priori* knowledge of a subject (treat *a priori* as all one word) is knowledge capable of being had about that subject independently of any experience with that subject. For example, you can know *a priori* that if you roll two six-sided dice, the probability of getting a seven is one in six. (Here is the proof. There are six ways the first die can come out and six ways the second die can come out. That means there are thirty-six possible combinations for the sum of the two dice. Of those thirty-six possibilities, six of them add up to the number seven: 1 + 6, 2 + 5, 3 + 4, 4 + 3, 5 + 2, and 6 + 1.) So, in order to know that the probability of getting a seven is one in six, you do not need to spend hours and hours rolling dice. No experience of playing board games or casino games is necessary. You can work out the answer in your head or on a sheet of paper. In other words, you can know *a priori* that the probability of getting a seven is one in six.

Having said that, maybe you hate math but love playing games with two dice – games like Monopoly, Chutes and Ladders, and Three Man. After careful observation and lots of experience, you notice a pattern: the number seven rolls out about a sixth of the time. This shows that something that is knowable *a priori* might come to be known through experience. In this case, if you learned from experience that seven rolls out about a sixth of the time, you did it the hard way. You learned it from experience (and maybe wasted a lot of your valuable time and money), but you could have learned it just by doing some basic math.

For some propositions, however, there is no way to know them to be true except through observation and experience. Propositions that are knowable only this way are called *a posteriori* propositions. (Again, treat *a posteriori* all as one word.) So, for example, "Smoking causes lung cancer" is something humans came to know by applying the scientific method. You can know (i) what smoking is, (ii) what lung cancer is, and (iii) what it is for one thing to cause another thing, but you cannot know that smoking causes lung cancer just by reflecting on (i), (ii), and (iii). Humans had to employ the scientific method to come to know that smoking causes lung cancer. Likewise, "Bourbon Street in New Orleans smells awful in the morning" is something you can know only by experience (either by your own experience or by other people sharing their experiences with you). Neither proposition is one that you can know to be true just by thinking about it. Neither proposition is knowable *a priori*. Both are knowable only *a posteriori*.

We now have a basic sense of what propositions are. We have also seen that there are different kinds of propositions and different relationships in which propositions can stand to one another. Now, what do philosophers do with propositions?

1.2.2 Arguments

For philosophers, propositions are the building blocks of arguments. In philosophy, "argue" and "argument" are good words. To argue is not to shout or get angry, but to give reasons in support of a claim. In logic, an <u>argument</u> is a set of propositions. One of them, the conclusion, is the proposition being argued for. The rest, the propositions given in support of the conclusion, are the premises. Philosophers care deeply about arguments because arguments provide the basis for evaluating what other people believe. Arguments make it transparent to everyone what the reasons are that people have for what they believe. The provision of arguments is thus a powerful force for dialogue, discussion, understanding, and (hopefully) tolerance. As you will come to see while reading this book, the people on all sides of religious debates have surprisingly powerful arguments for their positions. A position you may think is ridiculous can suddenly start to make a lot more sense once you hear the arguments for it.

1.2.2.1 The Standard Presentation of Arguments

In ordinary life, arguments are presented in a wide array of forms. Sometimes the conclusion is stated at the beginning for effect. Sometimes the premises or the conclusion are presented using a rhetorical question. And sometimes, it is just not clear what the conclusion of the argument is supposed to be. Philosophers try to impose a degree of order on this confusion. As a matter of standard practice, they restate or paraphrase the argument so that it consists of only declarative sentences, with each sentence given a number and with the conclusion put at the end. In this book we will frequently present basic philosophical positions as arguments. When we do, we will follow this procedure. Doing so makes it easier to examine the reasons available for a position, see the weak spots, and possibly come up with a better argument.

1.2.2.2 Inductive Versus Deductive Arguments

Logicians divide arguments into two broad types. An inductive argument is one in which the premises are not put forth as guaranteeing that the conclusion is true, but only as providing grounds for thinking that the conclusion is probably true. In contrast, a deductive argument is one in which the premises are put forth as guaranteeing that the conclusion is true. The person making a deductive argument is saying this: "If you believe each of my premises, you absolutely must believe my conclusion. There is no wiggle room, no way out for you. All you can say is that one of my premises is false. There is no possible way all of my premises are true and yet my conclusion is false."

To illustrate the distinction, and to get a sense in general of what arguments are like, consider these two arguments for the conclusion that some Creator made the universe.

An Inductive Argument for the Existence of a Creator

(1) Computers are complex things, with all of their parts finely adjusted so that they can engage in computation.
(2) Computers do not just appear naturally, but rather are created by intelligent beings who have a plan in mind.
(3) Airplanes are complex things, with all of their parts finely adjusted so that they can fly.
(4) Airplanes do not just appear naturally, but rather are created by intelligent beings who have a plan in mind.
(5) Philosophy textbooks are complex things, with all of their parts finely adjusted so that they can impart wisdom.
(6) Philosophy textbooks do not just appear naturally, but rather are created by intelligent beings who have a plan in mind.
(7) The universe is an incredibly complex thing, with all of its parts finely adjusted so that it can produce life.
So, (8) Probably, the universe was created by an intelligent being who had a plan in mind.

Notice two things about this argument. First, each premise is a simple declarative sentence, and so is the conclusion. Furthermore, each sentence is given a number. Presenting arguments this way lays out each element of the argument piece by piece, making it easier to pinpoint exactly what is being talked about when the argument is examined closely. Second, notice the structure of the argument. The first six premises provide three instances of one property (complexity geared toward a purpose) going together with a second property (having been created by an intelligent being). The last premise says that the universe has the first property. The conclusion says that the universe probably has the second property. The key word here is "probably." Obviously, just because two things go together most of the time does not guarantee that they go together all of the time. So even if all of the premises are true, it does not guarantee that the conclusion is true, and the person making the argument surely does not mean the argument that way. Because of that, the argument is classified as "inductive."

Now compare that argument to the next one.

A Deductive Argument for the Existence of a Creator

(1) If the universe had a beginning in time, then the universe was created by some powerful being outside of the universe.
(2) The universe had a beginning in time.
So, (3) The universe was created by some powerful being outside of the universe.

Here, the argument has a simple form: if A, then B; A; therefore, B. (Logicians give a name to this argument structure: _modus ponens_.) The person putting forward this argument is saying that there is just no way for both premises to be true yet the conclusion false. The premises are claimed to guarantee that the conclusion is true. That is why this argument is classified as "deductive."

1.2.2.3   Valid and Invalid Arguments; Sound and Unsound Arguments

A deductive argument was just defined as one in which the premises are intended to guarantee the truth of the conclusion. But arguments do not always do what they were intended to do. Sometimes a person advances an argument that they think guarantees the truth of their conclusion, but in fact their argument fails to provide that guarantee. For example, imagine your friend tells you this: "Everyone who is going to be at Alayna's party tonight is a friend of Brittany. But everyone who is a friend of Brittany is a friend of Catie. Therefore, at least one friend of Catie is not going to be at Alayna's party tonight." Maybe your friend is right that at least one friend of Catie is not going to be at Alayna's party, but the premises do not guarantee that conclusion. Perhaps Alayna, Brittany, and Catie all have the exact same friends, including one another. So your friend has made a deductive argument that failed to do what a deductive argument is meant to do. It failed to guarantee that the conclusion is true if the premises are all true.

The term "valid" is a word of appraisal that is applied to deductive arguments. In saying that an argument is valid, we are not saying that its conclusion is, in fact, true. What we are saying is that, *if* the premises are true, the conclusion *must* be true. The argument about Alayna, Brittany, and Catie aspired to be valid, but it failed. It is an invalid deductive argument. Knowing that an argument is valid does not mean that the premises are true, nor does it mean that the conclusion is true. Maybe the argument is valid, but one of the premises is false. In that case, the conclusion could be true or it could be false. An old slogan in computer science was GIGO ("garbage in, garbage out"). The slogan meant that a program could be written perfectly, but the output could be bad if the data input was bad. The same applies to valid arguments. The reasoning in an argument may be perfect, but the excellence of the reasoning will not matter if one of the premises is false.

However, an argument may be invalid, but the conclusion might be true (by coincidence). In logic, a sound argument is a valid argument with all true premises. So, if an argument is sound, the conclusion must be true. If an argument is unsound, that means it either has at least one false premise or is invalid. For example, a deductive argument for the existence of a creator is valid, but (as we will see later on in this book), both of its premises are highly debatable. While it is clearly valid, it is not clearly sound.

Logic can be a difficult subject. If philosophy is your degree program, you will probably be required to take at least one course on logic. Since not everyone using this book will be a philosophy student, the arguments you see here will be simplified in this important respect. Unless explicitly labeled otherwise, all of the arguments that get displayed and given a name in this book will be deductive arguments that are valid. This way, you will be free to focus your attention on the premises of the arguments. You will have to decide whether the argument is or is not sound. But, unless you are told otherwise, you will not have to worry about whether the conclusion might be false even if the premises are all true.

1.2.3 Conceptual Analysis

In the course of thinking about arguments and the premises that occur in them, we often have to think quite carefully about the concepts being used. Consider this argument concerning abortion. "Every person has a right to life. A human fetus is a person. So, a human fetus has a right to life." The key concept in this argument is "person." There is considerable controversy over this concept. What does it take to be a person? Is being a person just the same as being a member of the species *Homo sapiens*? Not everyone agrees with that. For example, proponents of the rights of animals often claim that elephants, dolphins, and some primates have enough mental and emotional capacity to count as people. Meanwhile, artificial intelligence is advancing so rapidly that it is no longer just science fiction to wonder whether a computer might ever count as a person. But, if being a person does depend on one's mental abilities, just what abilities are necessary? Some say humans who have lost the ability to remember, to speak, and to direct their own lives (e.g. patients in long-term comas or with advanced Alzheimer's disease) no longer count as people. Others say personhood does not depend on the possession of these faculties.

As the personhood example shows, whether we judge a statement to be true or false and whether we judge an argument to be sound or unsound can depend on our beliefs about the concepts involved. To probe these beliefs, philosophers engage in conceptual analysis – the exploration and clarification of the most basic components of thought. Here are some of the most important tools philosophers use when engaging in conceptual analysis.

1.2.3.1 *Identifying Necessary and Sufficient Conditions*

A necessary condition is a requirement. It is a condition a thing must satisfy in order to qualify as being of a certain kind. A sufficient condition is a guarantor. It is a condition that is enough for a thing to qualify as being of a certain kind. For example, it is a necessary condition for being a University of Mississippi student that you submit an application to the University of Mississippi. Not everyone who submits an application is a University of Mississsippi student, but you cannot be a University of Mississsippi student without having submitted an application. It is a sufficient condition for being a University of Mississsippi student that you are a member of the University of Mississsippi Ethics Bowl team. If you are a member of the University of Mississsippi Ethics Bowl team, that fact guarantees that you are a University of Mississsippi student.

Statements of the form "if … then …" are called <u>conditional statements</u>. "If it is snowing, then it is below freezing" is a conditional statement. A conditional statement consists of an <u>antecedent</u> ("it is snowing") and a <u>consequent</u> ("it is below freezing"). For conditional statements, the consequent specifies a necessary condition for the antecedent. In this example, if it is not below freezing, it is not snowing. Below-freezing temperature is a necessary condition (a requirement) for it to be snowing. Likewise, if it is snowing, you are guaranteed that it is below freezing. Snowing is a sufficient condition for it being freezing. So the antecedent of a conditional specifies a sufficient condition for the consequent.

As part of conceptual analysis, philosophers will spend considerable effort trying to identify the necessary and sufficient conditions for a given concept. For example, we will soon look at the question of whether anyone is ever truly free if God exists. Supposedly, God is omniscient (all-knowing) and infallible (never wrong). But that seems to mean that God has foreknowledge of (knows ahead of time) every single thing everyone has ever done, is doing, or ever will do. And since God is never wrong, that means no one ever has done, ever does, or ever will do anything other than what God foresaw happening. So there seems to be a logical inconsistency between saying "God is omniscient" and "Humans have free will."

When we look at this problem more carefully, however, we will see significant differences in how philosophers analyze the concepts of omniscience and of free will. For example, some philosophers claim it is not a necessary condition for being omniscient that God knows future events. They agree that God knows everything that happens *as it happens*, and that God remembers everything that has ever happened, but God does not know anything *before it happens*. Other philosophers claim it is not a necessary condition for having free will that we be able to do something other than what God foresees that we do. They say our being free is consistent with God's foreseeing what we do. So whether or not divine foreknowledge and human freedom are compatible will depend on how the concepts of foreknowledge and freedom are analyzed.

1.2.3.2 Generating Counterexamples

If someone claims that A is a necessary condition for B, or that A is a sufficient condition for B, a philosopher will oftentimes push back by offering a <u>counterexample</u> – a particular case that undermines or disproves the claim. For example, suppose someone says a necessary condition for something's being a religion is that it promotes belief in a single supreme being. If promoting belief in a single supreme being is a necessary condition for something being a religion, you will never be able to find something that counts as a religion but that does not promote belief in a single supreme being. There are counterexamples to that claim. For example, in most forms of Buddhism, there is little discussion of God. Belief in God is certainly not promoted, and in some key texts powerful arguments against the existence of God are advanced. For Buddhists, belief in God is not necessary for achieving the central goal: enlightenment and release from suffering. Yet Buddhism is pretty clearly a religion. So the case of Buddhism is a counterexample to the claim that religions, by definition, promote belief in a single supreme being. (As we will see later in the book, the case of Buddhism provides counterexamples to a number of claims made about the nature of religion.)

The ability to generate counterexamples is an important aspect of conceptual analysis. When you read general claims in this book – for example, "Every event has a prior cause" – you ought to be thinking to yourself, "Is this generalization true or are there counterexamples to it?"

1.2.3.3 Creating Thought Experiments

The topics discussed in philosophy are often abstract and sometimes otherworldly. For example, metaphysicians who seek to understand the nature of time might consider the possibility of time travel. But there are no real-life cases of time travel. In situations such as this, philosophers will often construct <u>thought experiments</u> – imagined scenarios that bring out the thoughts and presuppositions underlying our judgments. Sometimes these scenarios are drawn from books, as in the case of Hermione's Time-Turner from the Harry Potter series. Sometimes they are drawn from movies such as *Avengers: Endgame*, *Looper*, or *Hot Tub Time Machine*. Sometimes they are drawn from television, as with Stewie's time machine from *Family Guy*. Other times, philosophers just make up their own scenarios. Either way, the point is to get us to put our concepts to the test – to see whether the concept we have identified really does work the way we expect it to work. In the case of time travel, for example, a common thought experiment is to imagine what would happen if you went back in time and found yourself in a position to interfere in such a way that you were never born. It seems that, somehow or other, something must happen to prevent you from doing this, because if you were to succeed, you would not exist and so you would not have been able to go back in time. As a result of thinking through these sorts of cases, some philosophers claim that the very notion of time travel makes no sense.

Thought experiments play an important role in the philosophy of religion. For example, in trying to understand concepts surrounding life after death – heaven, hell, reincarnation, and so on – philosophers will ask their readers to think about what they would say, do, or judge if they were in a certain hypothetical situation that no one we know of has actually experienced. You may be asked to think more deeply about movies such as *Heaven Can Wait* or *Down to Earth*. Suppose (as happens in these movies) that your last memories were of being terrified as a huge truck was coming right at you at full speed, and of everything going dark. Then suppose right now that you are experiencing walking on clouds, being told you have died and are in heaven, and so on. Would you automatically conclude that you were in the afterlife? Or might you think that there was some other explanation? Thinking through cases such as this is an important tool in the philosophy of religion, especially since many of the properties (e.g. omnipotence) and scenarios (e.g. life after death) that we discuss are ones that we have never experienced.

1.3 What Religion Is

Now that we have gained a basic understanding of what philosophy is and of what tools we will use when we "do philosophy," let us turn to the subject of our philosophical attention: religion. What is religion? Can we define it? As you might expect, this will be quite a challenge. There is almost certainly no short, clean definition of "religion." Some concepts are narrow enough and precise enough that we can articulate the necessary and sufficient conditions for their application – for example, the concept of "triangle." Religion is not one of those concepts.

Indeed, just using the noun "religion" suggests that we are thinking in terms of concrete things – Hinduism, Buddhism, Judaism, Christianity, Islam, and so on. Thinking of religion in that way may lead us to focus on doctrines – sets of beliefs that, say, Christians have but Buddhists lack. But maybe thinking in terms of "religion" is the wrong way to start. Perhaps we should focus on the adjective "religious" and the adverb "religiously." What is it for something – a person, a thought, a way of life – to be religious? What is it for someone or some group to do something religiously? Framing the question this way moves our focus away from the doctrines people believe and toward the experiences people have and the practices in which they engage. And that could be a good thing, because religion is at least as much about what people do and feel as about what they say and believe.

Instead of seeking necessary and sufficient conditions for something being a religion, the philosopher of religion William Alston proposed we search for "religion-making characteristics" – characteristics that "help make something a religion." Here are the characteristics he came up with.

1   Belief in supernatural beings (gods).
2   A distinction between sacred and profane objects.
3   Ritual acts focused on sacred objects.
4   A moral code believed to be sanctioned by the gods.
5   Characteristically religious feelings (awe, sense of mystery, sense of guilt, adoration), which tend to be aroused in the presence of sacred objects and during the practice of ritual, and which are connected in idea with the gods.
6   Prayer and other forms of communication with gods.
7   A world view, or a general picture of the world as a whole and the place of the individual therein. This picture contains some specification of an over-all purpose or point of the world and an indication of how the individual fits into it.
8   A more or less total organization of one's life based on the world view.
9   A social group bound together by the above.[1]

As you can see, that is quite a long list of religion-making characteristics, which makes it hard to say just what is and what is not a religion. Clearly something does not need to have all of these characteristics to count as a religion. On top of this flexibility, every item on the list is pretty abstract. It is not clear how they apply in concrete cases.

If you want to get a better sense of the concrete reality of religion – of what religion is, of what it is for something or someone to be religious, and of what it is for someone to act religiously – you really ought to take some religion cours-es at your college or university. Far too many people are familiar only with their own faith tradition, and some of them are familiar with it in only a narrow way. For example, someone who is a Lutheran may have only a vague idea about other Protestant denominations, almost no idea of Roman Catholicism, and no idea at all of Hinduism. Taking a world religions course may help correct this problem. Whether you adhere to some set of religious beliefs or to none, you can hardly understand history or current events if you do not have a basic sense of the major world religions. Only with a background in world religions will you be in a position to say whether a proposed definition of "religion" is adequate or not.

What is quite clear about religion in all of its forms is that religions raise philosophical questions for themselves. Indeed, philosophical problems are so prevalent in religions that, for almost every world religion, there is a sep-arate academic study of the philosophical aspects of that religion. There are academic journals and Library of Congress classifications devoted to Hindu

---

[1] William P. Alston, "Religion," in Paul Edwards (ed.), *The Encyclopedia of Philosophy* (New York: Macmillan, 1967), vol. 7, pp. 141–142.

philosophy, to Buddhist philosophy, to Jewish philosophy, to Christian philosophy, to Islamic philosophy, and so on. The sorts of philosophical questions arising within these religions span almost every branch of philosophy: metaphysics, epistemology, ethics, and even logic. Considered from this perspective, the range of philosophical issues concerning religion is vast. The range is so great that it is impossible to cover all of the philosophical issues in just one textbook.

1.4 What Philosophy of Religion Is

Now that we have gotten a sense of what philosophy is and of what religion is, we can define philosophy of religion as the subfield of philosophy that addresses the big questions raised by or within religions and that makes use of the tools of philosophy (e.g. logic, conceptual analysis, thought experiments) to do so. The big questions are numerous, and the answers to them can vary dramatically from religion to religion. Does God exist? If so, what is God's relationship to us? Do we have free will? What is justice? Is there a purpose to the universe? Is there life after death? What is the meaning of an individual human life? What do we have to do to lead ethical lives? How should society be organized? This is only a sample of the philosophical questions that arise within religions.

But with that definition of "philosophy of religion" in place, we now come to an important realization about this book. There is no way to cover in a single, average-sized book all of the questions and topics that legitimately fall under the heading "philosophy of religion." There are just too many religions in the world and just too many fundamental questions they raise. We are going to have to narrow down the topic considerably. So while the title of this book is *This Is Philosophy of Religion*, you should really think of it as a book about selected topics in the philosophy of religion. Here are some of the ways in which the focus has been narrowed.

The primary focus of this book is on issues that arise within the major monotheistic religions: Judaism, Christianity, and Islam. All of these religions are instances of theism. They all promote belief in just one supreme being – a being that is perfect in every way. That being goes by different names (Yahweh, God, Allah), but in each of these religions that being is said to have the same basic properties: omniscience, omnipotence, moral perfection, necessary existence, eternal existence, and freedom. In this book, we will just use the term "God" for that being.

In Chapter 2, we will spend considerable effort trying to understand the properties of God more clearly. We will try to determine whether they all cohere – that is, whether it is logically consistent to maintain that God has all of them. And we will try to see whether the existence of God is consistent with other things we know or believe – for example, that humans have free will. In Chapters 3 and 4, we will try to see whether there are any good arguments for thinking that God exists. In Chapter 5, we will look at two arguments for thinking that God does not exist. In Chapter 6, we will examine whether there is anything wrong with a person believing in God if that person has no good evidence for thinking God exists. In Chapter 7, we will look at a number of theories about why people believe God exists (or believe in any gods at all). Only in the postscript will we look at the philosophical issues arising within a non-theistic religion, Buddhism.

The scope of this book is thus wide in one sense (about half of the people in the world adhere to at least one of the major religions we will cover), but narrow in another sense. We will neglect a good number of religions – for example, Hinduism, Confucianism, Taoism, alternative spiritualities/new religious movements, and traditional religions from various parts of the world. For coverage of those religions and the philosophical problems connected with them, you may want to take one or more courses on them – for example, Eastern religions or Eastern philosophy. This neglect should not be construed as a judgment that there is greater philosophical depth, sophistication, and profundity in the monotheistic religions than there is in other religions. It is just that we can cover only so much in one textbook.

Even with our restricted emphasis on the issues raised within theism, there are still many important questions that we will just not cover because of the limitations of space. Here are some of the important topics in the philosophy of religion that will not be addressed in this book.

Religious language: Can finite and imperfect beings like us ever successfully talk about and refer to God, a perfect and infinite being?

Death and the afterlife: Is life after death possible? If so, how? What forms might it take? And why should we care about what happens to us in the afterlife?

Divine hiddenness: If God exists, why is it not completely obvious to everyone that God exists? That is, why does God stay hidden from us?

Marxist, feminist, and race-theoretical criticisms of theism: Is the concept of God shared by the monotheistic religions itself best understood as a reflection of underlying social forces such as class domination, sexism, and racism? For example, is routinely referring to God as "he" a way for men to continue ruling society?

These are just a few of the many questions that could be covered in a book on the philosophy of religion. You may find that your teacher for this course wants to cover some or all of these topics. Do not think they are any less important just because they do not show up here. They are not being covered mostly for the practical reason that if they were all covered, this book would be much too long, your teacher would probably not assign it, and it would be so expensive you probably would not buy it.

Now that we have gotten a clearer sense of the meaning of "philosophy of religion" and of the scope of this book, let us take a close look at our first topic: the concept of God.

Annotated Bibliography

Copi, Irving M., Carl Cohen, and Kenneth McMahon (2011). *Introduction to Logic*, 14th edn (New York: Prentice Hall).
    There are many introductory logic textbooks on the market. This is one the oldest, most comprehensive, and most polished.

Hales, Steven D. (2013). *This Is Philosophy: An Introduction* (Malden, MA: Wiley Blackwell).
    The first book in the *This Is Philosophy* series, it covers basic philosophical problems concerning ethics, freedom, personal identity, the mind, and knowledge, as well as God and religious belief. It is an excellent starting point for the beginner.

Rauhut, Nils Ch. (2011). *Ultimate Questions: Thinking about Philosophy*, 3rd edn (New York: Prentice Hall).
    Another introductory philosophy book, this one begins with two helpful chapters. The first is on what philosophy is, while the second is on basic philosophical tools. Both chapters contain useful exercises.

2

THE CONCEPT OF GOD

2.1 Logical Consistency Problems for Theism

2.1.1 God Versus Zeus and Thor

The gods Zeus and Thor were said to possess superhuman powers such as the ability to change shape and the ability to direct bolts of lightning. While no human has such abilities, we can at least visualize what it would be like to exercise them. The powers of God, however, are said to go beyond any powers possessed by limited deities such as Zeus and Thor. While Zeus can do amazing things, such as take the form of a bull or a swan, supposedly God can do anything. And it is not just God's power that is unique. The table of divine properties lists some – but not all – of the one-of-a-kind properties of God. These properties would make God unlike any other being in reality. The technical name for each property is given on the left, with a brief description on the right.

Table of Divine Properties

Omnipotence	Unlimited power; the ability to do anything
Omniscience	Unlimited knowledge; knowledge of everything
Eternality	Eternal existence; existence at all times; alternatively, existence outside of time
Immutability	Unchangingness; perfect constancy
Omnibenevolence	Perfect goodness; complete lack of vice, evil, or moral deficiency

This Is Philosophy of Religion: An Introduction, First Edition. Neil A. Manson.
© 2021 John Wiley & Sons, Inc. Published 2021 by John Wiley & Sons, Inc.

It is these properties that make the concept of God such a powerful one in comparison to that of Zeus, a god with none of the properties listed in the table. It is not true that Zeus can do anything whatsoever. For example, Zeus cannot annihilate the universe. Likewise, there are things Zeus does not know in full, such as the plans of his fellow Greek gods. He is certainly not morally perfect; in myth, he took the form of a swan and seduced Leda. He came into being when Kronos, his father, created him, which means he is not eternal. It also means he changed over time. So, while Zeus is a pretty tough customer (probably even Wonder Woman would not want to mess with him), you can do better than Zeus if you are looking for a god to worship. God, the supreme being, is supposed to be absolutely perfect. As the medieval Christian theologian **St. Anselm**[1] put it, God is the being than which none greater can be conceived. It is from this absolute perfection that all of God's particular perfections (omnipotence, omniscience, and so on) flow. It is this absolute perfection that supposedly makes God the one being in all of reality that is truly worthy of worship.

2.1.2 The Importance of a Logically Consistent Concept of God

The divine properties are not properties of any of the things we normally encounter in day-to-day existence. Might it turn out that, in fact, nothing could have all of these properties? Perhaps closer inspection would reveal, for example, that being omnipotent makes no more sense than being a round square or being able to travel back in time. Perhaps, on closer thought, we might come to think that God could not be both omniscient and perfectly free. To put the matter a different way, we might come to think that the proposition "God is omnipotent" contains a hidden contradiction, or that the pair of propositions "God is omniscient" and "God is perfectly free" are logically inconsistent with one another. Let us call questions about whether the divine properties make sense (considered individually or in combination) "logical consistency questions," and let us call the problem of whether any being can have all of the divine properties the logical consistency problem for theism. Historically, philosophers, and theologians have spent a lot of time worrying about the logical consistency of theism and addressing logical consistency questions. Some have done so because they wish to attack theism. Some have done so because they wish to defend theism.

For some logical consistency questions, the right answer may be "no." If the answer to even one of the logical consistency questions is "no," it seems pointless to address any remaining questions about theism – questions such

---

[1] https://www.britannica.com/biography/Saint-Anselm-of-Canterbury.

as whether there is any evidence that God exists or whether it is rational to believe that God exists if there is no evidence that God exists. If the very idea of God is logically inconsistent, it seems that there cannot be any evidence for the existence of God, nor can it be rational to believe in God. So addressing the logical consistency problem seems to be the first order of business before we look at any other philosophical problems concerning theism.

An analogy will illustrate the point that addressing the logical consistency problem is the top priority. Imagine that there has been a crime and you are a detective investigating it. You have gathered some evidence about the crime and are now at the stage of formulating hypotheses. A fellow detective suggests that perhaps the crime was committed by someone from the future who traveled back in time. Should you entertain this hypothesis? Should you seek to gather evidence either to support it or refute it? Well, if you think the very idea of traveling back in time just makes no sense, it seems pointless to entertain the hypothesis and useless to gather evidence either for or against it. Likewise, if you think it really makes absolutely no sense that something possesses all of the divine properties, there would be no point in looking for evidence of the existence of God or in addressing whether it is rational to believe in God without evidence. Either you should explore alternative conceptions of God – conceptions on which God does not possess all, or perhaps even any, of the divine properties – or you should just give up on the idea of God altogether. These considerations show why any philosophical examination of theism should begin by addressing the logical consistency problem.

2.2 Voluntarism

2.2.1 An Easy Solution to the Logical Consistency Problem?

A logical consistency problem is a problem concerning the relationship between concepts – either between one concept and a different one or between a concept and itself. For example, the concept of a round square – a two-dimensional figure that is both a square and round – just does not make any sense. The very description is self-contradictory. When you think about roundness and squareness, you see that no two-dimensional figure can be both at the same time. The concepts of roundness and squareness just do not go together. Likewise, the logical consistency problem for theism is that it seems not all of our concepts of the divine properties can be combined into one coherent concept – that is, nothing can be everything that God is supposed to be.

To take one example – one to which we will return in section 2.3 (on "Omnipotence") – it seems that nothing can be omnipotent, since there are some powers that, by their very nature, imply a limit on other powers.

For example, a person with typical physical abilities can make a stack of books and also lift a stack of books. But there are limits to both of those abilities. You can make a stack only so high, and you can lift a stack only so heavy. These limitations mean that it makes sense to say that you can make a stack of books so high that you cannot lift it. But if God has unlimited lifting power, that implies a limit on God's stacking power. God cannot make a stack of books so high that God cannot lift it. So it seems that two concepts cannot fit together: the concept of unlimited stacking power and the concept of unlimited lifting power. But both of these concepts fall under the more general concept of omnipotence. So, it seems, the concept of omnipotence is logically inconsistent, and therefore the concept of God is logically inconsistent.

But a concept is simply something in your mind that enables you to grasp things in the world outside of your mind. Because concepts are human possessions, they seem as able as any other human thing to be defective. Because we are mere humans, it seems we are just as liable to be wrong about the logical consistency of concepts as we are about anything else – even if we are thinking about fundamental, basic concepts. For example, many of history's smartest humans thought carefully about the concepts of space, time, and geometry, and concluded that **parallel lines could never intersect**.[2] Yet in the last two centuries other smart humans delved deeply into the concepts of geometry and concluded that, however unintuitive it may seem, **it is logically consistent to say that parallel lines can, indeed, intersect**.[3] What if those who examine the concept of God and see logical inconsistency in it are like the smart people from many centuries ago who thought parallel lines could never intersect? In that case, the concept of God may be perfectly consistent logically. It is just that we humans have limited minds.

This approach to the logical consistency problem for theism goes all the way back to medieval times in both Christian and Islamic theology. The seventeenth-century French philosopher **Rene Descartes**[4] took this sort of approach – a position called voluntarism. Voluntarism is the idea that nothing – not the structure of space, not the laws of geometry, not even morality or mathematics or truth or logic – is beyond the will of God. (The word "voluntary" is from the Latin word *voluntas*, which means "will.") If we think something is impossible, says Descartes, that is only because of a limitation of our minds. It is not because there is any limitation on God.

---

[2] A brief explanation and history of Euclid's parallel postulate can be found at http://mathworld.wolfram.com/ParallelPostulate.html.

[3] Two brilliant nineteenth-century mathematicians, János Bolyai and Nikolai Lobachevsky, called into question Euclid's parallel postulate: http://www.storyofmathematics.com/19th_bolyai.html.

[4] https://www.britannica.com/biography/Rene-Descartes.

I do not think that we should ever say of anything that it cannot be brought about by God. For since every basis of truth and goodness depends on his omnipotence, I would not dare to say that God cannot bring it about that there is a mountain without a valley, or bring it about that 1 and 2 are not 3. I merely say that he has given me such a mind that I cannot conceive a mountain without a valley, or a sum of 1 and 2 which is not 3; such things involve a contradiction in my conception.[5]

What Descartes is suggesting here is that logical consistency and inconsistency are just in our heads. When we say certain complex concepts are not logically consistent – such as the concept of 1 and 2 adding up to 7, or the concept of a mountain that never bottoms out into a valley – we are merely reporting a limitation on our own ability to conceive things. These limits do not apply to God. They only apply to the minds that God gave us. According to Descartes and to the voluntarists, what properties or propositions are or are not logically consistent with one another is really just a function of our minds. Since the structure of our minds depends on the will of God, logical consistency and logical inconsistency (as well as the modal properties of necessity, possibility, and impossibility) themselves depend upon the will of God.

If voluntarism is correct, we would have a solution to any logical consistency problem for theism. According to the voluntarist, anytime anyone asks a logical consistency question about theism, the theist can declare that the conflict is only in our minds. For example, if you think that the idea of unlimited stacking power conflicts with the idea of unlimited lifting power, or if you think that God could not make a mountain without making a valley, or if you think that there is no number God can let 1 and 2 add up to besides 3, the right response, according to the voluntarist, is to remember your mental limitations, not to doubt the existence of God or the scope of God's power.

2.2.2 The Problem with Voluntarism

Voluntarism looks like a powerful weapon in the arsenal of the theist. For any apparent logical consistency problem confronting theism, the voluntarist can say it is no problem because logical inconsistency is just in our heads. Attractive as it seems, however, voluntarism has a number of odd – indeed, preposterous – consequences. If voluntarism is true, then God can make it the case that God does not exist, or that night is day, or that good is evil, or that you are God. Let

---

[5] Descartes's letter to Arnauld, repr. in *The Philosophical Writings of Descartes*, vol. 3, trans. John Cottingham, Robert Stoothoff, Dugald Murdoch, and Anthony Kenny (Cambridge: Cambridge University Press, 1991), pp. 358–359.

us take that last one as an example. Here is an argument for the conclusion that possibly, you are God.

The Argument from Voluntarism to the Possibility that You Are God

(1) Everything whatsoever depends upon the will of God.

So, (2) What it is to be God depends upon the will of God.

So, (3) Possibly, God wills that what it is to be God is to have exactly the set of properties and powers that you have right now, including being mortal, being ignorant of many things, being of limited power, reading *This Is Philosophy of Religion*, and thinking you are certainly not God.

So, (4) Possibly, you are God.

This looks like a preposterous conclusion, but it follows directly from the voluntarist's claim that everything whatsoever depends upon the will of God. It is preposterous conclusions such as this that have led almost all theologians and theistic philosophers to reject voluntarism.

2.2.3 Why Voluntarism Is Tempting

If believing in voluntarism is such a mistake, why would any theist commit it? Here are two suggestions as to why someone might mistakenly endorse voluntarism.

First, two temptations can combine to incline someone toward voluntarism: reification and being overly committed to one's favorite slogans. Reification is the act of turning an abstraction into a concrete thing. For example, someone who thought the way to beat the high cost of textbooks is to get a gun and shoot the high cost of textbooks is guilty of reifying the high cost of textbooks. When we discuss divine properties such as omnipotence, we use nouns such as "property" and "omnipotence." This language tempts us to think that there is a concrete thing, omnipotence. That, in turn, tempts us to think that God controls omnipotence, since God controls every thing and omnipotence is a thing. But this is a mistake if there just is no concrete thing corresponding to the noun "omnipotence."

The second temptation is clear enough. Careless thinkers hear an attractive slogan, support it or the cause behind it, and eventually come to feel that they must defend the slogan at all costs. "Everything is relative," some say. Well, that is an attractive slogan and believing it might serve some useful purposes. For example, it might encourage people to be more tolerant and open-minded. But if it is taken literally and without qualification, it leads to absurd conclusions – for example, that the earth is not really a sphere, but is spherical only relative to the people who believe it is a sphere and flat relative to the people who believe it is flat. Surely there is a way to preserve the spirit of tolerance and open-mindedness that motivates saying "everything is relative" without actually believing and insisting that every single thing is relative. Surely there is a better way to preserve the spirit of awe and respect for God that motivates people to say "God can do anything" or "with God, all things are possible" without actually maintaining that God can do anything whatsoever, where "anything" includes preposterous stuff like making God not be God, making good be evil, making 1 and 2 add up to 7, and so on.

When reification combines with a tendency to adhere to slogans, it leads some people to reason as follows: "I am a faithful believer in God. All of my life I have been told that God can do anything. I have been taught that with God all things are possible. If I give that up, I give up my belief in God. So, at all costs, I must insist that God controls everything. But wait! Mathematics, logic, ethics, the divine properties – these are all things. So, if I want to continue counting as a faithful believer in God, I must say that God controls mathematics, logic, ethics, and so on." Hopefully you see now that this line of thought is not a good basis for voluntarism.

Second, some might mistake constitutive rules for constraints. Constitutive rules are rules that define a thing or activity. Consider, for example, the rule in chess that says the bishop can move only diagonally. Does it make any sense to say that this rule is holding back the full potential of the bishop and is constraining real chess? No. Rather than holding the bishop back, the rule about moving only diagonally makes the bishop the piece it is. Rather than constraining real chess, the rule that there are exactly two pieces per side that can move only diagonally helps make chess the game it is. (Imagine how boring chess would be if every piece had the power of the queen!) The rule helps constitute chess. That is why we call the the-bishop-can-move-only-diagonally rule a constitutive rule. Another example is American football. If you change the rule that the ball carrier must be tackled in order to be down, so that merely touching the ball carrier is enough to make the ball carrier down, you create an entirely different game: touch football.

Now consider, for example, the laws of logic. These include the law of the excluded middle (the rule that, for any proposition P, either P is true or P is false) and the law of noncontradiction (the rule that, for any proposition P, P cannot be both true and false). In addition to all of God's other properties, theists say that God is perfectly rational. Let us suppose that this is right. So God will never believe of some particular proposition P both that it is true and that it is false. Also, for any proposition P, either God will believe that P is true or God will believe that P is false. Would this mean that God, being rational, is "constrained" by the laws of logic? No. It is better to say that following these laws is just part of what it is to be rational. Adhering to them helps constitute perfect rationality. As the English philosopher and political theorist **John Locke**[6] said, "Where there is no law, there is no freedom." Likewise, without laws of logic, there can be no rationality. Rather than holding God back, the "constraint" of logic actually helps define what it is to be rational.

If theists reject voluntarism, they deprive themselves of very easy answers to all of the logical consistency questions for theism. But that does not mean that there are no good answers to those questions. Instead of trying to answer all of them in one fell swoop, we can tackle them one by one. That is how we will proceed in the remainder of this chapter, looking at just the divine properties mentioned in the table. We will begin with omnipotence. Does the idea of being all-powerful even make sense?

2.3 Omnipotence

2.3.1 Paradoxes of Omnipotence

The concept of **omnipotence**[7] faces the paradox of the stone. We have already seen this paradox, except we expressed it in terms of stacking books instead of lifting stones. Creating a stone so heavy that you cannot lift it is a power a being could have. Yet the very having of that power has built into it a limitation on power. If you have the power to create such a stone, you lack the power to lift such a stone. If you lack the power to create such a stone, you have a limitation on your creative power. Either way, there is a limitation. So it looks like no being can have unlimited power. That means no being can be omnipotent, and that means no being can be God. Does this show that the concept of God is logically inconsistent?

Puzzles like this can be multiplied. Can God commit suicide? If not, there is a limitation on God's power, right? Or, again, creating a being with the ability to defeat or overrule its creator is a power a being could have. After all, Frankenstein created a monster that eventually killed him. In the *Star Wars* movie franchise, the emperor, Darth Sidious, trained and empowered Darth Vader, yet Darth Vader eventually turned on his master and killed the emperor. (Or did he?) Yet this seems to lead to a paradox when it comes to a supposedly omnipotent being. If God cannot create a God-defeating being, there is a limitation on God's power. But, if God can create such a being, then God would be unable to defeat the being that God created, and so again there would be a limitation on God's power. Yet many philosophers have thought these paradoxes can be avoided if we refine our concept of omnipotence.

---

[6] https://www.britannica.com/biography/John-Locke.
[7] https://plato.stanford.edu/entries/omnipotence.

2.3.2 A Refined Concept of Omnipotence

In his book *The Coherence of Theism*, contemporary philosopher Richard Swinburne suggests several clarifications of our concept of omnipotence. First, we should follow the suggestion of **St. Thomas Aquinas**[8] and restrict omnipotence to what is <u>logically possible</u> – to what does not involve a contradiction. What philosophers now call "logically possible" Aquinas called "absolutely possible," in contrast to what is only "relatively possible" – possible in the sense that it lies within the power of some particular kind of being. For example, flying is possible relative to birds but not to humans. Some would-be actions – making 1 and 2 add up to 7, creating a round square, and so on – are not just relatively impossible. It is not just that they are impossible for a few people here and there. They are absolutely impossible. Not even God can do them. To put it another way, to say that not even God can do these things is not to say that God is at a disadvantage relative to some other being. It is not like making 1 and 2 add up to 7 is something that somebody could do, but not God. No one could do it. So, despite how great the slogan sounds, it is just not true that "with God, all things are possible." The logically impossible – the absolutely impossible – is impossible for everyone, including God.

Saying that God cannot do what is absolutely impossible is in conflict with Descartes's voluntarism, according to which what we call "absolutely impossible" is really only relatively impossible – only impossible relative to our limited way of conceiving things. As we saw in section 2.2, however, voluntarism leads to deeply strange results, such as that possibly you are God. Aquinas's view that God does not control what is and is not logically possible seems much more reasonable.

Second, according to Swinburne, we should understand omnipotence, not in terms of performing possible actions, but in terms of making things happen. This is a subtle change to the definition, but making it helps us to avoid a good number of problems. Many actions are specific to certain kinds of thing. If God is not that kind of thing, God cannot perform that kind of action. For example, the verb "photosynthesize" picks out something plants do. Since God is not a plant, God cannot photosynthesize, and so there is something God cannot do. But is this really a problem for the concept of omnipotence? Is this really a limitation? It does not seem so.

Consider more examples. You can slap your forehead, but God cannot slap God's forehead. God also cannot get in shape by joining CrossFit, simply because God is not the sort of thing that gets in shape. (We will set aside here

---

[8] https://www.britannica.com/biography/Saint-Thomas-Aquinas.

the possibility of incarnation – of God becoming human, as Christians claim happened in the case of Jesus.) Are these cases really problems for the concept of omnipotence? Not really. Think of it this way. If we say God cannot photosynthesize, slap God's forehead, or join CrossFit to get in shape, that does not mean God cannot make something else do those things. The things that God cannot do here are actions that are restricted to specific kinds of being – beings distinct in kind from God. In other words, these actions are not logically possible after all. So, for the sake of having a clear concept of omnipotence, we should not understand omnipotence in terms of performing actions, but in terms of making things happen. It is consistent to say that God can make the world be any (logically consistent) way God wants it to be, yet also to say that God cannot perform every single kind of action performed by the beings in the world. God could make every person in the world get in shape, even if God cannot do the same.

Third, says Swinburne, it could be that there are ways the world can be, but that it is not logically possible that God *makes* the world be one of those ways. Consider acts done of your own free will, such as hitting yourself. You might think that, if an act is done of your own free will, by definition it is not the result of any outside influence. You, and only you, made that thing happen. So it is logically possible that you hit yourself of your own free will. It is also logically possible that God makes you hit yourself. God could take control of your nervous system and make that happen. God hardened Pharoah's heart (Exodus 9:12), so surely God could make you hit yourself. But perhaps it is not logically possible that God *makes* you hit yourself of your own free will. That is because, if God made you do it, you would not have done it of your own free will. (This idea will turn out to be very important when we discuss the problem of evil and the response that evil is due to human free will.)

Finally, notes Swinburne, there can be restrictions on God's power arising from God's other perfections – omniscience, moral perfection, and so on. A restriction of this sort is called a <u>limitation of perfection</u>. For example, suppose that God, being morally perfect, cannot torture innocent puppies for fun. Is it really a limitation on God – a reduction in God's greatness – that God cannot do this? On the contrary, it looks like this inability enhances, rather than reduces, God's greatness. This limitation brings God closer to perfection. Suppose that you just cannot bring yourself to kill your parents in cold blood, but the person next door to you can. Who is the better person? Likewise, suppose that Zeus can fail to know what your favorite movie is but God cannot. Who is the greater deity? The limitations of perfection flow from the greatness of God, not from any deficiency. They are good limits to have, not bad ones.

2.3.3 Resolving the Paradox of the Stone

Now that we have made some of these refinements to the definition of "omnipotent," can we use them to resolve the paradox of the stone? We can. The inability to create a thing so heavy that the creator cannot subsequently lift it seems to be a limitation of perfection – in this case, a limitation that results from God's unlimited power. We humans are capable of piling stacks of books so heavy that we cannot subsequently lift those stacks, but that is because our lifting powers are limited. But as the philosopher George Mavrodes has argued, God's lifting power is unlimited, so no stone could ever meet the description "not liftable by God." For any sized stone you like, God can create it, and for any sized stone you like, God can lift it. Can God create a billion-kilogram stone? Yes. Can God lift a billion-kilogram stone? Yes. And the same is true for any specific mass you can name for a stone. There can be no answer to the question "What is the mass in kilograms of the stone so heavy that God can create it but cannot lift it?" That is a good hint that such a stone cannot exist, and so the paradox of the stone is not really a problem for the logical consistency of theism.

We have just been asking a logical consistency question about theism – the question "Can anything be omnipotent?" And we have just examined one problem – the paradox of the stone – that has led some people to answer "no" to that question. But we also glimpsed a way to resolve the paradox of the stone. Does this show that the concept of omnipotence is logically consistent? No. The concept of omnipotence may have other insoluble problems, even if the paradox of the stone is not one of them. However, we have learned two important things from our discussion of the concept of omnipotence. First, the concept is a lot more complex than it first appears. Simple slogans such as "God can do anything" or "with God, all things are possible" mask serious difficulties. In order to have a workable conception of omnipotence, we need to introduce important qualifications. Second, careful attention to details can pay off when problems such as the paradox of the stone are posed. As we will see, these two lessons are reinforced when we address other properties of God.

2.4 Omniscience, Eternality, and Freedom

What does "omniscience" mean? Does it just mean "knowledge of everything"? It would be nice if matters were that simple, but, as you may have come to suspect by now, things are more complicated than that. First, the word "know" has a number of very different senses. Given God's other perfections and some obvious facts about us humans, perhaps God could not know everything there is to know for each of these different senses of "know." Second, if God knows the future, then God knows both what God will do beforehand and what we will do beforehand. That seems to mean that God is not free and neither are we. Let us take these problems one at a time.

2.4.1 Kinds of Knowledge

The table shows three kinds of knowing, each with a sample sentence illustrating a particular sense of the word "know."

Three Kinds of Knowledge

"Know-that" knowledge; knowledge of propositions	"I know that France is in Europe."
"Know-how" knowledge; possession of abilities	"I know how to tie my shoes."
Knowledge by acquaintance; familiarity with an object, a person, or a state of being	"I served with Jack Kennedy. I knew Jack Kennedy. Jack Kennedy was a friend of mine. Senator, you are no Jack Kennedy."

When we say that God is omniscient, do we mean that God knows everything there is to know in all three senses of "know"? It turns out that each of these three ways of knowing poses problems when it comes to God.

2.4.1.1 Ability Knowledge

The problem with know-how has, in a way, already been covered in our discussion of omnipotence. Just as some sorts of action are restricted to certain sorts of being (e.g. photosynthesizing is restricted to plants), so too with some sorts of ability. Suppose you know how to drive when you are sleepy. You do it by rolling the windows down, drinking some coffee, and putting your car stereo on full blast. Does that mean that the theist has to say that God knows how to drive while sleepy? But God is not the sort of being who drives a car, gets sleepy, drinks coffee, or listens to loud music. Of course, God surely knows for each driver what they must do in order to drive when sleepy. But that is different from God possessing the know-how for driving while sleepy. Admitting that God does not know how to drive when sleepy, however, does not seem to be a very big problem for saying that God is omniscient, any more than admitting that God cannot photosynthesize is a very big problem for saying that God is omnipotent.

2.4.1.2 Acquaintance Knowledge, Impassibility, and Competing Conceptions of God

The problem with acquaintance knowledge is much more serious for an important religious reason. You are almost certainly acquainted with all sorts of negative emotional states: sadness, hatred, frustration, envy. You may also know what it is like to be in severe physical pain. Is God acquainted with these sorts of things? On the one hand, it seems that God, being perfect, is never sad, hateful, frustrated, or envious. If God does not have a body, it seems God cannot feel severe physical pain. (Again, let us set aside the possibility of incarnation – the Christian doctrine that God became a flesh-and-blood, physical being.) So we want to say that there are all sorts of states of being with which God just cannot be familiar. On the other hand, if we want to say God loves us, and if we think loving a person requires fully understanding – if not outright sharing – the emotional states of that person, then it seems that God cannot love us. If God cannot know what it is like to be sad, to hate, to be frustrated, or to feel severe physical pain, it seems that God cannot relate to us when we are in such states. God never feels sad at our sadness or hurts for our hurting.

Philosophers and theologians use the word "impassible" to name the property of being incapable of suffering or pain. (The word "passible" means "capable of suffering or pain"; the word "passion" goes back to the same Latin root. That is why the movie about the day leading up to Jesus's crucifixion was called *The Passion of the Christ*.) Although it was not on our original list of properties of God, many theologians have thought that, in addition to being omnipotent, omniscient, and so on, God is also impassible. So let us narrow down the problem of God having acquaintance knowledge to the problem of impassibility – the problem of how a being who cannot know what it is like to suffer can truly understand beings who do suffer. It is a fact that we suffer. Being impassible, however, seems to mean that God cannot know what it is like to suffer. But in that case, how can God be omniscient if there is a what-it-is-likeness to suffering and we can know it but God cannot? Furthermore, how can God be perfectly loving if God cannot relate to our suffering?

The problem of impassibility is a deep and difficult one for the theist. It is an instance of a more general problem with theism. On the one hand, there is the conception of God that comes from the scriptures within the monotheistic religious traditions. As the concept of God is actually taught to most people through scripture, God has many human characteristics. God grieves and is sorry (Genesis 6:5–8). **God gets angry.**[9] God can be negotiated with (Genesis

---

[9] One of the most famous items of early American literature is the 1741 sermon from the preacher Jonathan Edwards, "Sinners in the Hands of an Angry God," which is quite vivid! https://www.blueletterbible.org/comm/edwards_jonathan/sermons/sinners.cfm.

18:16–33), loves us, sacrifices for us, and so on. Call this "the scriptural conception of God." On the other hand, there is the conception of God we come up with when we create God from scratch (so to speak). If you are asked to conceive of the greatest being that you possibly can and then you write down the specific characteristics of that being, you will probably come up with a list that is very much like the table of divine properties. On this conception, God has very unhuman characteristics. God knows everything. God can do anything. God was never born and never dies. And so on. Call this "the philosophical conception of God." One general problem with theism is the conflict between the scriptural conception of God and the philosophical conception of God. The scriptural conception of God (sometimes called "the God of Jerusalem") clashes with the philosophical conception of God (sometimes called "the God of Athens"). The problem of impassibility is an instance of this conflict. On the scriptural conception, God loves us, understands us, feels our pain, and so on. On the philosophical conception, God is incapable of suffering or dying and thus can never know what it is like to suffer or feel pain.

No solution to the problem of impassibility will be offered here. Does that mean there is no solution to the problem? No. Just because a problem is posed and no solution is offered does not mean that the problem is insoluble. Nor does it mean the problem is soluble. What it means is that, as with many of the other problems posed in this book, you will have to make a decision. You may decide that the problem of impassibility cannot be solved, and therefore the whole idea of God just makes no sense. Maybe that is what you believed before you even heard of the problem of impassibility. Or you may decide that you must find a solution to the problem of impassibility, and so begin to inform yourself better on the topic. Maybe you will decide to read more deeply in theology and philosophy. Maybe you will consult with some religious authority you respect. Maybe you will just think through the problem on your own and come up with a brilliant, utterly original solution to it. Or you may decide just to ignore the problem and to continue believing whatever you believed before. If you are reading this book as part of a philosophy class, almost certainly your instructor is not trying to get you to make any one of these decisions in particular. The point of the discussion is not to get you to believe some specific thing. It is not to get you to become a theist or an atheist. It is to make you think. Posing difficult questions and letting you work out the answers for yourself is a great way to make you think.

2.4.1.3 Propositional Knowledge

We will set aside the problem of impassibility, which grows out of the idea that God has acquaintance knowledge, and move on to problems arising from the third kind of knowledge we mentioned: propositional knowledge. Here is a proposition: "The person reading this sentence will have cereal for breakfast tomorrow." Does God already know it definitely to be true or definitely to be false? If God does already know it, then it looks like you cannot do anything but what God definitely knows, and so you are not free regarding what you have for breakfast tomorrow. If God does not already know it, then there is a proposition God does not know – namely, the proposition about what you will have for breakfast tomorrow. In that case, God does not know every true proposition and so is not omniscient. This problem – the <u>problem of fore-knowledge and human freedom</u> – is one of the oldest, most difficult questions facing theism.

2.4.2 Foreknowledge and Freedom

2.4.2.1 Foreknowledge of Future Contingent Propositions

In order to make this question more precise, we need to grasp some terminology. As we saw in Chapter 1, a contingent proposition is a proposition that is both possibly true and possibly false. For example, "Barack Obama is the 44th US president" is a contingent proposition. Although it is true, it might have been false. Obama might have lost the 2008 election, he might have lost his bid to be the nominee of the Democratic Party in 2008, he might never have run for US president, he might never have been born, and so on. A contingent proposition is contrasted with a necessary proposition, which either cannot possibly be false (e.g. "If I weigh over 200 pounds, I weigh over 100 pounds") or cannot possibly be true (e.g. "If I weigh under 100 pounds, I weigh over 200 pounds").

Some propositions about the future seem to be contingent. That is, whether they are true or false, it seems they could turn out the other way. Call such propositions <u>future contingents</u>. "Barack Obama will eat cereal for breakfast on April 18, 2029" appears to be a future contingent. It is not necessarily true that he will eat cereal then, and it is not necessarily false that he will eat cereal then.

If God is omniscient in the sense of having complete propositional knowledge, then God knows every single true proposition. But that means God knows every single true future contingent. Since these future contingents are future, that means God knows these truths ahead of time. Call knowledge of future contingents <u>foreknowledge</u>. In some scriptures, God is portrayed as foreknowing things. For example, God foreknows how Pharaoh will behave in response to the miracles Moses performs (Exodus 6:28–12:36). Jesus, too, is said to foreknow things – for example, that the 12 disciples will disown him (Matthew 26:30–35). Many theists will find it hard to deny that God fore-knows things.

2.4.2.2 The Apparent Incompatibility of Foreknowledge and Free Will

If God has foreknowledge, it seems humans are never truly free. Let us assume that Barack Obama eats cereal for breakfast on April 18, 2029 and use that to illustrate the <u>argument for incompatibility</u> – the argument for the conclusion that it is logically inconsistent to say both that God has foreknowledge and that humans are free.

The Argument for Incompatibility

(1) God knew on April 18, 1929 that Obama would have cereal for breakfast on April 18, 2029.
(2) If God knew on April 18, 1929 that Obama would have cereal for breakfast on April 18, 2029, then Obama cannot do otherwise than have cereal for breakfast on April 18, 2029.
(3) If Obama cannot do otherwise than have cereal for breakfast on April 18, 2029, then Obama eating cereal for breakfast on April 18, 2029 is not a free act.
So, (4) Obama eating cereal for breakfast on April 18, 2029 is not a free act.

This conclusion is not specific to Obama, to eating cereal for breakfast, or to April 18, 2029. It applies generally to all people, all actions, and all times. That seems to mean that, if God exists, no one ever performs a free act. Divine foreknowledge is incompatible with free will. This is an astounding conclusion. Should theists want to avoid it? If so, how can they avoid it?

Some Christian theologians in the **Calvinist tradition**[10] not only say that God does, indeed, foreknow all human actions, but that, in fact, God willed from the beginning of time – **predestined**[11] – who would and who would not achieve salvation. So at least some theists seem to have no reason to resist the conclusion of the argument for incompatibility. Other Christian theologians – notably, those in the **Arminian tradition**[12] – say that salvation requires free choice. For at least some theists, then, the argument for incompatibility reaches an unwelcome conclusion and needs to be resisted. This difference in belief regarding free will is not merely academic. In the history of Protestantism, it became a source of deep doctrinal difference, leading to the formation of large, influential denominations such as Methodism.

---

[10] https://www.theopedia.com/Calvinism.
[11] http://www.theopedia.com/predestination.
[12] https://www.theopedia.com/arminianism.

If you are a theist who does not like the conclusion of the argument for incompatibility, how should you respond to it? As with any argument, if you want to deny the conclusion, you will either have to show that at least one of the premises is false, or you will have to show that, even if all the premises were true, the conclusion does not follow due to an error in reasoning. In this case, the form of reasoning in the argument for incompatibility is as follows.

The Form of the Argument for Incompatibility

(1) P.
(2) If P, then Q.
(3) If Q, then R.
So, (4) R.

That reasoning is perfectly valid. It simply involves two applications of *modus ponens*. That leaves the three premises. Is there any reason to think that even one of them is false? Let us go through them one by one.

2.4.2.3 God and Time

The first premise is that God knew on April 18, 1929 that Obama would have cereal for breakfast on April 18, 2029. But saying God knew it *on* April 18, 1929 implies that God *existed* on April 18, 1929. That, in turn, implies that God exists at particular times. Do theists have to say that? Maybe not. One of the items on our original list of divine properties was eternality, but we did not see a precise definition of the term then. Instead, we were given two options: (i) God exists at all times and (ii) God exists outside of time. The theist could argue that God's being eternal means (ii), not (i). That, in turn, would mean the first premise of the argument for incompatibility would be false, simply because it would be false that God knew anything at all on April 18, 1929. It would be false, not because God is ignorant of anything, but because God does not know *at* times or *within* time.

Sempiternity is the property of existing at this current time, existing at all past times, and existing at every future time. Atemporality is the property of existing outside of time. If God is sempiternal, God is like us in that God's life can be divided into past, present, and future. It is just that there is no beginning to God's life and no end to it either. If God is atemporal, however, God's life cannot be divided into past, present, and future, because these are not features of God's way of existing. God is not the sort of thing that has temporal properties. So one way to deny the argument for incompatibility is to say that God is atemporal, not sempiternal.

Can we even conceive of atemporal existence? An analogy may help us picture it better. Imagine an old-style movie composed of distinct frames. The appearance of motion is generated by rapidly projecting a sequence of different images by shining a light through a succession of film cells. This movie, however, is unlike any other in that it is of infinite length. In this scenario, think of the "now" as just whatever frame is being projected. If the entire life of a human were captured on that film, there would be a finite number of frames with that person in it, from birth to death. The "now" would proceed from the birth frame toward the death frame, frame by frame. If God is sempiternal, then God appears in every single frame of the film. Yet God still appears in individual frames and there is a "now" frame for God too. Whether a being is mortal or sempiternal, then, that being still exists from moment to moment and experiences the world one frame at a time.

If God is atemporal, however, then God views all of the frames as the same – without one frame being picked out as the one that is "now" to God. We are strongly tempted to say God views the frames "all at the same time" or "simultaneously," but that is expressing the matter using temporal language, which is exactly the wrong way to express atemporality. It is better to say that God grasps the entirety of every frame all in a single act of understanding. If it is hard to make sense of this idea, that shows just how strongly our understanding of experience and of knowledge is tied to temporality.

Saying God is atemporal has some attractions to theists. Many theists want to say God displays immutability – that God never changes. Well, what is it for something to change? Suppose that what it is for something to change is for it to have one property at one time and then to not have that property at a later time. For example, suppose what it is for you to get drowsy is for you to have the property of alertness at an earlier time and come to have the contrary property of tiredness at a later time. In that case, God could never change, since there would be no such things as "earlier" and "later" for God. Automatically, then, God's being atemporal would make God immutable. If this line of thinking is correct, then, saying God is atemporal would not only enable the theist to avoid the conclusion of the argument for incompatibility. It would also support the idea that God is immutable.

However, saying that God is atemporal and immutable also has drawbacks. One criticism is that taking God outside of time does not eliminate the problem of foreknowledge. If God is atemporal but still omniscient, that just means God will timelessly know what happens at every moment in time. What we call the future will be just as fixed and as real to God as the present and past are to us. And that means the future is real, fixed, and unalterable from the one perspective that really matters: God's. Another criticism is similar to the problem of impassibility. How can God relate to us if we are inside of time and God is not? How can God interact with us if we change and God never does?

Consider God's relationship with Moses, as depicted in the book of Exodus (6:23–28). God is said to speak to Moses. God makes a covenant with Abraham, hears the groaning of the Israelites, and calls the covenant to mind. If God is outside of time and never changes, how could God speak, make covenants, hear groaning, and bring that covenant to mind in response? All of these actions seem to be things that can happen only inside of time. Think, especially, of the part about God calling the covenant to mind. Recalling things, focusing one's attention on things – these are mental activities with which we are all familiar, and we know they happen in succession, one thought followed by another. How could God do any of these things – remember, focus, respond – if God's mental life does not involve any change over time? It seems that any atemporal, immutable being would be incapable of relating to temporal, mutable beings like us, or of having a mental life anything at all like ours. That is a real problem for the theist who wants to say that God is atemporal and yet loves us, hears our prayers, gives us strength when we are down, and so on.

God's relationship to time is a great conceptual puzzle. Too many solutions have been proposed for us to survey all of them here. Before we move on to the other premises of the argument for incompatibility, however, it is worth reflecting on what just happened. We began with the intention to discuss a specific divine property: omniscience. We ended up bringing other divine attributes – atemporality and immutability – into our discussion. We also had to reflect on the nature of time itself, as well as the nature of human experience. What this shows is that thinking about the concept of God can force us to consider broader philosophical questions. This is why some of the most important work in philosophy has been done by theologians. Historically, questions about the nature of time, freedom, necessity, and causation (to name just a few topics!) perplexed theologians trying to understand the nature of God. So even if you think that, ultimately, the concept of God is not logically consistent, you can still find value in the work of those who have struggled to make sense of it.

2.4.2.4 The Fixity of the Past

The second premise of the argument for incompatibility is that, if God knows what Obama will have for breakfast 100 years in advance, Obama cannot do otherwise than have that thing for breakfast 100 years later. This premise presupposes that it makes sense to say that God knows things *in advance*. That, in turn, presupposes that God is sempiternal. Let us, indeed, presuppose that God is sempiternal and knows what actions we will perform before we perform them. Does that mean Obama cannot do otherwise than eat the breakfast that God foresaw? The reason for saying "yes" is quite strong. Suppose Obama *could* eat something other than cereal for breakfast that day. Then he could do one of two things: make God wrong or change what God believed 100 years ago. But Obama cannot make God wrong since God is infallible – that is, incapable of being wrong or making a mistake. And Obama cannot change what God believed 100 years ago because the past is fixed. It is over and done with. If the past is over and done with, however, the past is out of Obama's control, which means what God's breakfast beliefs about Obama were 100 years ago are out of Obama's control. Since he cannot make God wrong or change what God believed, Obama cannot do anything but eat cereal for breakfast on April 18, 2029.

Some philosophers and theologians, however, have questioned whether the past is, indeed, fixed. They claim that what God believed in the past is merely a "soft fact" about the past, and is thus not fixed. <u>Soft facts</u> are those that are not genuinely and solely about a past time, whereas <u>hard facts</u> are genuinely and solely about a past time. For example, while "Commodus ruled Rome" is a hard fact about 180 CE, "Commodus was the Roman emperor upon whose actions the movie *Gladiator* was based" is only a soft fact about 180 CE. The movie *Gladiator* might never have been made, it might have been based on the life of a different emperor, and so on. Thus, this fact about Commodus was never fixed – never settled – until *Gladiator* was actually made. (If it helps you to remember the distinction, think of it this way: The fact was sitting there in 180 CE, softly waiting century after century for the movie to be made. Once the movie was made, the fact firmed up. It became a hard fact.)

Another way to draw the distinction between hard and soft facts is that hard facts about a time do not entail anything about how the world is after that time, whereas soft facts do. The soft fact that Commodus was the Roman emperor upon whose actions the movie *Gladiator* was loosely based entails various things about times after 180 CE – that there will be movies, that some movies will be loosely based on history, and so on. But "Commodus ruled Rome in 180 CE" entails nothing about times after 180 CE.

While there is nothing any of us could do after 180 CE to make Commodus not have ruled Rome, perhaps there is something that someone could have done after 180 CE to make Commodus not be the Roman emperor whose actions were portrayed in *Gladiator*. Likewise, while Obama has no control over hard facts, God's believing on April 18, 1929 that Obama would have cereal for breakfast on April 18, 2029 is a soft fact. If so, then there would be something Obama could have done after 1929 to make God not have believed that Obama would have cereal for breakfast 100 years later. If this is correct, the argument for incompatibility fails because the second premise is not true. If God has foreknowledge of what we will do, that does not mean we cannot do otherwise than what we in fact do, since what God foreknows is under our control and can be changed.

This is the idea, at least. You will have to decide whether it makes sense to you. Take as a particular case the Gospel story that Jesus foretold that his disciples would disown him (Matthew 26:30–35, 69–75). Peter says "Not me!" Jesus replies that Peter will disown him three times before the end of the night. And then Peter does, in fact, disown Jesus three times before the end of the night. Let us grant that, if Peter had not disowned Jesus three times, Jesus would not have known that Peter would disown Jesus three times and so would not have foretold it. Nonetheless, once Jesus's declaration is made – once it is out there in the world, heard by Peter and the other disciples – it seems there is nothing Peter can do to make Jesus's statement disappear. Either Peter can make Jesus wrong or he cannot. Assuming he cannot, Peter *must* deny Jesus three times. If he must do it – if he has no control over denying Jesus – then it seems Peter did not deny Jesus of his own free will. Or did he?

2.4.2.5 *The Definition of "Free"*

The third premise of the argument for incompatibility is that, if Obama cannot do otherwise than have cereal for breakfast on April 18, 2029, Obama's eating cereal for breakfast on April 18, 2029 is not a free act. The idea is that, if you can only do one thing – if you only have one option – your doing that thing is not free. But why should we agree with that? Maybe if we analyze the concept of human freedom, we will see that having only one option does not necessarily make an act unfree. Suppose you have only one option, but you do not know that you have only one option. Suppose, furthermore, that this option is what you wanted to do anyway. Would you perceive your action as free in that case? If you would, then maybe there is a solution to the problem of foreknowledge and freedom.

The case of the sleepy roommate illustrates this scenario. Unbeknown to your roommate, you enact a nefarious plot to keep the door to your room locked from the outside. You penny the door at 10 p.m., thus locking them in without their knowledge. At midnight you remove the pennies. Your roommate hears you and comes out. "Why are you fiddling with our door?" says your roommate. "I have been trying to sleep since 9:30." Did your roommate stay in your room freely? Remember, your roommate was doing what they wanted to do: stay in the room and sleep. If you say "yes," you agree that acting freely is perfectly compatible with having only one option. And if you agree with that, you have no reason to think that the third premise of the argument for incompatibility is true.

Let the phrase "the incompatibilist conception of freedom," or just "incompatibilism," stand for the idea that acting freely requires that a person have more than one option open to them. Let us use the phrase "the compatibilist conception of freedom," or just "compatibilism," to stand for the idea that an action is done freely if it is what the person wanted to do. What we see now is that the argument for incompatibility presupposed incompatibilism. If compatibilism is right, this presupposition is false, and the argument for incompatibility fails.

Are there any reasons to prefer compatibilism to incompatibilism? Here are two. First, some compatibilists argue that all that we mean when we say "Obama ate cereal freely" is "Obama ate cereal because Obama wanted to eat cereal," and all that that means is "*If* Obama had not wanted to eat cereal, he *would not have* eaten cereal." The last sort of statement is what philosophers call a <u>counterfactual conditional</u> statement – a statement about what *would* have happened *if* other things had been different. (Remember that a conditional statement is a statement of the form "if … then …") But an "if … then …" statement can be true even if the antecedent (the "if" part) is false. For example, it is true that if Obama had never run for US president he would not have been elected US president, even though it is false that Obama never ran for US president. Now look at the breakfast example in this light. The statement "If Obama had not wanted to eat cereal, he would not have eaten cereal" can be true even if it is false that Obama did not want to eat cereal. Indeed, it can be true even if it is impossible that Obama did not want to eat cereal. So it is consistent to say both that Obama ate cereal of his own free will and that Obama could not have done otherwise than eat cereal, so long as the reason for his eating cereal for breakfast is that he wanted to do so.

In response, incompatibilists offer counterexamples to the compatibilist account of human freedom. They ask us to consider cases in which what a person wants or desires is produced in the wrong way – say, by hypnotism, brainwashing, or threats of force. Suppose a criminal organization hypnotizes you so that you will rob a bank for them. (In a famous case from the 1970s, the lawyers defending Patty Hearst said this is what the Symbionese Liberation Army did to her.) They change what you want, so that you go from being a person who does not want to rob any banks to being a person who does. Then it will be true that you would not have robbed a bank if you had not wanted to, but it will be false that you robbed a bank of your own free will. Or suppose the sleepy roommate actually has a severe case of agoraphobia. She just hates going outside of her room because she has a compulsive fear of open spaces. Now suppose the door to her room is unlocked. Nonetheless, she stays in her room. It is true that, if she did not want to stay in the room, she would not stay in the room. Does this mean she is staying in the room of her own free will? Maybe not. After all, she cannot want to leave the room; that is why she counts as an agoraphobe!

But if God foreknows everything, God also foreknows everything you want. Just as you cannot go back in time and change what God believes you will *do*, and just as you cannot make God wrong in what God believes you will *do*, you also cannot go back in time and change what God believes you will *want to do*, and you cannot make God wrong in what God believes you will *want to do*. You can do what you want to do, but you cannot want to do other than what God foreknows you will want to do. We are back to the original problem in a slightly modified form, the incompatibilist will say.

The problems generated by the idea that God has foreknowledge are not limited to the issue of human freedom. Suppose that God is omniscient and is sempiternal, that God is responsible for creating the world in the first place, and that God knew from the beginning of time exactly what everyone would ever want and do. This means that, even if the worst people in the world are doing exactly what they want when they do the horrible things that they do, God knew from the beginning of time that they would want to do those horrible things. Those awful people could not do anything but those horrible things without going back in time or making God wrong – both of which are impossible. So it looks as if God knowingly created a world in which those awful people were guaranteed to do those horrible things. How, then, can we blame the awful people for doing those horrible things? And why would God create a world like this in the first place? Divine foreknowledge thus figures heavily in other deep theological puzzles, including the problem of evil.

2.4.2.6 Concluding Thoughts on Foreknowledge and Freedom

As we noted, thinking about the concept of God forces us to consider broader philosophical questions. In this case, asking whether omniscience is incompatible with free will forces us to carefully consider exactly what we think it is to have free will. It also forces us to think about the nature of time and of causation. Your decisions on these philosophical questions will ultimately determine your attitude toward the problem of foreknowledge and human freedom. Maybe in the end you will think it cannot be solved and so either God does not exist or we are not free. Maybe in the end you will think it can be solved and so it is possible both that God exists and that we are free. Your teacher and this book cannot tell you what to do, except to tell you to decide for yourself. It is up to you.

2.5 Omnibenevolence

The central criticism we gave of voluntarism was that, if it were true, all sorts of preposterous things could happen. God could make 1 and 2 add up to a billion. God could make night be day. And God could make evil be good. Let us focus on this last possibility. Is it possible that rightness and wrongness, goodness and badness, are just whatever God says they are? Is it possible that God commands us to do something we all think is morally wrong, but that it would be morally right simply because God commands it? This scenario actually arises in the biblical story of Abraham and Isaac (Genesis 22:1–18). God puts Abraham to the test by commanding him to sacrifice his only son, Isaac. Abraham is about to go through with it when God sends an angel to stop him. Suppose God had not sent an angel to stop Abraham. Would Abraham have done the right thing by killing his son? After all, Abraham would have been following a direct command by God. And if you say "God would never actually let Abraham go through with it, because God cannot do anything morally wrong," does that mean there is something – moral goodness – that constrains what God does?

2.5.1 Divine Command Theory

To address these questions, let us articulate a view called <u>divine command theory</u>. According to divine command theory, what makes wrong acts wrong is that God forbids them, and what makes right acts right is that God commands them. There is nothing else to rightness and wrongness, goodness, and badness, other than being commanded or forbidden by God. So if God had not had an angel intervene, Abraham would have done the right thing in sacrificing Isaac. And nothing forced God to send an intervening angel, since nothing has power over God. On this theory, the term "morally right" simply means "commanded by God" and the term "morally wrong" simply means "forbidden by God."

Divine command theory seems motivated by just one thing: the desire to maintain that nothing has power over God, that everything depends on God's will. In this particular case, it is morality that is the threat to unlimited divine power. Yet, as we have already seen in our discussion of voluntarism, enormous problems arise for theists when they interpret omnipotence to imply control over logic, mathematics, and so on. Might the divine command theorists be making the same mistake, but this time in the case of morality? Many philosophers and theologians have thought so (even though there are intelligent theists who defend divine command theory).

2.5.2 Four Problems with Divine Command Theory

Here are four strong reasons for rejecting divine command theory.

2.5.2.1 Might Does Not Make Right

First, it involves the "might makes right" fallacy. Take as an example the story of the issuance of the Ten Commandments (Exodus 19:1–20:21). God is described as descending atop Mount Sinai in a dense cloud. There was lightning, smoke, fire, and the sound of trumpets. Israelites who merely touched Mount Sinai perished. The Israelites were terrified. God then delivered the Ten Commandments. So we see a demonstration of might, followed by a declaration of what is right.

But is that what made the Ten Commandments morally right – the fact that a tremendously powerful being commanded them? By that reasoning, if aliens in gigantic spaceships landed on earth, put on an impressive light show, scared all of us with their advanced technology, and then gave us rules to follow, we would be morally obliged to follow those rules. That just cannot be right. It cannot be that mere power is what gives God's commands their authority.

2.5.2.2 It Makes God Arbitrary

Second, divine command theory represents God's commands as arbitrary and unreasonable. If God had commanded the Israelites "Thou shalt stuff pebbles in thine ears every other day," that would have been *morally* obligatory. Now, in this case, there does not seem to be any independent reason for God issuing this command, but, according to the divine command theorist, reason has nothing to do with morality. Right and wrong, good and bad, are all determined by God's will *and nothing else*. This implication of divine command theory is unacceptable to those theologians and philosophers who think that one of God's essential properties is to do everything for a reason. There certainly seem to be good reasons for most of God's commands. For example, a good reason to forbid stealing is that widespread theft leads to social instability and chaos. Perhaps that is not the only reason, or even the main reason, God would forbid stealing, but that is not the point. The point is that each of the commandments is the sort of thing for which a good reason can be given. That is an enormous coincidence if divine command theory is correct, since God could have arbitrarily selected ten totally different commands instead – ones that seem totally unreasonable to us.

The seventeenth-century German philosopher **G. W. F. Leibniz**[13] pointed out in his work **Discourse on Metaphysics**[14] that God's being reasonable is a big component of our finding God worthy of worship. By separating morality from reason, divine command theorists are diminishing the concept of God, not enriching it:

> If you say, as Descartes did, that things are good not because they match up to objective standards of goodness, but only because God chose them, you will unthinkingly destroy all God's love and all his glory. For why praise him for what he has done, if he would be equally praiseworthy for doing just the opposite? Where will his justice and wisdom be if there is only some kind of despotic power, if reason's place is taken by will, and if justice is tyrannically defined as what best pleases the most powerful?

---

[13] https://www.britannica.com/biography/Gottfried-Wilhelm-Leibniz.

2.5.2.3 "God Is Good" Becomes a Tautology

Third, divine command theory makes the statement "God's commands are good" completely uninformative. If for something to be good is to have been commanded by God, saying "God's commands are good" just amounts to saying "God's commands are commanded by God." This just means that on divine command theory the proposition "God's commands are good" turns out to be a tautology – a statement that is true in virtue of logic alone. Other tautologies are statements such as "If you lose, you lose" and "Either it is Monday or it is not Monday." Tautologies do not really tell us anything. Theists want the statement "God is perfectly good" really to tell us something important about God. If so, goodness must be determined by something other than the arbitrary will of God.

2.5.2.4 It Conflicts with Scripture

In addition to purely logical arguments against divine command theory, some theologians offer scriptural ones. Here is a puzzling passage for the divine command theorist. In Genesis 1:3–4 it says "God said, 'Let there be light', and there was light; and God saw that the light was good, and he separated light from darkness."[15] If whatever God creates is automatically good, to say that God saw that the light was good is really just to say that God saw that the light was created by God. But if God created light, God *knew* that God had created light and so did not need to *see* that God had created light. The passage only makes sense if there is some standard of goodness that is independent of God, so that God can compare that creation to the standard and say, "Yes, my creation is good." This is precisely what Leibniz was getting at when he said in the same section of *Discourse on Metaphysics* that "If [divine command theory] were true, God, knowing that he is the author of things, would not have to regard them afterwards and find them good, as the Holy Scripture witnesses."

2.5.3 God's Role in Morality

If divine command theory is wrong, that does not mean God could have no role in human morality. First, it might be that we need God to reveal certain especially hard-to-grasp moral truths to us. Here is an analogy. There is a very

---

[14] The full text of Leibniz's *Discourse on Metaphysics* can be found at http://www. earlymoderntexts.com/assets/pdfs/leibniz1686d.pdf. The passages quoted here and later are from section 2.

[15] *The New English Bible* (New York: Oxford University Press, 1971). All biblical quotations are from this translation.

quick method for adding up very large strings of consecutive numbers. So, for example, if you ask a person who knows the method to calculate the sum of all the whole numbers between 1 and 100, she can give you the answer very quickly: 5,050. Suppose you ask her to do just that, and she gives you the answer. Did she make the answer be 5,050? No. The answer is 5,050 whether she figures it out or not. So do not thank her for *making* the answer be 5,050, but (if you want to) thank her for *telling you that* the answer is 5,050. Likewise, perhaps there are some questions about morality that are just too hard for us to answer. God can step in and convey the right answers to us. The right answers are what they are independently of God, but without God we would never know what they are.

Second, there is the obvious role for God of enforcer. There are people who know that stealing is morally wrong, but they do it anyway, since they do not fear being caught. If God exists and enforces the rules of morality, God is playing an enormous role in human morality. Even if God is not creating the rules, God can give people a practical reason not to break the rules. For example, God might create heaven and hell, and God might decide who gets sent where. The point here is not that theists must believe in a punisher God who sends wicked people to hell. It is simply that a theist could reject divine command theory but still think that God plays a unique and crucial role in our moral lives.

2.6 Concluding Thoughts on the Concept of God

We have just finished a survey of some important concepts: omnipotence, omniscience, eternality, and moral perfection. We will see in Chapter 3 that there are other concepts connected with the idea of God – concepts such as existing necessarily and being the creator of all of reality. We have not definitely concluded that these concepts make sense, nor have we definitely concluded that they do not. But at this point you may be getting impatient. Even if we grant that the concept of God does make sense, that does not show that there really is such a thing as God. Is there any reason to think, not just that the idea of God makes sense, but that God really does exist? That question is the topic of the upcoming chapters.

Annotated Bibliography

Adams, Robert Merrihew (1999). *Finite and Infinite Goods: A Framework for Ethics* (New York: Oxford University Press).
      Sophisticated and philosophically rich, Adams's book argues for a system of ethics and value grounded in God's existence. He makes a strong case for a modified version of divine command theory.

Almeida, Michael (2008). *The Metaphysics of Perfect Beings* (New York: Routledge).
    This book ranges widely over some of the most difficult of the logical consistency problems for theism. It touches on divine command theory as well as Rowe's argument, from *Can God Be Free?*, that, if God is morally perfect, God is not free.

Fischer, John Martin, ed. (1989). *God, Foreknowledge, and Freedom* (Stanford, CA: Stanford University Press).
    This volume brings together some of the central essays in analytic philosophy on foreknowledge and human freedom. Fischer's introduction maps the philosophical terrain masterfully.

Gale, Richard M. (1991). *On the Nature and Existence of God* (New York: Cambridge University Press).
    This is a comprehensive survey and evaluation of the literature on the attributes of God, as well as arguments for the existence of God.

Hoffman, Joshua and Gary Rosenkrantz (2002). *The Divine Attributes* (Malden, MA: Blackwell).
    The authors cover all of the attributes discussed in this chapter, as well as several others, with unsurpassed technical precision.

Rowe, William (2004). *Can God Be Free?* (New York: Oxford University Press).
    While this chapter covered whether humans can be free given that God is omniscient, Rowe develops an argument that God cannot be free given that God is morally perfect. Given God's moral perfection, God is unable to do anything less than the very best. Thus, God created this world of necessity. An original and important book, it also highlights the sometimes surprising conflicts that can arise among the standard divine attributes.

Sobel, Jordan Howard (2004). *Logic and Theism: Arguments For and Against Beliefs in God* (New York: Cambridge University Press).
    Sobel approaches the concept of God (and arguments for the existence of God) from a skeptical perspective. He devotes Chapters 9 ("Romancing the Stone") and 10 ("God Knows") to the paradoxes associated with omnipotence and omniscience.

Swinburne, Richard (1977). *The Coherence of Theism* (New York: Oxford University Press).
    This is the first of Swinburne's trilogy on the philosophy of religion. The other two titles are *The Existence of God* and *Faith and Reason*. They are all classics in analytic philosophy of religion. Students seeking a deeper understanding of the logical consistency problems facing theism could hardly do better than start here.

Wierenga, Edward (1989). *The Nature of God: An Inquiry into Divine Attributes* (Ithaca, NY: Cornell University Press).
    This is a thorough and detailed discussion of the main attributes of God, including all of those discussed in this chapter.

Wilson, Margaret Dauler (1978). *Descartes* (New York: Routledge).
    In part 3, section 3 Wilson provides the central passages from Descartes in favor of voluntarism. She notes: "This doctrine seems to have provoked mainly bewilderment in Descartes's correspondents; from Leibniz to the present it has occasioned shock reactions as well."

3

THE ONTOLOGICAL AND COSMOLOGICAL ARGUMENTS FOR THE EXISTENCE OF GOD

3.1 Natural Theology

In this chapter we will explore the idea that God's existence can be proven using reason, evidence, and basic philosophical principles. Initially you may be skeptical of this idea. Everyone knows that religious belief is all about faith, right? While this attitude toward religious belief is very common nowadays (among both believers and nonbelievers), it is not universal. In fact, historically many theologians held that reason could prove many things about God – prove them to anyone, even the nonbeliever. This effort to gain knowledge of God simply through reason and observable evidence they called natural theology. They contrasted natural theology with revealed theology. Revealed theology is the effort to learn about God by studying the information God revealed to humans, either directly or through prophets.

Take the case of the Roman Catholic theologian **St. Thomas Aquinas**.[1] He held that even pre-Christian pagan thinkers – people like the ancient Greek philosopher **Aristotle**,[2] for example – could (and sometimes did) know that God existed, just by thinking carefully about the world around them. Only through God revealing it to us, however, could we know the doctrine of the Trinity (the idea that God is three persons in one). Theologians like Aquinas thought that seeing that God exists is like seeing that the Pythagorean theorem is true or understanding that the earth is round. It is not something so obvious that every person understands it immediately, but, if your mind is working well and you pay attention to the reasons, you will see it – even if you have never been taught to believe in God.

[1] https://www.britannica.com/biography/Saint-Thomas-Aquinas.
[2] https://www.britannica.com/biography/Aristotle.

This Is Philosophy of Religion: An Introduction, First Edition. Neil A. Manson.
© 2021 John Wiley & Sons, Inc. Published 2021 by John Wiley & Sons, Inc.

In the previous chapter, we engaged in natural theology by using reason and philosophical principles to get clear on some of the divine properties. In this chapter, we will engage in natural theology in a different way. We will see whether some combination of scientific evidence, reason, and philosophical principles can show that God exists. We will look carefully at three specific arguments for the existence of God. The first two are in this chapter and the last is in Chapter 4. While there are many other arguments for the existence of God, these three are among the oldest, most common, and most interesting philosophically. Each one focuses on a particular set of divine properties, including some properties that were not discussed in Chapter 2. What these additional divine properties are will be explained as we go along. For now, we will just name the arguments, the specific divine properties with which each is associated, and the basic idea behind each one.

Arguments for the Existence of God

Argument name	Associated divine properties	Basic idea
Ontological argument	Being the greatest conceivable being and existing necessarily	Existence is included within the very concept of God, so God exists of logical necessity.
Cosmological argument	Existing necessarily and being the creator *ex nihilo* of the universe	Only God's existence explains why there exist any other beings.
Design argument	Omnipotence, omniscience, and omnibenevolence	God's existence is the best explanation of the apparent design of the universe and some of its parts.

3.2 The Ontological Argument

If you think again about the properties of God we discussed in Chapter 2, they all derive from a more general property: absolute perfection. God is supposed to be the greatest being we can think of. As the medieval theologian **St. Anselm**[3] put it, God is "the being than which none greater can be conceived." Anselm developed a deductive argument for the existence of God based on this idea. It is called the **ontological argument**.[4] (The word "ontological" derives from the

---

[3] https://www.britannica.com/biography/Saint-Anselm-of-Canterbury.
[4] https://plato.stanford.edu/entries/ontological-arguments.

Greek root *ontos*, which means "being.") It is an *a priori* argument. That is, for each of the premises, if you can know it to be true at all, you can know it to be true without the aid of sense experience. You do not need to see, smell, touch, taste, or hear anything to know that the premises of the argument are true. You do not need to perform any scientific experiments to support the premises. All you need to do is think the argument through in your head. Anselm claimed that, if you just thought clearly about the idea of God, you would see that God must exist, because existence is contained within the very concept of absolute perfection.

3.2.1 The Basic Strategy of the Ontological Argument

Anselm employs an unusual but very effective logical strategy: <u>*reductio ad absurdum*</u> (which is Latin for "reduction to absurdity"). The maneuver is to assume the opposite of what you are trying to prove, then show that this assumption leads to a logical contradiction – an "absurdity." Since a logical contradiction must be false, whatever assumption led to the logical contradiction must also be false, meaning that the denial of that assumption must be true. Anselm asks us to assume for the sake of argument that the atheist (whom Anselm calls "the fool") is correct in saying that God does not exist. Anselm also assumes that, when the atheist says "God does not exist," they mean the same thing by "God" that the theist means when they say "God does exist." That is, Anselm assumes that both the atheist and the theist agree on the concept of God. It is just that the atheist thinks there does not actually exist anything that matches the concept of God, while the theist thinks there does.

For an analogy, consider that both you and a young child can agree on what Santa Claus is supposed to be. You both have the same idea in mind when you think about Santa Claus: old, fat, jolly, long beard, gives out free gifts, and so on. It is just that the child thinks Santa Claus really does exist, while you do not. Likewise, Anselm thinks the atheist and the theist have the same idea in mind when they think about God. It is just that the theist thinks God really does exist while the atheist does not.

Anselm says that, if the atheist were to reflect carefully on the concept of God, they would see that they contradict themselves by saying God does not exist. A God that existed merely in our minds, Anselm thought, clearly would be less great than a God that existed in reality too. In other words, the atheist who *says*, "I know what God is supposed to be; I just think there is no God," does not *really* know what God is supposed to be. The atheist's concept of God includes omnipotence, omniscience, being the creator of everything else, and so on, but it is missing a key ingredient: existence. Although Anselm works out this argument in considerable detail, we can restate it briefly as follows.

Anselm's Ontological Argument

(1) God, the greatest conceivable being, exists in the mind but does not exist in reality. (This is the assumption for the sake of *reductio ad absurdum*. It represents what the atheist believes.)

(2) We can conceive that God, the greatest conceivable being, exists in reality as well as in the mind. (Anselm assumes even atheists admit this.)

(3) A being that existed both in reality and in the mind would be greater than a being that existed only in the mind.

So, (4) We can conceive that the greatest conceivable being could be greater than it actually is. (This is the "absurdity" necessary to complete the *reductio ad absurdum*.)

So, (5) The assumption made in (1) must be false, and so its negation must be true.

So, (6) God, the greatest conceivable being, exists in reality as well as in the mind. That is, God really does exist.

Anselm uses the analogy of a painting. A painter can have the idea in his mind of a beautiful work of art. This idea is a beautiful thing, but it is not as beautiful as the completed painting. The completed painting has something that the artist's idea does not have: existence in reality. Likewise, says Anselm, a God that exists in reality is clearly superior to a God that is just an idea in our minds. So if we really do think God is the greatest conceivable being, we must admit that God cannot exist merely in our minds. God must exist in reality as well. Thus, God exists.

3.2.2 Criticisms of the Ontological Argument

If you are puzzled by the ontological argument, you are not alone. It draws wildly varying reactions, from "This is just a word game – you cannot prove God exists that way!" to "This is a work of genius; it is really deep and important." Have you ever heard someone – a small child or perhaps a friend who has had too much to drink – say something strange that catches your attention, and you cannot decide whether it is totally stupid or utterly brilliant? The ontological argument is like that. Instead of just gaping at it, however, philosophers and theologians have articulated specific responses to it.

3.2.2.1 First Response: The Argument Proves Too Much

A contemporary of Anselm, a monk named **Gaunilo**,[5] wrote a reply to Anselm's argument entitled "In Behalf of the Fool." He claimed that, if we

---

[5] https://www.britannica.com/biography/Gaunilo.

substituted "island" for "being" in Anselm's argument, we would see that Anselm's argument must be mistaken. Try conceiving of the greatest possible island. It will have perfect weather, lovely palm trees, stunning mountain landscapes, waterfalls, beautiful beaches, no mosquitoes, and so on. Now which island would be better: a "perfect" island that existed only in your mind, or a perfect island that existed in reality? The one that existed in reality, of course! So, says Gaunilo, Anselm's reasoning proves the existence of all sorts of objects besides God, including ridiculous things like the most perfect island. Gaunilo thought that surely this showed something was wrong with Anselm's argument.

A variant of Gaunilo's objection is to consider the worst conceivable being. It would surely be worse if such a being existed in reality than if it existed only in our minds. Therefore the concept of the worst conceivable being includes existence, and so the worst conceivable being exists. Anselm's reasoning not only proves God exists. It proves that Satan exists too!

Two things are interesting about Gaunilo's objection. First, it illustrates a powerful method of logical analysis (one we saw in Chapter 1): refutation by counterexample. If you want to show someone that their argument is a bad one, make another argument of exactly the same form, but that leads from true premises to a clearly false conclusion. This shows that something is wrong with the logical structure of the argument. Although refutation by counterexample does not necessarily show where the mistake in reasoning lies, it shows that there is a mistake somewhere. Second, Gaunilo was a Christian just like Anselm, yet he put effort into disproving Anselm's argument for the existence of God. Why? Shouldn't Gaunilo have been on Anselm's side? From Gaunilo's perspective, however, Christians should not endorse just any old argument for the existence of God. Otherwise, they risk looking like fools if the argument is later refuted; that is bad for the strength and the spread of the faith. This is a common theme in the history of religious thought. Some of the most heated debates in philosophy of religion and in theology are not between believers and nonbelievers, but rather are internal to a particular faith, because the believers think so much depends on getting things exactly right.

3.2.2.2 Second Response: Existence Is Not a Property

Anselm's argument relies on a peculiar distinction: the distinction between existing in reality and existing in the understanding. Anselm describes a painter planning his painting in his mind as the painting existing in the painter's understanding. When he finishes painting it, the painting exists in reality. We do, indeed, talk in this way. You may have said of a deceased person, "She lives on in our hearts." Or suppose a secret admirer has a crush on you. (Such a person at least exists in your understanding.) That person might say, "I cannot get [your name] out of my mind." The important question here is whether this is more than just a manner of speaking. It seems not. The deceased person, being dead, no longer exists, and so cannot live on in any sense, much less in someone's heart. If you believe in the afterlife, then the deceased person does exist – but in heaven or hell, not in your mind. Likewise, you cannot fit into anyone's mind – not even your secret admirer's. Otherwise your secret admirer's skull would explode, or something material would come to occupy something immaterial.

To Anselm, the thing-in-the-understanding and the thing-in-reality differ in only one small respect: the thing-in-reality has the property of existence. This makes existence out to be a property that can be added to concepts to produce objects, like adding hot water to turn dry ramen noodles into soup. Contrary to Anselm, however, it seems that concepts differ from concrete objects in ways far greater than just existence. Your thought of Obama does not weigh anything (it is either an immaterial thought or an organized neuronal pattern), whereas Obama weighs about 180 pounds. Your thought of Obama does not have, and never did have, the power to send US troops into combat. Your thought of Obama never served in the US Senate. And so on. The dissimilarity between your concept of Obama and Obama himself could not be more radical.

The mistake here, as the eighteenth-century German philosopher **Immanuel Kant**[6] argued, is the notion that existence is a property. To say "Jack the Ripper existed" is not analogous, logically, to saying "Jack the Ripper murdered." To say that Jack the Ripper existed is to say that there was some person who met the description given for Jack the Ripper, but it says nothing about what that description is and nothing about who Jack the Ripper is supposed to have been. If you have no idea who or what Jack the Ripper is supposed to be, you do not learn anything more by being told that Jack the Ripper exists. Likewise, to say "The Higgs boson exists" is not analogous to saying "The Higgs boson is a subatomic particle that is responsible for giving mass to matter." The first statement adds nothing to your concept of the Higgs boson. If you never knew what the Higgs boson was in the first place, you did not learn anything from being told that it exists.

So saying "X exists" is not like saying "X is green" or "X is left-handed." Saying "X exists" is not really predicating anything of X. That is, existence is not a predicate. Existence just is not a property something has or lacks. If Kant is right, then Anselm's ontological argument fails. Omniscience, omnipotence, omnibenevolence, eternality, immutability – these are all eligible to be entries on the table of divine properties in Chapter 2. Since existence is not even a property, however, it does not belong on the list.

---

[6] https://www.britannica.com/biography/Immanuel-Kant.

3.2.2.3 Third Response: There Is No Logically Consistent Concept of the Most Perfect Being

Premise (1) of the ontological argument – the assumption of *reductio ad absurdum* which gets the whole thing going – is a conjunction. Logicians classify a conjunction as any complex proposition formed by joining together two simpler propositions using a coordinating conjunction such as "and" or "but." Premise (1) says two things: (A) the concept of God exists in our minds *but* it is not the case that (B) God exists in reality. In conclusion (5) Anselm claims to have shown that (1) is false. In conclusion (6) he claims that this means God exists in reality. One response to the ontological argument is to say that the transition from (5) to (6) is not logically valid. If we deny the two-part claim – that God does exist in our minds *and* does not exist in reality – perhaps we should conclude that God does not even exist in our minds.

To see the force of this response, we need to appreciate a basic fact of logic: if a conjunction is false, that means at least one, *but possibly both*, of the conjuncts is false. For example, if your friend tells you tonight that they are going out but that they will not go dancing, there are three things you could find out tomorrow that would show they did not tell you the truth. First, you could find out that they went out and went dancing. Second, you could find out that they stayed home and did not do any dancing. Finally, you could find out that they stayed home and danced. Likewise, if the first premise of the ontological argument is false (the conjunction "A and not-B"), that leaves three possibilities: (i) A and B (God exists in the mind and in reality); (ii) not-A and not-B (God does not exist in the mind and does not exist in reality); and (iii) not-A and B (God does not exist in the mind but does exist in reality). Presumably neither the atheist nor the theist is going to be satisfied with (iii). Instead of going for (i), however, the atheist has the option of (ii). That is, instead of saying that God exists in reality as well as in the mind, the atheist can say that God does not even exist in our minds – that we do not *really* have a concept of God.

This response sounds pretty strange. It says we think we have a concept in our minds, but we do not. How is that even possible? How could we be wrong about what is in our own minds? Here is how. In the previous chapter we looked at the concept of God. We saw that some people think that the concept of God is just not logically consistent. That is, they think that, although the idea of an absolutely perfect being – a being that is omnipotent, omniscient, omnibenevolent, and so on – sounds as though it makes sense, on closer inspection it turns out not to. According to this second response to the ontological argument, if you say the concept of the most perfect being includes the idea that the most perfect being really exists, then that only shows that there is something defective about the concept of the most perfect being. But what? The answer, according to this line of criticism, is the idea of necessary existence. Since this idea has not been explained yet, and since it also figures crucially in the next argument for the existence of God, let us turn our attention to that idea now.

3.3 Necessary Existence

As we noted in Chapter 1, to say a proposition is necessary is to say that it must be true. To say that a proposition is impossible is to say that it cannot be true. And to say that a proposition is contingent is to say that it could be true and it could be false; it is neither necessary nor impossible. Likewise, a necessarily existing being is a being that could not fail to exist; its nonexistence is impossible. A contingently existing being is a being that does not exist but could, or that does exist but could not. These concepts all rely on modal notions – the notions of what could be, of what could not be, and of what must be. So far, however, we have not explained just what modality is. What exactly do we mean when we say that a necessarily existing being *must* exist? It turns out that how we answer this question is crucial to understanding the third response to the ontological argument. We will distinguish two senses of necessary existence.

3.3.1 Aseity

In one sense, a being that was not and could not have been created by any other being, and that will not be and can never be destroyed by any other being, is a necessarily existing being. After all, there is nothing any other being can do to make such a thing come into or go out of existence. Such a being is completely independent of any other being. Let us use the term aseity for this first sense of necessary existence – complete independence from any other being, including the impossibility of being either created or destroyed. Clearly, theists want to affirm God's aseity. Otherwise they would be admitting that some other being could have power over God. We humans lack aseity. If our parents had not gotten together, we would never have existed. Furthermore, we will all die someday. It is interesting to note that many of the gods of ancient mythology also lacked aseity. For example, Zeus would not have existed if Kronos had not fathered him. Supposedly God is not like that. God's existence is supposed to be completely independent of the existence of any other being. That is part of what supposedly makes Zeus such an inferior deity compared to God.

3.3.2 Logically Necessary Existence

Some theists want to say that God is more than just completely independent of any other being, however, because saying only that still leaves open the possibility of God's nonexistence. If we think of God as merely possessing aseity, then it is still conceivable that God does not exist. In addition to aseity, according to these theists, God must have <u>logically necessary existence</u>. That is, God's nonexistence must be inconceivable or logically impossible.

To grasp this point, consider as an analogy what most atheists believe about the physical universe. According to many of them, the physical universe is all that there is. Therefore, nothing else made the physical universe come into existence. Furthermore, nothing else can make it cease to exist, since there is nothing outside of the physical universe to do the destroying. Nonetheless, say these atheists, it is not true that the universe *must* have existed. It very well might not have. The existence of the universe is, they think, an accident (perhaps a lucky one). If you were to ask "Why does the physical universe exist?" many an atheist would reply "There is no reason why it exists; it just does." So, for most atheists, the physical universe possesses aseity, but that does not mean it must have existed or that there is a reason why it exists.

Philosophers would describe this atheistic position as the view that the existence of the physical universe is a <u>brute fact</u>. Brute facts have no explanation at all for *why* they are true. For example, consider the speed of light. It is approximately 300,000,000 (3×10^8) meters per second (about 186,000 miles per second). As far as contemporary physicists know, there is no reason in physical theory that the speed of light is exactly what it is. For all they know, it could have been twice as fast or twice as slow. So it is not part of the very meaning of "the speed of light" that the speed of light is 3×10^8 meters per second. Furthermore, the speed of light seems to be independent of all other physical factors. So it seems that the speed of light *just is* 3×10^8 meters per second. It is just a brute fact that the speed of light is 3×10^8 meters per second. More generally, for any fact X, if the real, ultimate, final answer to the question "Why is X a fact?" is "It just is, and that's that," then X is a brute fact.

Many theists really dislike this idea that God's existence is a brute fact – that God exists, but for no reason whatsoever. To deny this, they have to say that God's existence is no accident. They have to say that there is a reason why God exists. But, since God possesses aseity, this explanation of God's existence cannot be in terms of any other being. Therefore, God's existence must be explicable in terms of God's essence. It must be part of the very nature of God to exist. So, for these theists, not only is it impossible that anything other than God creates God or destroys God. It is impossible that God does not exist. And that is what it is to have logically necessary existence.

3.3.3 Logically Necessary Existence and the Ontological Argument

Now we are in a position to better appreciate the third response to the ontological argument – the response that there is no coherent concept of the most perfect being. According to these respondents, when theists like Anselm say God exists necessarily, they are putting more than just aseity on the list of divine properties. They are putting logically necessary existence on that list too. For those making the third response to the ontological argument, however, the very idea of logically necessary existence makes no sense. For them, whatever the fundamental being in reality is – whether that being is God, the physical universe, or something else – it will be a brute fact that that being exists. If God is the fundamental, ultimate reality, then the answer to the question "*Why* does God exist?" will be "God just does exist, and that's that." And if the physical universe is the fundamental, ultimate reality, then the answer to the question "*Why* does the physical universe exist?" will once again be "It just does." The idea of logically necessary existence – of a thing existing because it is in the nature of that thing to exist – just makes no sense to those making the third response to the ontological argument.

3.3.4 Aseity and the Cosmological Argument

We have just seen some powerful reasons for rejecting the ontological argument. Even if that argument fails, however, that does not mean that all arguments for the existence of God fail. Perhaps there is some other way to establish that God exists – a way that still brings in the idea that God exists necessarily. We will see in section 3.4 that some philosophers think that we can prove the existence of a being possessing aseity. They think they can prove that, if the universe exists, there must exist an ultimate cause of it – one that is incapable of being either created or destroyed and that is independent of all other beings. This argument is one of the most popular philosophical arguments for the existence of God. It is called the cosmological argument.

3.4 The Cosmological Argument

The **cosmological argument**[7] attempts to move from the existence of the cosmos (the totality of material things) to the existence of a cause of or reason for

---

[7] https://plato.stanford.edu/entries/cosmological-argument.

the cosmos. Cosmological arguments have a great deal of intuitive appeal. It is very natural to ask, "Where did it all come from?" According to proponents of the cosmological argument, this fundamental question has an answer: "God." As we try to clarify this line of reasoning, however, we will see that there is more than one way to represent the argument. Some ways are better than others. For example, consider this argument.

The Cosmological Argument (Initial Version)

(1) The cosmos exists.
(2) Everything that exists has a cause.
(3) There cannot be an infinite series of past causes.
So, (4) There must be a first, uncaused cause (God).

There are two problems with this argument. First, there is a contradiction in it. If (2) is true, then God has a cause, too, because God is a being that exists and, according to (2), everything that exists has a cause. This version of the argument elicits a commonly asked question. "If God made everything, who made God?" So, for the cosmological argument to work, premise (2) cannot be included. Instead, some premise that is like (2) but that does not apply to God must be used.

Second, there is a big leap in the conclusion. Why are we entitled to assume that the first, uncaused cause (whoever or whatever that is) is God? No reason has been given for thinking that any being that is a first, uncaused cause must also be all the other things that God is supposed to be (omnipotent, omniscient, morally perfect, and so on). This is an instance of the identification problem – the problem of identifying whatever it is that these purely philosophical arguments point to with God. Why identify the first, uncaused cause with God? Perhaps the first, uncaused cause is one thing while God is something else entirely.

The problem is that we are using the term "God" here as a description of whatever thing it is that has a certain group of properties. It is sort of like the term "the Unabomber." The Unabomber was simply the name given to a person (later discovered to be Ted Kaczynski) who, in the 1980s and 1990s, sent mail bombs to people at *un*iversities and *a*irlines (hence "Un-a-bomber"), had bizarre theories about industrial-technological society, and so on. Now, if the FBI had found a particular person who espoused bizarre theories about industrial-technological society, this would not be enough to conclude that that person was the Unabomber. Maybe lots of people other than the Unabomber believed in similarly bizarre theories. So someone could have partially matched the description given of the Unabomber without having actually been the Unabomber. Likewise, finding a partial match (by showing that there exists a being that is the first, uncaused cause of the cosmos) is not enough to establish that there actually exists a being possessing all of the divine characteristics. Further arguments are necessary for identifying that being with God.

Since the identification problem is a general problem with most arguments for the existence of God, we will set the identification problem aside for now. Our main focus will be on whether there are good arguments for the existence of a being whose description even just partially matches our description of God (rather than perfectly matches it). Specifically, is there a good argument for thinking that there exists outside of the universe a creator of the universe?

3.4.1 The Causal Version of the Cosmological Argument

Here is a better version of the cosmological argument, logically speaking. It avoids one of the problems that faced the initial version.

The Causal Version of the Cosmological Argument

(1) There are things that come into existence.
(2) Whatever comes into existence is caused to exist by something else.
(3) There cannot be an infinite series of past causes.
So, (4) There was a first cause (God).

This version does not run into the logical inconsistency of our initial version of the cosmological argument. This is because premise (2) is not that everything whatsoever has a cause, but only that everything that comes into existence has a cause. If God is eternal, God never came into existence, and so the rule in (2) does not apply to God.

Now we can see a little more clearly the thinking behind the causal version of the cosmological argument. Look around you. What do you see? A book, some furniture, maybe some trees if you are outdoors. Have those things always existed, or was there a time at which they did not exist? None of them have always existed. All of them came into existence at one time or another. So, it is pretty clear that premise (1) is true. We know this by experience; that is, we know it *a posteriori*. Well, what else can we say about our experience with those sorts of things – things like books, furniture, and trees?

They all came into existence at some time or other, yet none of them just popped into existence ("poof!") or created themselves. (Self-creation does not seem even to make sense.) No, all of those things were caused to exist by something else. Your book came from a publisher. Your furniture came from a manufacturer. The tree came from a seed that fell off a prior tree. What about the book publisher, the chair manufacturer, and the seed-producing tree? It is the same thing with them; each of them also came into existence at a particular point in time, and all of them were caused to exist by something else. So it seems like premise (2) of the causal version of the cosmological argument is true.

Could it be that this series of causes goes back in time without end? Think about the last tree you saw. Could it be that that tree came from a seed that came from a tree that came from a seed that came from a tree that came from a seed that … and so on, forever? If premise (3) of the causal version of the cosmological argument is true, then no, it is not possible that there is an infinite series of past causes. And that means that there has to have been an initial cause – a first being back to which everything else traces. This first being would be the first cause of everything else in the universe. But that role – being the cause of everything else in the universe – is precisely the role God is said to play. God is supposed to be the creator _ex nihilo_ of the whole universe. (The phrase _ex nihilo_ is Latin for "out of nothing.")

According to this argument, then, our experience with the world, coupled with our reasonable intuitions regarding creation and infinity, lead us to conclude that there exists a special kind of being: the first cause. God is supposed to be the first cause, the creator. So, it looks like a combination of reason and experience shows us that there exists a being meeting (at least in part) the standard description of God. And so we now have another argument for the existence of God.

Of course, if it were that easy to prove that God exists, there would probably not be so much controversy and disagreement on the issue. If you disagree with the conclusion of the causal version of the cosmological argument, you must think one of the premises is false. But which one? It cannot be (1). It is undeniable that there exist things that have not always existed. So what about premises (2) and (3)? Let us look more carefully at them now.

3.4.1.1 Coming into Existence Out of Nothing

Despite how natural premise (2) of the causal version of the cosmological argument may seem, there is an important scientific objection to it. According to **quantum physics**,[8] the world is fundamentally indeterministic. Some events at the smallest levels of reality – among things that are smaller even than atoms – not only are unpredictable, but are not fully caused. At the subatomic level, the way things are at a given time does not completely determine how things will be at a later time.

---

[8] https://www.britannica.com/science/quantum-mechanics-physics.

Instead, the way things are at a given time only makes some future states more or less probable. For example, in a uranium atom, radioactive decay does not happen in an entirely predictable way. Instead, it is a matter of probability. Radioactive decay is not guaranteed to happen in a certain span of time; instead, what is true is something like that, for one gram of uranium, there is a 20% chance that it will emit a single beta particle in the next 10 minutes. This quantum indeterminacy might extend to the very beginning of the universe. There is a theory in physics called **quantum cosmology**.[9] According to it, at the very beginning – at the Big Bang – **the universe just popped into existence out of nothing.**[10]

There is considerable debate within physics about how exactly we ought to understand quantum mechanics. Not all of the considerations are just scientific ones; some are philosophical (both metaphysical and epistemological). There is just as much debate about quantum cosmology. So we cannot say here that premise (2) is definitely false. What we can say is that it is not undeniably true. Since the causal version of the cosmological argument needs premise (2) to be true if it is going to be a sound argument, that argument has, if not a huge hole in it, at least a chink in its armor.

But suppose premise (2) is true. We are still not done. If premise (3) is false, then the causal version of the cosmological argument will be unsound. If there are just reasonable grounds for doubting premise (3), we cannot be sure the argument is sound. So let us take a closer look at premise (3).

3.4.1.2 Infinity

Several defenses have been given of the claim that there cannot be an infinite series of past causes. For example, Aquinas argued that if there were an infinite series of causes, there would be no first cause and hence no intermediate causes, meaning that there would be no series of causes at all. Others have argued that the series of causes in the cosmos does have one temporal endpoint (namely, now) and so it cannot be infinite. And still others have argued that the very concept of infinity is incoherent.

Yet all of these defenses face a fundamental problem. There is a concept of infinity from mathematics that has been precisely articulated. It is known to be logically consistent and it figures into a vast number of mathematical applications. The mathematicians are perfectly fine with this concept of infinity. So, as

---

[9] A more detailed account of how quantum cosmology is supposed to undermine the causal version of the cosmological argument can be found at https://plato.stanford.edu/entries/cosmology-theology/#4.

[10] Here is a blog entry explaining how the Big Bang might have arisen from nothing: Richard Yonck, "Is All the Universe from Nothing?," *Scientific American*, May 22, 2014, https://blogs.scientificamerican.com/guest-blog/is-all-the-universe-from-nothing.

far as mathematicians are concerned, infinities are possible. If they are possible mathematically, why think they are impossible in reality?

To see how infinities are possible mathematically, we need to look to **set theory**,[11] a branch of mathematics that was developed in the late nineteenth century. It provides a common foundation for arithmetic, calculus, algebra, and all the other branches of mathematics. A set is simply any collection of items. For example, Congress and Parliament can be thought of as sets of elected officials. In your mathematics classes you have probably talked about sets. For example, you may have spoken of an algebraic function like "$x = 5y + 19$" as being a set of ordered pairs: $\{(24, 1), (29, 2), (34, 3), ...\}$. A proper subset of a set S is a set that is included within, but is not identical to, S. For example, the set of all University of Mississippi soccer players is a proper subset of the set of all University of Mississippi students, while the set of all University of Mississippi students who weigh more than three pounds is not a proper subset of the set of all University of Mississippi students.

The notions of set and subset help us generate the following definition: a set S is infinite if and only if there is a proper subset of S whose members can be put into a one-to-one correspondence with the members of S itself. For example, consider the set of all positive integers and one of its proper subsets, the set of all positive multiples of 7.

1	2	3	4	5	6	7 ...		
↓	↓	↓	↓	↓	↓	↓	→	∞
7	14	21	28	35	42	49 ...		

As you can see, every member of the first set can be matched uniquely with a member of the second set. That is what we mean when we say that they can be put into a one-to-one correspondence. The positive integers can be matched uniquely with the positive multiples of 7 even though the set of positive multiples of 7 is a proper subset of (i.e. is included within) the set of positive integers. Such a matching could not occur for the set of whole numbers from 1 to 7,000 because, if we tried to match up the numbers in that set with the multiples of 7 that lie between 1 and 7,000, we would be left with 6,000 unmatched whole numbers. Thus the set of all positive integers is infinite, while the set of all positive integers from 1 to 7,000 is not.

Note that the word used in the definition is "infinite," not "infinity." That is, mathematicians use the adjective, not the noun. "Infinity" is not a number. For the mathematician, there is only the property of being infinite, and only sets can have this property.

---

[11] https://www.britannica.com/topic/set-theory.

Now that we have a grasp of the notion of an infinite set, we are in a position to address a common criticism that has been leveled against the notion of an infinite collection. Suppose there can be sets with an infinite number of members. Suppose, for example, there are two jars of marbles. Jar 1 contains an infinite supply of both red marbles and blue marbles, while jar 2 contains an infinite supply of just red marbles. If both jars contain an infinite supply of marbles, then jar 1 cannot contain more marbles than jar 2. Yet it seems that there must be twice as many marbles in jar 1 as there are in jar 2. Does this show that the notion of an infinite collection is logically inconsistent? No, it does not. The marbles in jar 1 can be put into a one-to-one correspondence with the marbles in jar 2.

jar 1:	red 1	blue 1	red 2	blue 2	red 3	blue 3	red 4	blue 4	...
	↓	↓	↓	↓	↓	↓	↓	↓	→ ∞
jar 2:	red 1	red 2	red 3	red 4	red 5	red 6	red 7	red 8	...

That is, for every marble in jar 1, there is a marble in jar 2. Contrary to appearances, jar 1 does not contain twice as many marbles as jar 2, and so no logical inconsistency arises in saying that both jars have an infinite number of marbles. Thus this objection to the notion of an infinite collection is easily handled by set theory.

Also, there can be infinite sets that are bounded or limited in some way. For example, it is easy to put the positive integers (1, 2, 3, 4, ...) into a one-to-one correspondence with all of the nonzero integers (..., −3, −2, −1, 1, 2, 3, ...). Just match 1, 2, 3, 4, 5, 6, 7, 8 ... with 1, −1, 2, −2, 3, −3, 4, −4 ... So even a series of things with an endpoint can be infinite. Remember, one of the defenses of premise (3) of the causal version of the cosmological argument was that the series of causes could not be infinite because it had "now" as an endpoint. Well, mathematicians are fine with the idea that a series can have an endpoint but still be infinite. The positive integers are just such a series.

Let us review our discussion of infinity. For the causal version of the cosmological argument to be sound, premise (3) must be true. But what we see from mathematics is that there is no good mathematical defense of premise (3). If mathematics alone is our guide to the truth of premise (3), then, we have to judge premise (3) to be false and the causal version of the cosmological argument to be unsound. In other words, if mathematics alone is our guide, it is possible that the universe has no beginning in time and so there is no first cause of it.

It should be noted that some defenders of the causal version of the cosmological argument respond that there is a big difference between a potential infinity and an actual infinity. While potential infinities are possible, they say, actual infinities are not. This is a recurrent theme in the formulations of the cosmological argument that are common in classical Islamic theology. Due to limited space, we will not address this response here.

3.4.2 The Contingency Version of the Cosmological Argument

In response to the difficulties with the claim that there cannot be an infinite series of past causes, some philosophers shift from talking about causes to talking about reasons or explanations. The idea here is that the universe – whether it has a beginning in time or instead has existed forever – is not self-explanatory. Even if the universe has been around forever, it might not have existed at all, or it might have been very different. In a short essay entitled **"The Ultimate Origin of Things,"**[12] the seventeenth-century German philosopher Leibniz conducts a classic thought experiment. He asks us to imagine that a certain book has always existed, with one copy made from the previous copy, and that one from a prior one, and so on, forever.

> It is obvious that although we can explain a present copy of the book from the previous book from which it was copied, this will never lead us to a complete explanation, no matter how many books back we go, since we can always wonder why there have always been such books, why these books were written, and why they were written the way they were. What is true of these books is also true of the different states of the world … however far back we might go into previous states, we will never find in those states a complete explanation for why, indeed, there is any world at all, and why it is the way it is.

Behind Leibniz's intuition is the idea of a <u>contingent being</u> – a thing that, though it does exist, might not have existed. You, for example, are a contingent being. Consider how easily you might not have existed. Your parents might never have been born. They might never have met. The particular egg (one of hundreds of thousands) and the particular sperm (one of millions) that combined to form you might never have done so. The insight of Leibniz is that, even if the universe is eternal, it is still contingent. It might have been very different. It might have been very different even if it is eternal in the same way that the series of books might have been very different even if it has been around forever.

For example, the universe has three spatial dimensions. Why? Well, "because it has always had three spatial dimensions" is not a satisfactory answer. We can imagine a universe with more or fewer spatial dimensions. For another

---

[12] Leibniz's short essay "The Ultimate Origin of Things" can be found at http://www. earlymoderntexts.com/assets/pdfs/leibniz1697b.pdf.

example, the force of gravity is exactly what it is, not much greater (so that we would all get squished) or less (so that we would all float away). We can imagine a universe in which gravity is much stronger than it actually is. So why is the force of gravity what it is and not something else? We can even imagine that there is no universe at all. So why is the universe the way it actually is rather than some other way? These all seem to be perfectly sensible questions. And that is why Leibniz (and many others) regard the universe as contingent.

Connected with the notion of a contingent being is the notion of a dependent being. Let us say that a being X depends on another being Y when X cannot exist unless Y exists. For example, waterfalls depend on water; waterfalls could not exist unless water exists. Note that dependence is not always a two-way street. Water could exist even if there were no waterfalls. Note also that this relationship of dependence can exist even if the related things are eternal. Here is another thought experiment to show that. Suppose that somewhere there is a garden that has existed for all of eternity. This garden is fed by a natural spring. The plants in the garden would die if they were not constantly being watered by the natural spring. Luckily, the natural spring has also existed for all of eternity. If there were no spring, there would be no garden, but without the garden there would still be a spring – even though both are eternal.

3.4.2.1 The Principle of Sufficient Reason

Leibniz thought that, even if the cosmos is eternal, it still would be contingent. It would depend on something other than itself. This other thing would have to be God. Why did he think that? Maybe the universe just is, without any explanation or reason. Maybe it is just a brute fact that there is a cosmos with precisely the features of our universe.

Leibniz rejects this possibility. He endorses something he called the principle of sufficient reason: for every truth there is a sufficient reason for why it is true, and for every being there is a sufficient reason for why it exists rather than not. (The word "sufficient" here is being used in the sense defined in Chapter 1. Your being over two feet tall is a sufficient reason for your being over one foot tall just because being over two feet tall guarantees being over one foot tall.) According to the principle of sufficient reason there are no brute facts. It is important to note that Leibniz is not saying that we humans can find a complete reason for everything. Some things happen for reasons we can never know. Leibniz is fully aware of that. He is just saying that there is a reason, whether or not we can discover it.

3.4.2.2 From the Principle of Sufficient Reason to God

If we grant that the principle of sufficient reason is true and that the cosmos is a contingent being – a thing that might not have existed – we can, says Leibniz, conclude that there exists a noncontingent being. That is, we can conclude that there exists a <u>necessary being</u> – a being that not only does, in fact, exist, but that could not have failed to exist. This being is not contingent and its existence is not just a brute fact. And this being, Leibniz thought, just is God. Here is his argument.

The Contingency Version of the Cosmological Argument

(1) The cosmos exists and is contingent.
(2) There is a complete explanation for why the cosmos exists. (This is a consequence of the principle of sufficient reason.)
(3) The cosmos cannot be explained in terms of an infinite series of contingent beings behind it, because there would be no explanation for the existence of the entire series.
So, (4) There must be a noncontingent being – a necessary being – in terms of which the existence of the cosmos is explained (God).

We have already talked about the reasons for saying premises (1) and (2), but notice this new premise (3). What is the justification for that?

Well, suppose that every being *were* contingent and that every being depends for its existence on some other contingent being. Then we would have an infinite series of contingent beings, each one explained in terms of the one before it. Leibniz's imaginary infinite series of books is supposed to be analogous to this. We can think of all the contingent beings as forming an infinite chain. The cosmos would itself be a link in this chain. According to the principle of sufficient reason, there must be a complete explanation for why that chain exists, as opposed to some other chain, or no chain at all. That is, there must be some being on which the chain depends. But that being cannot be a part of the chain itself. If it were, the chain would depend on only itself and nothing else. It would be an <u>independent being</u>, not a dependent being. So the chain must depend on some being that is not a part of the chain. But since the chain contains all and only the dependent beings, any being that is not on the chain must not be dependent. That is, it must be an independent being and not a contingent one.

The opposite of a contingent being is, as we have seen, a necessary being – more specifically, a *logically* necessary being. A logically necessary being not only exists, but *must* exist. A logically necessary being could not fail to exist and does not depend for its existence on any other being. Logically necessary existence, then, is a stronger concept than aseity. Aseity is just uncreatability combined with inde-structibility. But aseity is compatible with the possibility of nonexistence. Aseity is compatible with God's existence just being a brute fact. As we have seen, many theists are not satisfied with the notion that God's existence is just a brute fact.

Now it just so happens that God – at least as God is traditionally thought of by many theists – is also supposed to be a necessary being. So here we have a partial match between our description of God on the one hand and the being mentioned in the conclusion of the contingency version of the cosmological argument on the other. So the contingency version of the cosmological argument seems to give us a strong reason to believe that God exists. Of course, it is a leap to go from the conclusion that there is a necessary being to the conclusion that the necessary being is God. Perhaps the necessary being that explains the cosmos is ignorant of many things, is evil, or is of limited power. However, we will set this problem (which is just the identification problem we mentioned earlier) aside and consider other objections to the argument instead.

3.4.2.3 Objections to the Argument

The eighteenth-century Scottish philosopher **David Hume**[13] objected that, if we can explain the existence of each individual member of the chain of things that do or ever have existed in the universe, it is unreasonable to go further and demand an explanation for the chain as a whole. To see what he was getting at, consider the following fictional dialogue:

Ancil: Where did you come from? What is the story about your existence?
Booze: That is an interesting question! Hmmm. My mom and my dad got together, and, well … you know. They "did it." You know the rest of the story: conception, pregnancy, childbirth. And that is why I am here!
Ancil: Of course! But where did *they* come from?
Booze: Well, my mom came from my mom's mom and my mom's dad, and my dad came from my dad's mom and my dad's dad. After that, the story is the same as the one I just gave you.
Ancil: Listen, Booze, you are not grasping what I am getting at. You can tell me your ancestry every step of the way, listing two people, then four, then eight, then sixteen, and so on as long as you like. But no matter how far back you go, you will not be answering my question. I want a complete explanation of where you came from. You are not giving it to me.
Booze: Well, Ancil, that is not what any normal person would mean by asking me that question. You mean your question in a very weird way. I cannot answer it, I do not even see how I could possibly answer it to your satisfaction, and I do not see why you are bothering to ask me it. Either ask me a different question or leave me alone.

Hume shares Booze's attitude. The sort of explanation being demanded by Ancil is not a normal one. Likewise, says Hume, the question for which Leibniz

---

13 https://www.britannica.com/biography/David-Hume.

wants an answer is just a bad question. There is no need to answer it. Why does the universe exist at all? Why is it the way it is and not some other way? Hume thinks these are abnormal questions, and furthermore that any answer we give to them will just raise the same questions all over again.

However, saying that the questions motivating the contingency version of the cosmological argument are bad ones is not a refutation of the argument. A much stronger criticism is offered by the contemporary philosopher Peter van Inwagen. He says that the argument is implicitly self-contradictory. The conclusion of the argument is that there exists a necessary being, and that this necessary being is the sufficient reason for the existence of the cosmos. But if the existence of God is a sufficient reason for the existence of the cosmos – if God's activity completely explains the existence of the cosmos – and if it is necessarily true that God exists, then it is necessarily true that the universe exists and is the way it is. This contradicts the initial premise of the argument, premise (1), that the universe is contingent rather than necessary.

This is a difficult point to grasp, but maybe another thought experiment can help us understand things better. Suppose you believe just what Leibniz believed. You believe in the principle of sufficient reason. That is, you believe that there is a complete explanation for everything, whether we know it or not. This means that there is a complete explanation of why God created the universe and of why the universe is precisely this way and not some other way. Likewise, however, there must be a complete explanation for all of God's decisions. The principle of sufficient reason does not have an exception built in for God.

In that case, though, there would have to be a complete explanation of every particular fact about God's relation to the world. For example, there would have to be an explanation of why God made Moses the leader of the Israelites rather than picking someone else for that job. If you asked God "Why Moses?", God would have an answer. (You may not get it if you asked, but God would have an answer.) And the same goes for every other activity, decision, and utterance of God. But if we keep applying this way of thinking, we reach the conclusion that God had a sufficient reason for doing everything God has ever done, ever does, and ever will do, and for doing it exactly the way God did, does, and will do it. God was guaranteed to do exactly what God did and could not have done anything differently. But (given that God necessarily exists) this would just mean that the cosmos could not have failed to exist and could not have been in any respect different from the way it is. In that case, though, the cosmos would be a necessarily existing being, not a contingently existing being as was originally supposed.

It seems that, if the principle of sufficient reason were true and applies to all aspects of God, and if everything were dependent on God, then nothing could be different in the slightest. Trying to avoid the objection by saying God's activities and decisions are an exception to the principle of sufficient reason is *ad hoc*. So it seems we have a dilemma: either the principle of sufficient reason is false or necessitarianism is true. Necessitarianism is the view that every feature of reality, down to the smallest detail, is necessarily what it is and could not have been the slightest bit different. Some notable philosophers have been necessitarians – for example, Baruch Spinoza and (perhaps) Leibniz himself. But for most philosophers necessitarianism is a very big pill to swallow. If the choice is between being a necessitarian and abandoning the principle of sufficient reason, most philosophers will abandon the principle of sufficient reason. And if that goes down, then so does the contingency version of the cosmological argument.

3.5 Concluding Thoughts on the Ontological and Cosmological Arguments

We have just looked carefully at two classical arguments for the existence of God. As we saw, while both of them rested on intuitively plausible ideas, both of them also fell victim to very serious criticisms. In retrospect, the criticisms all stemmed from a feature common to both arguments: both were highly abstract and very detached from ordinary experience. The ontological argument is entirely *a priori*. None of its premises are such that you need to experience anything to know that they are true. Meanwhile, although both versions of the cosmological argument are technically *a posteriori*, the empirical evidence needed to get them going is minimal. You do not need to know much to know that there are things that exist! If theists want a more successful argument for the existence of God, perhaps they ought to look in a different direction. Perhaps they ought to look to concrete experience, and to science in particular. As we will see in Chapter 4, that is precisely the approach taken by proponents of the design argument.

Annotated Bibliography

O'Connor, Timothy (2008). *Theism and Ultimate Explanation* (Malden, MA: Blackwell).
    This is a novel reformulation of the cosmological argument. The author takes care to address the identification problem at length in chapter 4.

Oppy, Graham (2006). *Arguing About Gods* (New York: Cambridge University Press).
    This is a comprehensive and critical analysis of just about every philosophical argument for the existence of God. Chapter 2 covers the ontological argument, while chapter 3 covers the cosmological argument.

Rowe, William (1998). *The Cosmological Argument* (New York: Fordham University Press).

Rowe thoroughly analyzes the cosmological argument, including the principle of sufficient reason and the idea of a necessary being.

Sennett, James, ed. (1998). *The Analytic Theist: An Alvin Plantinga Reader* (Grand Rapids, MI: William B. Eerdmans).

This is a collection of some central essays from Alvin Plantinga, one of the most important contemporary philosophers of religion. Essay 3 is "The Ontological Argument," and essay 8 is "Necessary Being."

Sobel, Jordan Howard (2004). *Logic and Theism: Arguments For and Against Beliefs in God* (New York: Cambridge University Press).

This book was mentioned in Chapter 2. Chapters 2–4 are concerned with versions of the ontological argument, and chapters 5 and 6 with versions of the cosmological argument.

Taylor, Richard (1983). *Metaphysics*, 3rd edn (Englewood Cliffs, NJ: Prentice Hall).

This is an excellent introduction to basic topics in metaphysics. For students seeking a deeper understanding of the cosmological argument, chapter 10 is a great place to start.

van Inwagen, Peter (1993). *Metaphysics* (Boulder, CO: Westview Press).

This introductory book is engagingly written and has many provocative thought experiments. Chapter 5 covers the ontological argument, and chapter 6 the cosmological argument.

4

THE DESIGN ARGUMENT FOR THE EXISTENCE OF GOD

We have just looked carefully at two arguments for the existence of God. Both of them are deductive arguments. The ontological argument is also an *a priori* argument – that is, all of the premises are knowable by reflection and intuition alone. In that sense, the ontological argument does not at all depend on the results of observation and experience. In particular, it does not depend at all on what science tells us. The cosmological argument is not, strictly speaking, an *a priori* argument. But, for each version, the *a posteriori* premise in it is a very general statement. For the causal version, it is "There are things that come into existence." For the contingency version, it is "The cosmos exists and is contingent." In both cases, you do not need to do any sort of detailed scientific investigation to discover that the premise is true. Even before the scientific method was developed, people knew that the cosmos existed and that there were things that came into existence.

The last argument for the existence of God that we will examine is very much unlike these other two arguments. It is inductive, not deductive. Furthermore, it relies heavily on the discoveries of science – indeed, on some of the most advanced science in the world. The central idea is that, through scientific investigation, anyone can see that the universe is not the sort of place that could have arisen by chance. Its overall structure, as well as certain specific structures within it, had to have been designed by some being outside of the universe. That being, it is argued, is probably God.

4.1 The Basic Idea Behind the Design Argument

If you have taken a college biology class, or just watched the television channel Animal Planet, you may have been struck by the startling complexity and

---

This Is Philosophy of Religion: An Introduction, First Edition. Neil A. Manson.
© 2021 John Wiley & Sons, Inc. Published 2021 by John Wiley & Sons, Inc.

adaptation of living organisms. **Lyre birds have the ability to imitate perfectly any sound they hear.**[1] **Cuttlefish can camouflage themselves to near perfection.**[2] **Aeronautical engineers could learn a thing or two from eagles.**[3] From the grandest mammal to the lowliest cell, life displays an intricacy and structure that would put a high-paid design team to shame. How could such fantastically organized, complex structures arise at all? How could life emerge out of unintelligent matter?

Speaking of matter, why is *it* the way it is? Although it is unimaginably vast, our universe has precise features. So does the matter within it. A glance at the inside back cover of a college physics textbook shows that **there are extremely precise numbers describing the fundamental properties of matter.**[4] These include numbers for the speed of light in a vacuum, for the masses of the fundamental particles (electron, proton, neutron, etc.), and for the strengths of the forces (gravity, electromagnetism, etc.) that act on those particles. These numbers seem completely arbitrary. For all we know, they could have been totally different. Yet they turn out to be exactly what a universe needs in order for complex life to emerge in it.

Likewise, the cosmology section of an astronomy course will teach you that there are very precise values for the temperature of the universe, for how much matter there is per cubic centimeter in the universe, for the rate at which the universe is expanding, and so on. And those numbers also need to be just right if our universe is to be habitable by beings like us. How did those numbers get to be what they are? Were they just magically pulled out of a cosmic hat at the Big Bang? Or did someone choose them for a purpose?

If you have ever asked yourself these sorts of questions, you are not alone. Scientists, philosophers, and theologians throughout much of history have asked the very same questions. And throughout that history one of the most popular ways to answer them has been in terms of God. On this way of thinking, just as an arrow in a bull's-eye requires a skilled archer, a universe with the just-right properties of ours requires an intelligent being to pick them out. Just as a watch requires a watchmaker, goes the thinking, life requires a designer. This is the basic idea behind what philosophers call the **teleological argument**[5] (from the Greek word *telos*, meaning "end" or "purpose"). It is more widely known as the design argument for the existence of God.

---

[1] A lyre bird can imitate, among other sounds, that of a chainsaw: see https://www.youtube.com/watch?v=VjE0Kdfos4Y.

[2] https://www.youtube.com/watch?v=pgDE2DOICuc.

[3] A bird's-eye view of life as an eagle: https://www.youtube.com/watch?v=G3QrhdfLCO8.

[4] A handy all-in-one-place list of the constants of physics: https://physics.info/constants.

[5] https://plato.stanford.edu/entries/teleological-arguments.

Proponents of the design argument say that the universe and the intricate structures in it could not have arisen by chance. Chance making our universe would be like a magical whirlwind blowing through a dorm room – a whirlwind that left every bed made and put every empty pizza box in a trashcan. Such an event is just far too improbable to happen by chance. If chance is not an option, then only intelligence is left as an explanation of all of the apparent design in the universe. This intelligence would have to exist outside of our universe in order to act upon it, and would have to be immensely powerful and knowledgeable in order to create something as vast, complex, and orderly as our universe. According to proponents of the design argument, a supernatural, super-powerful, super-knowledgeable intelligence who created our world – a world of tremendous richness and beauty – would almost certainly have to be God.

4.2 William Paley's Analogical Version of the Design Argument

Variants of this line of thinking can be found as far back as the ancient Greek era, but the classic statement of the design argument was by an English priest and philosopher, **William Paley**,[6] in his book *Natural Theology* (published in 1802). Paley spelled out the <u>analogical version of the design argument</u>. (We saw a variant of that argument in Chapter 1, where we called it "An Inductive Argument for the Existence of a Creator.")

The Analogical Version of the Design Argument

(1) Devices like watches are complex things: all of their parts are finely adjusted so that they can perform functions such as keep time.

(2) Complex devices do not just appear naturally, but rather are created by intelligent beings who engineer them with the goal of their fulfilling particular purposes.

(3) Organisms are complex things: all of their parts are finely adjusted so that they can perform functions like seeing, hearing, and flying.

So, probably, (4) Organisms were created by an intelligent being who engineered "them with the goal of there being living things."

Note that, in the conclusion, the statement is prefaced with "probably." Paley did not say that the conclusion follows with logical certainty. That is why the argument is classified as inductive rather than deductive. But, Paley thought, the premises very strongly point toward the conclusion, and any reasonable

---

[6] https://www.britannica.com/biography/William-Paley.

person ought to accept the conclusion given the premises. Let us now look more carefully at his reasoning.

Paley started with an analogy between finding a watch out in the middle of nowhere and finding intricacies in nature such as eyes, wings, and circulatory systems. Think of an **old-style wind-up watch with gears and springs**.[7] It is a finely calibrated, complex item that serves a function. Complex functional objects clearly do not just pop into existence naturally in the middle of nowhere. If you find a watch, you can infer that an intelligent creator of the watch exists or existed.

Furthermore, you should infer this even if there are some imperfections in the watch and even if the watch has some functions that are unknown to you. If the watch does not keep perfect time, or if it has a small, useless-seeming knob on it, you would still think the watch was designed. What if it somehow happened that we discovered the watch was actually reproduced from a prior watch? Paley imagines that we found a watch with a hatch in the back. Somehow, inside the watch, there is a mechanism for creating a smaller watch – a "baby" watch – so that the "mother" watch occasionally spits out a miniaturized duplicate of itself. Would that explain away the existence of the mother watch? Perhaps the mother watch came from a prior watch, just as the baby watch came from the mother watch. But would that be a satisfactory explanation? Paley says it would not be, because we would still need an explanation of how the original watch got *its* structure. If anything, we would have even more to explain – not just how a watch got to be out in the middle of nowhere, but how any watch got to have the ability to reproduce itself.

Paley said analogous reasoning justifies us in concluding that there is or was a designer of the intricate functional objects found in nature. We can conclude there was a designer acting in the biological realm even if certain structures within an organism are imperfect. (Biology is full of imperfect structures such as the human back, which is not quite ideal for walking erect and which is highly susceptible to injury.) And Paley also thought that we can conclude that there was a designer acting in the biological realm even if certain structures within an organism have no function (like the human appendix). For much of the rest of his book, Paley went through case after case of intricate, organized, and well-designed biological structures.

To see what Paley was thinking, consider the mammalian eye. The similarity between the structure of the eye and the structure of a camera is uncanny. From a design standpoint, it is practically just like a camera. Both have lenses, light sensors (rods and cones for the mammalian eye versus film for a camera),

---

[7] The inside of a pocket watch is dissected in this video. It is pretty amazing how humans could make such intricate devices such a long time ago: https://www.youtube.com/watch?v=QWboEcgVdTk.

and so on. Paley saw all of this functional detail in biology as screaming out "design!" He was not alone. Particularly because of the development of microscopes, the biologists of the seventeenth and eighteenth centuries were stunned at the geometric regularity and apparent design of the parts of living creatures. They just could not see how these intricate, machine-like structures could arise by natural processes. From their perspective, conscious design by God was the only alternative.

4.3 David Hume's Criticisms of the Analogical Version of the Design Argument

We will consider an alternative, scientific explanation of design in nature (namely, evolution by natural selection) shortly. But, in terms of pure philosophy, there is still plenty of room to criticize Paley's argument. These criticisms were spelled out by the Scottish philosopher **David Hume**[8] in his book *Dialogues Concerning Natural Religion*[9] (published posthumously in 1779). Note that Hume's work was published nearly a quarter-century before Paley's. Versions of the design argument were quite popular even before Paley's book was published.

4.3.1 The Identification Problem

Many of Hume's criticisms are instances of what we have already called the identification problem (in Chapter 3). Why think that the terms "the designer of the universe and the life within it" and "the supreme eternal being who knows everything and can do anything" refer to one and the same individual? Why should we identify the designer with God? The evidence of design does not rule out designers other than God. Indeed, when we consider the imperfections of the world, says Hume, the analogy should lead us to conclude that the designer of the world is an imperfect being, not a perfect one like God. Hume suggests in *Dialogues*, part 5, that the universe might even be the product of some "infant deity" or of "several deities [who] combine in contriving and framing the world." To Hume, our universe looks as though it could have been designed by a committee of juvenile architects!

---

[8] https://www.britannica.com/biography/David-Hume.
[9] The full text of *Dialogues Concerning Natural Religion* is available at http://www.earlymoderntexts.com/assets/pdfs/hume1779.pdf.

In connection with this, Hume imagines inspecting a really bad, run-down building – a building that is drafty, poorly lit, and poorly ventilated, with crooked steps and doors that do not fit into the doorframes. If we had to guess, we might grudgingly admit that someone or other designed the building. But we would never infer that the world's greatest architect had done the designing (maybe a malicious or incompetent architect, but not a great one). The building is not nearly good enough. If we were told that **I. M. Pei**[10] designed the building, well, *maybe* we could reconcile that with what we observe. As one of the world's greatest architects, Pei might have had a building plan we nonarchitects just cannot understand. Pei knew a lot more about architecture than we do. So, if we had some independent evidence that Pei had designed the building, such as a plaque on the building with his name on it, then maybe we could manage to believe that the building was designed by one of the world's greatest architects after all. But if we did not have any independent evidence – if all we had to go on was the building itself – then there is no way we would say it was designed by one of the world's greatest architects.

Hume suggests that the same point works against the design argument. People like Paley are not asking us to *reconcile* the observed world with belief in God. They are asking us to *infer* the existence of a perfect being from the observed world. It is not that people like Paley are calling our attention to the universe – a universe that includes coronaviruses, catastrophic hurricanes, deadly wildfires, devastating earthquakes, and other horrors – and saying, "It is *not impossible* that God created this world." They are calling our attention to the universe and saying "God *almost certainly* created this world." Hume insists we cannot draw this conclusion. He thinks a perfect being could and would have made a much better universe.

4.3.2 Anthropocentrism

Hume also suggests that the design argument involves another mistake. To see what that mistake is, think first about a different mistake: egocentrism. Some time in your life – maybe after you acted in a particularly selfish way – you may have heard someone say "You think the whole world revolves around you." At that moment, you were just accused of egocentrism. A person is guilty of egocentrism if they overrate their own importance in the grand scheme of things. Likewise, a person is guilty of anthropocentrism if they overrate the importance of human beings in the grand scheme of things (*anthropos* is Greek for "human").

Hume alleges that proponents of the design argument mistakenly regard human beings, or human attributes such as intelligence and thought, as the be-all and end-all of the universe. Proponents of the design argument think

---

[10] https://www.britannica.com/biography/I-M-Pei.

they see design in the universe, but Hume suggests that they are just projecting design upon the universe. They see intelligence and thought as the most important aspects of the universe, but in reality intelligence and thought are no more special than anything else – in the grand scheme of things. "What peculiar privilege has this little agitation of the brain which we call *thought*, that we must thus make it the model of the whole universe?" Hume asks in part 2 of *Dialogues*: "Our partiality in our own favor does indeed present it on all occasions, but sound philosophy ought carefully to guard against so natural an illusion." Hume illustrates this point at the end of part 7 with an analogy: If there were talking spiders, he suggests, they would say that the universe was created for spiders by a spider-like being; we would say that those spiders are just projecting their own preferences and biases onto the universe. Hume thinks that we humans do the same thing when we endorse the design argument.

Indeed, Hume goes so far as to suggest that the reasoning behind the design argument is theologically offensive. The basic idea behind the design argument is that the universe is very unlikely to be the way it is if it had arisen by chance, but that it is extremely likely to be the way it is if God had created it. But who are we to say what God would or would not be likely to do? None of us is God, so none of us can say what God would or would not be likely to do. Hume suggests that, when a person tells us what God would do, they are really telling us what *they* would do if *they* were God. That, he suggests, would be presumptuous – as believers in God should agree. The source of that presumptuousness is, once again, anthropocentrism. "By representing the Deity as so intelligible and comprehensible, and so similar to a human mind," Hume writes at the end of *Dialogues*, part 3, "we are guilty of the grossest and most narrow partiality, and make ourselves the model of the whole universe." If we did not have such an inflated opinion of ourselves and of our species, he suggests, we would never go along with the design argument.

4.4 The Theory of Evolution

Some philosophers regard Hume's objections to the design argument as completely devastating. Yet, however convincing his philosophical rebuttals may be, they still do not explain where biological complexity came from. For many people, Hume's objections do not put the design argument to rest. Indeed, the biologist **Richard Dawkins**,[11] one of the world's foremost defenders of the theory of evolution by natural selection, says that it was hard to be an atheist prior to the publication of **Charles Darwin**'s[12] book *On the Origin of Species*. However

---

[11] https://www.britannica.com/biography/Richard-Dawkins.
[12] https://www.britannica.com/biography/Charles-Darwin.

right Hume may have been on an abstract level, organisms certainly *look* like they were designed, says Dawkins, but Darwin showed us a mechanism for the development of life that made divine intervention unnecessary. After Darwin, Dawkins argues, all of the complexity of life could be understood in terms of a few basic principles operating over enormous periods of time. Eyes, wings, circulatory systems, and all of the other complex structures of life could now be explained as products of undirected nature alone, unaided by God. Through the process of evolution by natural selection, nature itself becomes "**the blind watchmaker.**"[13]

4.4.1 The Basic Principles of Evolutionary Theory

To see how evolutionary explanations work, consider an analogy. Suppose you were a con artist who wants to get an unsuspecting victim to give you a lot of money. What might your scam be? Here is a tried and true method. First, come up with the number of consecutive correct predictions about the daily overall performance of the Dow Jones Industrial Average ("the Dow") that it would take to convince someone that you are a brilliant stock market analyst. Suppose you were to convince someone you are a brilliant stock market analyst by correctly predicting for them whether the Dow increases or decreases in value every day for two weeks. Two weeks is ten business days. What could you do to ensure that you made 10 straight correct predictions about the Dow? Call up 2^{10} people (i.e. 1,024 people). Tell half of them that the Dow will go up tomorrow and half of them that it will go down. If it goes up, do not call back anyone in the second group; only call back people in the first group. If it goes down, do the opposite. Repeat this procedure until you get to the tenth day. At the end of the 10 days you will have progressed from 1,024 people who have heard *no* correct Dow predictions from you to one person who has heard *10* correct Dow predictions from you! That person may very well come to believe that you are a brilliant stock market analyst and be eager to give you a lot of money to invest.

If you were to do this, would it mean that you were a brilliant stock market analyst? Absolutely not. What you would be is an ordinary scam artist who has created the *appearance* of being a brilliant stock market analyst. How did you create this appearance? By using three tools. First, you employed a large number of trials. You gave yourself 1,024 customers to work with. By patiently making phone calls to such a large number of people, you generated enough chances for you to correctly predict the Dow 10 times in a row. Second, you introduced variation in your answers. Each day, you gave one answer to half of the people and

---

[13] Here is a retrospective on the publication of Richard Dawkins's *The Blind Watchmaker*: https://www.theguardian.com/science/2010/apr/30/richard-dawkins-blind-watchmaker.

a different answer to the other half. Third, you employed a selection mechanism. The actual performance of the Dow on a given day selected which people to call back. With these three tools, you generated the appearance of intelligence, even though in reality you were no better at predicting the Dow than a cat.

Darwin pointed out that these three factors operate in nature. First, there is a large number of trials, in that there is an enormous number of organisms produced via reproduction. For example, you may have heard the figures about how, if every fly egg survived to become an adult fly, in a few months the whole earth would be covered with flies. This would happen because flies reproduce at a rate far greater than is necessary just to replace the flies that die.

Second, in nature there is variation, and that variation is usually heritable. Just as no two humans are exactly alike, no two flies are either. We now know that this variation is caused by random mutations in DNA, but even in Darwin's time it was clear that an organism's offspring displayed considerable variation among themselves and that some of these variations were more or less suited to the environments in which the offspring found themselves. A classic example from Darwin concerned the **beak sizes of Galapagos finches**.[14] Longer beaks may be better suited than shorter beaks to extracting food from certain plants, while shorter beaks may be better suited than longer beaks for cracking open nuts. But since there is variation in beak size among finch offspring due to random mutations, both long beaks, which are suitable for food extraction. and short beaks, which are suitable for nut cracking, will be produced.

Third, resources are limited out in the wild. Some animals are better suited to getting hold of those resources than others. Thus there is a selection mechanism in place – **natural selection**[15] – for organisms that are better suited to their environments. If disease leaves only nut-producing plants on an island, the finches with beaks unsuited for cracking nuts will starve to death. Furthermore, these traits are heritable. The genes for short beaks will be passed on, while the genes for long beaks will not.

4.4.2 Evolution and Paley's Argument

Darwin gave a simple, elegant explanation for why the beaks of certain Galapagos finches are so perfect for cracking open nuts. If the beaks of their ancestors were

---

[14] William J. Cromie provides a more detailed explanation of the variation of beak sizes in Galapagos finches in "How Darwin's Finches Got Their Beaks," *Harvard Gazette*, July 24, 2006, https://news.harvard.edu/gazette/story/2006/07/how-darwins-finches-got-their-beaks.

[15] A more detailed explanation of natural selection can be found at https://evolution.berkeley.edu/evolibrary/article/evo_25.

not fit for cracking open nuts, those ancestors would have starved before they could reproduce. So we will see only finches that look as if they were designed for their environments. And this sort of explanation applies to life forms more generally. Just as, in our earlier example, you created the appearance of intelligence in your investment scam (in the form of Dow predictive ability) using a large number of trials, variation, and selection, so nature creates the appearance of design (in the form of extremely well-adapted organisms) by large numbers of offspring, genetic variation, and natural selection. Organisms will *look as though* they were designed by an extremely intelligent designer, but the appearance masks reality.

There is overwhelming evidence favoring Darwin's theory of evolution by natural selection, including the fossil record, the discovery of DNA, and observed cases of evolutionary adaptation. Evolution is the central organizing fact in contemporary biological science, and **Darwin's ideas have been profoundly influential both within and outside of biology.**[16] The theory of evolution by natural selection is not **just a theory.**[17] Given this support for evolutionary theory, it looks as though Paley's analogical version of the design argument fails. We cannot infer the existence of God from apparent biological design because, in light of the theory of evolution, we see that apparent design is really only that – apparent, not real.

4.5 Evolution and Belief in God

Does this failure of Paley's design argument show that God does *not* exist? No. All it shows is that the existence of apparent design in biology does not force us, intellectually, to believe that God *does* exist. The situation here is similar to that of a prosecutor who has failed to obtain a conviction. The failure of the prosecution just means that the prosecutor did not *prove* that the defendant was guilty. But the lack of a compelling case for guilt is not the same thing as a compelling case for innocence. So, for all that has been said thus far, the truth of the theory of evolution is perfectly consistent with belief in God. The truth of evolutionary theory does not show that God does not exist. It only shows that one widespread argument for God's existence – Paley's analogical version of the design argument – does not work.

---

[16] The evolutionary biologist Ernst Mayr explains in an accessible article how Darwin's theory revolutionized not just biology, but all of modern thought: "Darwin's Influence on Modern Thought," Scientific American, November 24, 2009, https://www.scientific-american.com/article/darwins-influence-on-modern-thought.

[17] The US National Academy of Sciences has an article rebutting the claim that evolution is "just a theory": "Evolution and Society: Introduction," http://www.nas.edu/evolution/TheoryOrFact.html.

4.5.1 Creationism

Are there any other reasons for thinking that one cannot believe both that the theory of evolution is true and that God exists? This question has provoked intense discussion ever since the theory of evolution gained wide acceptance. Creationism is the view that the biblical account of the six-day creation of the world presented in the book of Genesis is literally true, with God directly creating each type of plant and animal and the heavens and the Earth being less than 10,000 years old. (The position is sometimes also called "young earth" creationism, to reflect the belief that the earth is much younger than today's geologists tells us it is.) Creationism was quite a popular position before Darwin presented his theory of evolution, partially because God's having directly created life seemed to be the best explanation available of the sorts of structures in biology to which Paley called our attention. Even after Darwin, some theists defended creationism, and **there are still many creationists around today**.[18] Yet, even in ancient times, theists such as the fourth-century Christian bishop and theologian **St. Augustine**[19] recognized the enormous problems with the claim that the book of Genesis is literally true.

Creationism is clearly inconsistent with the theory of evolution, simply because the theory of evolution says that all living beings came to have the features they have by a process radically different than direct creation by God. However, creationism is also inconsistent with many other scientific findings. For example, our best geological theories tell us that the earth is around 4 billion years old, while the best current theory of the origin of the universe – the Big Bang theory – says the universe is about 13 billion years old. Both geology and cosmology imply that the age creationists assign to the earth and the universe is off by a factor of 1 million. If the scientific claims are correct, creationism is wrong. So evolutionary theory is not *uniquely* inconsistent with creationism. The creationist will have to see many theories of modern science as a threat to a literal interpretation of scripture, and not just evolutionary theory.

4.5.2 Theistic Evolutionism

Does belief in God require acceptance of creationism? If so, then the theory of evolution will be inconsistent with the belief that God exists. But whether it really does is a highly controversial matter. Theistic evolutionism is the view that God created the universe sufficiently many billions of years ago, allowing

---

[18] Perhaps the leading creationist organization online is the Answers in Genesis ministry: https://answersingenesis.org.

[19] https://www.britannica.com/biography/Saint-Augustine.

enough time for a long evolutionary process to produce all life eventually (without any special interventions or acts of creation by God). For the theistic evolutionist, God wanted there to be human life – or at least intelligent, conscious life of some sort – and God used the process of evolution by natural selection to bring about that goal. God set up the world so that the evolutionary process would happen and human life would come to exist eventually. Theistic evolutionists see design in the world, but at the level of the universe as a whole, not at the level of biological life. (Many of them thus support the fine-tuning argument; we will discuss that argument shortly.)

Theistic evolutionism obviously avoids inconsistency with the theory of evolution. The whole point of theistic evolutionism is to be the version of theism that fully accommodates evolutionary theory. The question for theistic evolutionists, though, is whether their approach effectively abandons core commitments that any believer in God should have. For example, if there was no special creation of humans by God (as indicated at the beginning of the book of Genesis), when exactly did our ancestors acquire souls? Theistic evolutionists typically respond to these sorts of questions by saying that not all parts of scripture were meant to be interpreted literally. These disputes about what is required for fidelity to scripture and for genuine belief in God are matters of the particular version of the monotheistic faith in question. As such, they lie beyond the scope of this book. The simple point to remember is that whether the theory of evolution is inconsistent with belief in God depends on a number of other religious presuppositions. The assumption that no one can believe in both God and evolution is not necessarily true.

4.6 Modern Versions of the Design Argument: Preliminaries

After Darwin, most philosophers, theologians, and scientists thought the theory of evolution removed any scientific basis whatsoever for belief in a designer of the universe. The design argument was dead, they thought, and Darwin had buried it. Since the 1960s, however, the design argument has undergone a tremendous resurgence. The developments have come on several scientific fronts, but we will focus on new discoveries about the universe as a whole from the scientific fields of particle physics, astronomy, and cosmology. These discoveries have fueled the claim that the universe was fine-tuned for life by God.

Before we look at this new argument, however, we must appreciate another way in which contemporary versions of the design argument differ from older ones such as Paley's. Modern varieties of the design argument typically are not arguments from analogy. Paley tried to show that parts of organisms were very similar in appearance and structure to various products of human design. However, modern versions of the design argument typically are framed in terms of numerical probabilities. More specifically, they are usually **Bayesian inferences**.[20] Learning about Bayesian inferences will help us understand not only these new versions of the design argument, but also a variety of other arguments that occur in contemporary philosophy of religion (some of which may come up in your "Philosophy of Religion" class). So let us take some time to understand those inferences more clearly.

4.6.1 Bayesian Inferences

Bayes's rule[21] is a formula in the mathematical theory of probability. It was discovered by **Thomas Bayes**,[22] an eighteenth-century English clergyman. Bayes's rule shows how we might revise, in the light of new evidence, the probabilities we initially assigned to competing hypotheses. Many contemporary philosophers think that we should (as much as we can) evaluate the impact of new evidence using Bayes's rule. They advocate what is called **Bayesian epistemology**.[23] To get a sense of **how Bayesian reasoning works**,[24] we are going to work through an example. It involves a little math, so be patient and attentive.

Imagine that you are following the final round of a low-level professional golf tournament – the Bayes Open – in which there are 100 golfers, one of whom you know is Tiger Woods, golf's greatest of all time (GOAT). In golf tournaments there is always a leader board, which tells you who is in the lead and by how much. Unlike the leader board of a typical golf tournament, however, imagine that the leader board for this tournament does not identify the players by name but rather by number. Next, imagine that you do not know Woods's number. Finally, suppose that the golfer at the top of the leader board

---

[20] Bayesian inferences are explained in this podcast: https://youarenotsosmart.com/2016/04/08/yanss-073-how-to-get-the-most-out-of-realizing-you-are-wrong-by-using-bayes-theorem-to-update-your-beliefs.

[21] https://plato.stanford.edu/entries/bayes-theorem.

[22] https://www.britannica.com/biography/Thomas-Bayes.

[23] https://plato.stanford.edu/entries/epistemology-bayesian.

[24] If you would like to hear someone walk you through an explanation of a similar case, watch this video explaining how Bayesian reasoning helps you to understand the significance of your getting a positive test for the coronavirus: "False Positives & Negatives for COVID-19 Tests: Using Bayes' Theorem to Estimate Probabilities," https://www.youtube.com/watch%3Dv%3FVuskwsIW02M.

is golfer 93, who is leading by 20 strokes. So imagine that the first four lines on the leader board look like this:

Leader Board

Player	Strokes	Place
Golfer 93	−24	First
Golfer 18	−4	Second
Golfer 51	−3	Third
Golfer 29	−2	Fourth

Now consider the following hypothesis (call it W for "Woods"), the following bit of data (call it L for "leading"), and the following statement of what you know about this golf tournament (call it G for "golf").

W = Golfer 93 is Tiger Woods.

L = Golfer 93 is leading by 20 strokes.

G = There are 100 numbered professional golfers, but none of them are especially good except Tiger Woods, the GOAT.

What is the relationship between W, L, and G? To answer this, it will be help-ful to use the following notation for conditional probability. Let $P(x \mid y)$ stands for the probability of x given that ("conditional on") y. For example, P(you get an A on your final | you got As on your midterm and on all of your quizzes) is simply the probability that you get an A on the final, given that you got As on your midterm and on all of your quizzes.

Now, knowing nothing else about golfer 93 except that they are one of 100 professional golfers, you think that Golfer 93 has one chance in 100 of being Woods. Woods is going to be assigned a number from 1 to 100, so he has the same chance of being assigned any particular number: one in 100. So, prior to getting any information about how golfer 93 is doing, you think

$$P(W \mid G) = 1\% = 0.01$$

This is what Bayesians would call the "prior probability" – the probability you assigned to the proposition that golfer 93 is Woods *prior to* acquiring the new information that golfer 93 has a 20-stroke lead.

But now you see on the leader board that golfer 93 is leading by 20 strokes. This is an extremely large lead for a professional golf tournament, so a golfer who could build such a lead would have to be much, much better even than the typical professional golfer. You think Tiger Woods could build such a lead because you think he is the GOAT, and you also doubt that anyone other than Woods could build such a lead. So you think the probability of a 20-stroke lead being built by golfer 93, conditional on golfer 93 being someone *other than*

Woods, is extremely low. Let us say that you think the odds of this are one in 10,000. So you think

$$P(L \mid \text{not-W \& G}) = .01\% = 0.0001$$

At the same time, you think the probability of a 20-stroke lead being built by golfer 93, conditional on golfer 93 *actually being Tiger Woods*, is fairly high. Let's say you think the odds of this are one in 100. So you think

$$P(L \mid W \& G) = 1\% = 0.01$$

In light of looking up at the leader board and gathering evidence L, you realize that you should assign a much higher probability to W than you did prior to looking at the leader board. In other words, you think that finding out that golfer 93 has built a 20-stroke lead is great evidence that golfer 93 is, in fact, Woods.

So, while you used to think that there was only a 1% chance that golfer 93 is Tiger Woods, now you think the chances are much greater that golfer 93 is Tiger Woods. This new probability is what Bayesians call the "posterior probability" – the probability that you assign *after* you get the new evidence about the identity of golfer 93.

But exactly how much higher should this posterior probability be? This is the crucial question that Bayes's rule helps you answer. Call the probability that golfer 93 is Woods and leads by 20 strokes the "particular probability," and call the probability that *any* of the golfers leads by 20 strokes the "total probability." Bayes's rule says that the posterior probability is simply equal to the particular probability divided by the total probability. In this case, the posterior probability is P(W | L & G); it is the probability that golfer 93 is Woods, given your background knowledge and the fact that golfer 93 has a 20-stroke lead. P(W | G) × P(L | W & G) is the particular probability; it is the probability that golfer 93 is Woods (given just your knowledge of the structure of the golf tournament) multiplied by the probability that Woods would build a 20-stroke lead in this tournament. The total probability is [P(L | not-W & G) × P(not-W | G)] + [P(L | W & G) × P(W | G)]; it is the probability that *any* golfer (whether or not it is Woods) would build a 20-stroke lead. In this case, the total probability is just the sum of two probabilities: the probability that golfer 93 is Woods and leads by 20 strokes, plus the probability that golfer 93 is *not* Woods and leads by 20 strokes.

Using Bayes's rule, we can now say what the new probability is:

posterior probability = particular probability/total probability
= (0.01 x 0.01)/[(0.0001 x 0.99) + (0.01 x 0.01)]
= 0.0001/0.000199
= 0.5025 = around 50%

That is, in light of the fact that golfer 93 built a 20-stroke lead, and given everything else you believe about the golf tournament, Bayes's rule tells you that there is about a 50% chance that golfer 93 is Tiger Woods. You started off thinking that there was only one chance in 100 that golfer 93 is actually Woods. But, after seeing how well golfer 93 is doing, you ought to bump it up to one chance in two that golfer 93 is actually Woods. By concluding that there is a 50% chance that golfer 93 is Woods, you just made a Bayesian inference.

Mathematicians, logicians, philosophers, and psychologists all agree that, if you want to reason well when it comes to probability, you ought to master Bayesian inferences. Some philosophers and psychologists go further. They advance the controversial claim that, subconsciously, we are making Bayesian inferences all of the time. It is not controversial to say that Bayesian inferential programs are and will remain at the heart of modern learning computers and artificial intelligence. If humans ever develop machines that think, you can be pretty sure that those machines will be exceptional at performing Bayesian inferences.

4.6.2 The Generic Bayesian Design Argument

Many contemporary proponents of the design argument say that new scientific evidence shows that the universe has very special features. These features, they say, are extremely improbable unless an intelligent designer like God has built them into the universe. In light of this new scientific data, they say, we should revise upward the probability that God exists. The general structure of their arguments is exactly like that of the argument for thinking that golfer 93 is Tiger Woods.

As with the Tiger Woods argument, these arguments are framed in terms of three statements. The first is some statement of our background scientific knowledge (call it K), regarding our best overall scientific understanding of the world, including physics, biology, astronomy, and so on. The second is a statement of the evidence of design (call it E), about how some feature of the universe had to be just right for there to be intelligent, conscious living beings such as ourselves. We will look at some of this alleged new evidence of design in section 4.7. The last is some design hypothesis (call it D), some statement about the nature, powers, and purposes of some supernatural intelligent being such as God. There are many possible design hypotheses. Perhaps a malevolent demon created the world. Perhaps a super-scientist in some alternative reality made a new universe come into existence. For ease of discussion, however, we will simply assume that the design hypothesis in question just is the hypothesis that God exists. The proponent of a Bayesian design argument would then make the following three claims.

First, the probability of the evidence of design, given our background scientific knowledge, and assuming that God does *not* exist – expressed symbolically as $P(E \mid K \,\&\, \text{not-}D)$ – is extremely low. It is exceptionally unlikely that the conditions of the universe and the life within it turned out right just by chance. Note that this is analogous to the claim that it is extremely unlikely that any golfer other than Woods would build a 20-stroke lead.

Second, the probability of the evidence of design, given our background scientific knowledge, and assuming that God *does* exist – expressed symbolically as P(E | K & D) – is quite high. In other words, it is pretty likely that things would turn out just right for the existence of life in the universe if God directed things. This is analogous to the claim that it is not too unlikely that Woods would build a 20-stroke lead.

Third and finally, it is *more* likely that God exists than that things in the universe turned out just right by chance; this is expressed symbolically as saying that P(D | K) is considerably greater than P(E | K & not-D). This is analogous to the claim that it is more likely that golfer 93 is Woods (1% chance) than that some golfer other than Woods built a 20-stroke lead (.01% chance). Claims (1), (2), and (3) together are the premises in a generic Bayesian version of the design argument.

The Generic Bayesian Design Argument

(1) P(E | K & not-D) is extremely low.
(2) P(E | K & D) is quite high.
(3) P(D | K) is considerably greater than P(E | K & not-D).
So, (4) P(D | E & K) is quite high.

In plain English, the argument is that the new scientific evidence of design strongly confirms the belief that God exists. So, whatever one's prior probability was that God exists, one's posterior probability – the probability one has *after* hearing about the new scientific evidence – ought to be much higher.

With this framework in place, a host of new versions of the design argument can be generated, with each particular version distinguished by the scientific evidence at the heart of that particular version. One notable version appeals to evidence from biochemistry and molecular biology. Its proponents argue that certain "irreducibly complex" structures within cells cannot be explained in terms of evolution by natural selection. The only way to explain these structures, according to this version, is in terms of the designing activity of a supernatural agent of great power and intelligence. This version of the design argument has come to be called *intelligent design theory*. It is scientifically controversial because it contradicts evolutionary theory. It is politically controversial (in the United States, at least) because teaching it in public schools as an alternative to evolutionary theory allegedly violates the separation of church and state. However, due to limited space, we will not discuss this particular version of the design argument in detail. Instead we will focus on the version that is turning into the most popular scientific argument nowadays for the existence of God: the fine-tuning argument.

4.7 The Fine-Tuning Argument

In the twentieth century a series of breakthroughs in physics and astronomy led to the development of the Big Bang theory of the origin of the universe – the theory that, about 13 billion years ago, the observable universe emerged from an unimaginably small, infinitely dense point. As they came to know the specific features of the universe much better, the relevant scientists (physicists, astronomers, and cosmologists) discovered that the universe is highly structured. It has precisely defined <u>cosmic parameters</u> – qualities such as the age, mass, curvature, temperature, density, and rate of expansion of the universe as a whole. Looking at the very precise values of these cosmic parameters, some of these scientists asked, "How would the universe have been if the values of these parameters had been slightly different?" The answer surprised many of them. The universe would not have been the sort of place in which life could eventually emerge. The numbers describing the universe, scientists discovered, were like the just-right spot on an old-style radio dial: you had to tune the radio just right to avoid the static and get meaningful sounds instead. As a result, many physicists started describing the values of the parameters as "fine-tuned for life." The overall discovery usually goes under the description "**cosmic fine-tuning**."[25]

4.7.1 Examples of Fine-Tuning for Life

To give just two of many possible examples of fine-tuning for life, the cosmological constant (symbolized by the Greek letter Λ) is a crucial term in **Albert Einstein's**[26] equations for the general theory of relativity. When Λ is positive, it acts as a repulsive force, causing space to expand. When Λ is negative, it acts as an attractive force, causing space to contract. If Λ were not exactly right, either space would have expanded at such an enormous rate that complex objects would never have had a chance to form any time after the Big Bang, or the universe would have collapsed back in on itself almost immediately after the Big Bang. Either way, life could not possibly have emerged anywhere in the universe. Some calculations put the odds that Λ has just the right value at well below one chance in a trillion trillion trillion trillion.

Similar calculations have been made showing that the odds of the universe having the right kind of stars is also unimaginably small. Amazingly, **every molecule in your body contains elements that were formed inside a star**.[27] Carbon, oxygen,

---

[25] https://plato.stanford.edu/entries/fine-tuning.

[26] https://www.britannica.com/biography/Albert-Einstein.

[27] Simon Worrall's article "How 40,000 Tons of Cosmic Dust Falling to Earth Affects You and Me" explains how all the heavier elements in your body were created inside stars: https://news.nationalgeographic.com/2015/01/150128-big-bang-universe-supernova-astrophysics-health-space-ngbooktalk.

iron, calcium – none of these elements existed at the beginning of the universe. They all came into existence only after the stars formed them and then ejected them when they eventually exploded. If the universe did not have the sorts of stars that engage in the process of nucleosynthesis, there would be no carbon, no oxygen, no iron, no calcium – and so no life like ours anywhere in the universe.

4.7.2 The Basic Reasoning Behind the Fine-Tuning Argument

How are these cases of fine-tuning for life supposed to support the belief in God? The reasoning goes like this. Having the cosmic parameters take values that lead to a universe that can support life is sort of like winning the Range Game on the television show *The Price Is Right*. But the odds of winning are much better on the television show than they are with the universe. To be more comparable, the winning window on the Range Game would have to be narrowed from $150 to one cent. And you would have to bid, not on a new car, but on the exact dollar value of all of the gold in Fort Knox, down to the last penny. The odds of winning that game are well over a trillion to one. If you were to win that guessing game, you may very well think that the game was rigged. The same line of thought applies to the universe. Instead of the universe being just right for life *by pure chance*, proponents of this version of the design argument suggest that the universe is just right for life *by design*.

This seemingly improbable adjustment of the cosmic parameters for life is the basis for a new version of the design argument. It is called the **fine-tuning argument**.[28] Note that it follows exactly the same logical structure as the generic Bayesian design argument.

The Fine-Tuning Argument

(1) The probability that the cosmic parameters take values that allow for life in the universe, given everything we know about physics and given that God *does not* exist, is extremely low.

(2) The probability that the cosmic parameters take values that allow for life in the universe, given everything we know about physics and given that God *does* exist, is quite high.

(3) If we set aside the evidence of fine-tuning, it is considerably more probable that God exists than that the cosmic parameters take values that allow for life in the universe just by chance.

So, (4) The probability that God exists, given that the cosmic parameters take values that allow for life in the universe and given everything else we know about physics, is quite high.

---

[28] The Fine-Tuning Argument Project: https://www.thefinetuningargument.com.

As with any version of the design argument, the basic idea is that we observe some special feature of the physical world that just cannot be explained as having arisen by chance. The better explanation, we are told, is that God is responsible for the special feature. In this case, the special feature is the life-permitting character of the universe as a whole. According to proponents of the fine-tuning argument, we should think that it is much more likely that God exists after we have learned the evidence of cosmic fine-tuning than we did before learning the evidence of cosmic fine-tuning. After all, if we believe in God, we will have an explanation of cosmic fine-tuning for life, whereas if we say that the universe is just right for life by pure chance we are stuck believing something incredibly improbable – namely, that we hit the **cosmic jackpot**.[29]

4.8 Miracles and the Fine-Tuning Argument

The fine-tuning argument is one of the most widely made arguments for the existence of God nowadays. One reason for this is that, compared to other arguments for the existence of God and to other versions of the design argument, the fine-tuning argument seems to be fully harmonious with a scientific worldview. In particular, it seems not to involve saying that, at some point in history, God miraculously intervened in the workings of the natural world. In this section, we will look a bit more closely at this supposed virtue of the fine-tuning argument. Before we do so, though, we need to answer a more basic question. What is it for some event to be a miracle?

4.8.1 Defining "Miracle"

A consequence of God's omnipotence is the ability to determine what the **laws of nature** are – things like the universal law of gravitation, the laws Albert Einstein laid out in his special and general theories of relativity, the laws of quantum mechanics, and so on.[30] As the fine-tuning argument presupposes, these laws are contingent. One of God's powers is the ability to determine these basic rules for reality. If the rules could not have been different, it would not make much sense to marvel at how they are exactly right for life to develop in the universe. But since God ordained those rules, it seems that God is not bound by them. **God could, if God wanted to, part**

---

[29] There is a book on the fine-tuning argument with precisely that title, Paul Davies's *Cosmic Jackpot* (New York: Orion).

[30] https://plato.stanford.edu/entries/laws-of-nature.

the Red Sea,[31] either for the sake of accomplishing some goal or just to send a message. And that is just what a **miracle** is supposed to be: an event that violates one or more of the laws of nature in such a way as to indicate some divine purpose.[32]

In ordinary language, of course, we use the word "miracle" much more loosely to talk about any good thing that is also surprising or unexpected. For example, there was the **Miracle on the Hudson**, which happened when all the passengers and crew survived a large plane making an emergency landing on the Hudson River in the middle of January 2009.[33] But, heartwarming and inspiring as the story of that event was, it was not a miracle. Commercial airliners are designed to survive emergency landings on water. Airline pilots are trained to perform such landings. The safe emergency landing was well within the realm of possibility. No laws of nature were broken in the course of it. However, if somehow both wings of an airplane fell off at 35,000 feet and, instead of crashing, the plane gently wafted straight down, landing right on time at its designated airport terminal and gate, that would be a miracle (especially the arriving-on-time part).

What this suggests is that mere improbability is insufficient for the occurrence of a good event to be considered a miracle. We talk about "the miracle of life" and "miracle babies" – babies who survived when they were not expected to (because of disease, a difficult pregnancy, war, and so on). But, on the strict definition of "miracle," pregnancy and childbirth do not count as miracles, since they are not in violation of the relevant (biological) laws of nature. And an infant's surviving a grave illness or birth defect, while a wonderful thing, is hardly surprising from a larger perspective. Suppose an infant were given a 1% chance of surviving an illness and did, in fact, survive. Surviving was certainly within the realm of possibility. Events with a 1% chance of occurring happen all the time, especially when we consider the large number of opportunities there are for the occurrence of a one-in-100 outcome. The notion of observational selection effects is relevant here. It is just not true that there are 99 news stories about infants who were given a 1% chance of surviving and then died for every news story there is about an infant who was given a 1% chance of surviving and then lived. If a child is predicted to die and does, we are considerably less likely to read about it. We should keep that in mind when we see stories of "miracle babies."

---

[31] The scene depicting this miracle from the classic Cecil B. DeMille movie *The Ten Commandments* can be found at https://www.youtube.com/watch?v=OqCTq3EeDcY.

[32] https://plato.stanford.edu/entries/miracles.

[33] Here is an explanation of how the pilots pulled off the feat of landing the plane safely on water: https://www.youtube.com/watch?v=4v7kASXPQMc.

The very idea of miracles has historically faced numerous objections. Here we will mention three. First, there is the metaphysical objection that violating a law of nature is logically impossible, since a law of nature is just a codification of whatever actually happens. On this way of looking at things, if we were ever to observe a "miracle," the appropriate response would not be to believe in God, but to revise our understanding of the laws of nature. Second, there is the epistemological objection that a person can reasonably believe that a miracle has occurred only if they think that it would be a bigger miracle that something is wrong with their evidence (e.g. that they are hallucinating or are being somehow tricked). The philosopher David Hume notably argued that this condition can never be met; he concluded that **no one could ever be justified in believing that a miracle had occurred**.[34] Third, there is the objection that the evidence for actual, particular miracle claims (from the most ancient to the most recent) that have been made in the name of the various world religions has never withstood critical scrutiny.

Addressing the metaphysical objection to miracles would involve us in some heavy-duty, oftentimes highly technical, discussion of just what it is for something to be a law of nature. For that reason, we will not look at it further. As for the epistemological objection, it is widely held that Hume's argument is a failure – at least on a straightforward reading of it (as opposed to one where Hume is working with some hidden premises). The final objection is not philosophical but <u>empirical</u>, so it is not appropriate to address it in a philosophy textbook. If you are interested in this, you can look into it yourself; there are many sources available online. **Debunking claims of paranormal activity**, including claims that miracles have happened, is an entire industry.[35] Instead of getting into the weeds regarding miracles, let us turn to the connection between miracles and the fine-tuning argument.

4.8.2 How Miracles Are Avoided by the Fine-Tuning Argument

There is a deep connection between the fine-tuning argument and Darwin's theory of evolution by natural selection. Darwin's whole point was to explain how life could arise without any special acts of creation by God. "No miracles necessary for life" may as well have been his slogan. If you look back at what

---

[34] Hume's argument for this conclusion is in "Miracles," section 10 of *An Enquiry Concerning Human Understanding*: http://www.earlymoderntexts.com/assets/pdfs/hume1748_3.pdf.

[35] The *Skeptical Inquirer*, for example, is a long-running magazine devoted to disproving claims about paranormal phenomena, including alleged religious miracles: https://skepticalinquirer.org.

we have said about the fine tuning argument, there is no mention of the actual, nuts-and-bolts processes by which life first arose and then grew in complexity. That is because, from the perspective of the proponent of the fine-tuning argument, those processes are the subject of modern biology, not of physics and cosmology. In other words, the proponent of the fine-tuning argument presupposes rather than contradicts the theories and discoveries of modern biology. The evidence of fine-tuning *just is* the fact that the universe is so well suited to the occurrence of the evolutionary processes that modern biology describes. Making the fine-tuning argument for God thus seems to be perfectly harmonious with fully accepting modern biology and its miracle-less view of life.

In this regard, it is instructive to compare the fine-tuning argument with intelligent design theory (briefly mentioned earlier in this chapter). Intelligent design theorists assert that, long ago in the mists of evolutionary history (and perhaps more recently), God miraculously assembled irreducibly complex biochemical systems. Without these divine interventions in the workings of nature, they say, complex organisms such as ourselves could never have arisen. If we could have observed with a microscope God's creating of irreducibly complex biochemical systems, we would have seen something happen on a molecular scale comparable to the parting of the Red Sea, or to a magical whirlwind tidying up a dorm room. This reliance on the idea that God miraculously redirected the trajectory of life largely accounts for the rejection of intelligent design theory as unscientific. The thinking is that, if God intervened in nature in this way millions of years ago, we cannot be sure God is not doing the same thing right now – in which case, we cannot do science. The activity of science presupposes that nature is uniform, lawful, and orderly. If intelligent design theorists are correct, that presupposition is wrong. In order to bring about life, God has acted within the universe over much of its history, tinkering with its molecules to bring about complex life.

Proponents of the fine-tuning argument, in contrast, do not locate the act of divine design *within* the universe but *prior to* it. Unlike creationists, they are not saying that God specially created humans in a single act under 10,000 years ago. Unlike intelligent design theorists, they are not saying that God fiddled around with molecules at various points over the last several billion years so that essential components of life would form. All of these would be interventions by God *within* the physical universe after it came into existence, and so would be occurrences that happened in violation of the laws of nature. They would be miracles. Instead, proponents of the fine-tuning argument say that the very structure of the physical universe was itself selected and created by God. Since the creation of the physical universe is not itself something that happens within the physical universe, and since the laws of nature apply only to what happens within the physical universe, it seems that God is not violating any laws of nature by creating a universe that allows for life to develop. In short, God's making the universe fine-tuned for life would not be a miracle. Thus it seems that the fine-tuning argument gives powerful scientific evidence of the existence of God without calling into question the integrity and universality of science. By backing the fine-tuning argument, it would seem that theists can have their cake and eat it too.

4.9 Criticisms of the Fine-Tuning Argument

On the basis of what we have seen so far, it looks as though the fine-tuning argument is a very strong argument for the existence of God. But closer inspection reveals some significant problems. First, there is disagreement about the calculations supporting the claim of fine-tuning. Some physicists say that, within the realm of theoretically possible universes, life-permitting universes are much more numerous than we initially thought. Furthermore, there is an important objection concerning the claim that fine-tuning is improbable. It seems that we cannot really say that fine-tuning is improbable since the range of possible values for the cosmic parameters cannot be well defined. While these objections are interesting, exploring them further would get us into technicalities that not all beginning philosophy of religion students are yet equipped to handle. Instead, we will focus here on three more easily understandable criticisms of the fine-tuning argument.

4.9.1 The Identification Problem Again

First, the fine-tuning argument still faces a problem that is common to all versions of the design argument: the identification problem, which was explained earlier in the chapter. Set aside temporarily any other problems with the fine-tuning argument. Even if all of the premises were true, the most that we can conclude from the evidence of fine-tuning is that some being (or beings) outside of the physical universe is (or are) responsible for the universe being just right for life. But why identify that being with God? Maybe there is more than one fine-tuner. Even if there were only one fine-tuner, maybe it is closer in characteristics to the Flying Spaghetti Monster (Google it!) than to God. Maybe the fine-tuner is not omniscient, omnipotent, and omnibenevolent, but is a mad scientist in another dimension. Some philosophers have even suggested that what we think is a physical universe is actually just a computer program, and **we are living in a simulation.**[36] If that were true, then the creator of the universe would just be some computer

---

[36] The idea that we are living in a computer simulation is explained by Clara Moskowitz, "Are We Living in a Computer Simulation?", *Scientific American*, April 7, 2016, https://www.scientificamerican.com/article/are-we-living-in-a-computer-simulation.

programmer in a higher reality. That these possibilities cannot be ruled out shows that the evidence of fine-tuning by itself does not narrow down the options just to God. So going from "the universe was designed" to "God exists" is a big leap.

4.9.2 Anthropocentrism Again

Another objection common to all forms of the design argument is the anthropocentrism objection, which we also saw earlier in the chapter. The objection, remember, is that the design argument relies upon assuming that conscious, intelligent, human life is special. But why think that? In the case of the fine-tuning argument, we are assuming that there is something special about a universe that allows for the development of the only sort of intelligent life we have ever experienced: carbon-based life. But what if non-carbon-based life forms are possible? What if life could emerge from silicon? What if there could be life on the surface of a neutron star? What if there could be life in a reality with a totally different set of rules of physics? If scenarios such as these are possible, then maybe the values of the cosmic parameters in another possible universe could be very different from the values those parameters take in our universe, and yet intelligent life could emerge in that other universe. Perhaps we think that our universe is fine-tuned for intelligent life only because we are focused on life that is like us. Maybe we are blind to those other possibilities because we are anthropocentric.

4.9.3 The Multiverse Hypothesis

Perhaps the most common criticism of the fine-tuning argument is that it assumes that our universe is the only universe. Some physicists deny this. They say that **the existence of other universes is a natural consequence of much of contemporary physics**.[37] According to the **multiverse hypothesis**,[38] there is a mechanism for the production of a vast multitude of universes. These universes vary randomly in their basic characteristics. Most of them are duds – for example, they recollapse a few milliseconds after the Big Bang. But there are

---

[37] Philip Ball, "Why There Might Be Many More Universes Besides Our Own," BBC, March 21, 2016, http://www.bbc.com/earth/story/20160318-why-there-might-be-many-more-universes-besides-our-own.

[38] A simplified account of the multiverse hypothesis: Tim Folger, "Science's Alternative to an Intelligent Creator: The Multiverse Theory," *Discover*, November 10, 2008, http://discovermagazine.com/2008/dec/10-sciences-alternative-to-an-intelligent-creator.

enough of them to make it likely that at least one of them has just the right conditions for the evolution of life. Just as with evolutionary explanations in biology, multiverse explanations in cosmology rely on three factors: a large number of trials, variation, and a selection mechanism.

4.9.3.1 The Anthropic Principle

But how would the existence of a multiverse explain why the cosmic parameters in *our* universe are just right for life? The answer is given in terms of a new kind of selection principle: not natural selection, but observational selection. An <u>observational selection effect</u> is any dynamic that filters a subject's experiences based on the need for certain conditions to be met in order for the subject to have those experiences. That definition is pretty abstract, but an example will help illustrate it. If you have ever watched a parkour or freerunning video, you may have wondered "How is it possible that all of those people completed all of those amazing stunts?" But that is not the right question to ask. The right question to ask is "How is it possible that I am observing a video of all of those people completing all of those amazing stunts?"

Once you frame the question that way, the answer is clear. The people you see make many videos of themselves. They try over and over until they get it right. The failures do not end up on the parkour videos you see; only the successes do. (Some of the failures do end up on parkour fail videos, and those are really funny!) A precondition for ending up on a parkour video is that the attempted stunt is completed successfully. If the attempt were not a success, you would not see it. Likewise, part of the reason a fashion model looks so good in the photographs you see is that the photographer takes a large number of pictures. The photographer selects only the best photos for publication. If a photograph is not good, you will not see it.

There is a similar observational selection effect that affects us humans when we engage in physics, astronomy, and cosmology. We are guaranteed to observe that the universe meets whatever conditions are necessary for there to be life in it, simply because if the universe did not meet those conditions, we would not be around to observe the universe! The **anthropic principle**[39] tells us that we should remain aware of this observational selection effect when we try to understand the significance of the observed fine-tuning of the cosmic parameters for life. According to proponents of the multiverse hypothesis, if there are many other universes, then probably at least one of them is just right for life. Keeping the anthropic principle in mind, they say, we will realize that a fine-tuned universe is the only kind of universe we could possibly observe.

---

[39] https://plato.stanford.edu/entries/cosmology/#AnthReasMult.

4.9.3.2 Undercutting the Fine-Tuning Argument

If this reasoning is solid, then it seems we have a non-religious explanation of the universe being just right for life. If the multiverse hypothesis is true, there is no need to bring God into the picture. There are countless other universes. Most of them do not permit life, but a few do. We observe a life-permitting universe only because, if it were not life permitting, we could not exist in it and so we would not be around to observe it. Notice that what we have here is an explanatory strategy very much resembling Darwin's. The multiverse plays the role of the massive replicator with random variations, but the things there are vast numbers of are not fly larvae or Galapagos finches, but universes! The anthropic principle alerts us to an observational selection effect that plays the same role in the multiverse theory that natural selection plays in evolutionary theory. Just as the appearance of design in biology was explained away by Darwin, the appearance of design in the universe is explained away by the multiverse plus the anthropic principle. In neither case does God figure in the explanation.

4.9.3.3 Evidence for the Multiverse Hypothesis

You may have noticed, though, that there is a big difference between the multiverse hypothesis and the theory of evolution. With evolution, we can see the fly larvae, the baby finches on the Galapagos Islands, and so on. We already know that there exist massive numbers of offspring that are necessary for the evolutionary explanation to make sense in biology. But do we have any independent evidence for the existence of the multiverse? Defenders of the fine-tuning argument (as well as many neutral observers) say we do not. They say that **the multiverse hypothesis is unscientific because it is untestable.**[40] Some go so far as to say that the multiverse hypothesis was dreamed up by irreligious physicists simply to avoid the obvious conclusion that God exists. It is, they claim, the last resort of the desperate atheist. Defenders of the multiverse hypothesis respond that it is perfectly scientific, and that it is possible to gain observational evidence of the existence of other universes. Some even say that **there is already evidence for the existence of parallel universes.**[41] Since this dispute is almost entirely scientific, we cannot address it here.

---

[40] Sarah Scoles's article illustrates the criticism that the multiverse hypothesis is untestable: "Think BIG! Can Physicists Ever Prove the Multiverse Is Real?" *Smithsonian Magazine*, April 19, 2016, https://www.smithsonianmag.com/science-nature/can-physicists-ever-prove-multiverse-real-180958813.

[41] Stuart Clark explains why some astronomers think they have already detected evidence of parallel universes in "Multiverse: Have Astronomers Found Evidence of Parallel Universes?" *The Guardian*, May 17, 2017, https://www.theguardian.com/science/across-the-universe/2017/may/17/multiverse-have-astronomers-found-evidence-of-parallel-universes.

4.10 Concluding Thoughts on Arguments for the Existence of God

In this and the previous chapters, we have addressed three arguments for the existence of God: the ontological argument, the cosmological argument, and the design argument. As we saw, all of them make intriguing points, but none is without weaknesses. So far, not one of them is convincing enough to change the mind of the philosophically astute atheist. Perhaps this is to be expected. A prominent philosophy professor once made a wry and wise observation. While philosophers may fantasize otherwise, a philosophical argument is never such that, if you read it and do not agree with the conclusion, your head explodes. Instead, the best you can hope for is that it bolsters the confidence of those who already agree with you, and maybe gives your opponents some reason to second-guess themselves.

So let us just stipulate that some theists have philosophical reasons for believing that God exists, but that there is considerable debate about whether these reasons are good or not. What about the other side? Are there good philosophical reasons for believing that God does not exist? What do the atheists have to say in defense of their position? We turn to these questions in Chapter 5.

Annotated Bibliography

Behe, Michael (1996). *Darwin's Black Box: The Biochemical Challenge to Evolution* (New York: Simon & Schuster).

This is the book that really started intelligent design theory. Behe articulates the irreducible complexity concept, argues that biochemistry shows that there are irreducibly complex biological structures, and claims that this is evidence of the existence of an intelligent designer.

Dawkins, Richard (1986). *The Blind Watchmaker: Why the Evidence of Evolution Reveals a Universe Without Design* (New York: W. W. Norton).

A notable atheist, Dawkins presents a powerful case that evolutionary theory upends the design argument in biology.

Holder, Rodney D. (2004). *God, the Multiverse, and Everything: Modern Cosmology and the Argument from Design* (Burlington, VT: Ashgate).

This is a comprehensive discussion of the fine-tuning argument from someone who is both an ordained priest and a physicist.

Leslie, John (1989). *Universes* (New York: Routledge).

Leslie exhaustively presents the fine-tuning data from physics and gives clever arguments for both the design hypothesis and the multiverse theory. It is the seminal book in philosophy on the fine-tuning argument.

Lewis, Geraint F. and Luke A. Barnes (2016). *A Fortunate Universe: Life in a Finely Tuned Cosmos* (Cambridge: Cambridge University Press).

Written by two physicists, this book contains the most up-to-date evidence of fine-tuning available. It is also engaging and written for a popular audience.

Manson, Neil A., ed. (2003). *God and Design: The Teleological Argument and Modern Science* (New York: Routledge).

This is a comprehensive anthology covering the science and the philosophy behind both the fine-tuning argument and intelligent design theory. It also includes a separate section on the multiverse theory.

Miller, Kenneth (2008). *Only a Theory: Evolution and the Battle for America's Soul* (New York: Penguin).

Miller, a biologist, opposes intelligent design theory and defends theistic evolutionism as an acceptable alternative for theists.

Plantinga, Alvin (2011). *Where the Conflict Really Lies: Science, Religion, and Naturalism* (New York: Oxford University Press).

Written by one of the foremost analytic philosophers of religion, this book addresses all of the issues that came up in this chapter. It includes a broader discussion of the relationship between Christianity and science, especially the theory of evolution.

Ruse, Michael (2000). *Can a Darwinian Be a Christian?* (Cambridge: Cambridge University Press).

The title is self-explanatory. Ruse is one of the foremost philosophers of biology and also has great historical knowledge of how Christian thinkers responded to Darwin's theory.

5

ATHEISM, THE PROBLEM OF EVIL, AND THE PROBLEM OF RELIGIOUS DIVERSITY

The word "atheism" derives from the Greek construction *a* + *theos* + *ism* – in English, "non" + "god" + "belief." Therefore an atheist is a nonbeliever in God. But how, precisely, does someone end up as a nonbeliever in God? Well, the situation with atheists is much the same as the situation with theists in this regard. Some people are theists because they were born and raised that way. The same is true with some atheists. Some people are theists because of the positive personal experiences they have had, either in direct encounters with other theists or with their synagogue, church, or mosque. Likewise, some people are atheists because of the negative personal experiences they have had with individual theists or with religious organizations. Finally, just as some people are theists because they have been convinced by at least one of the arguments for the existence of God, others are atheists because they see compelling arguments against the existence of God. Before we examine these arguments, however, let us look a little more carefully at the varieties of atheism.

5.1 Two Kinds of Atheism

As we saw, "atheism" means "non(God belief)." But that formulation presents an ambiguity. If your friend is a nonsmoker, does that mean that they just so happen not to smoke? Or does it mean that they are actively opposed to smoking? Likewise, if your friend is an atheist, does that mean that they just so happen not to believe in God? Or does it mean that they actively reject belief in God? Let us mark off these two different ways of being an atheist. We will call the first "absence-of-belief atheism" and the second "positive atheism."

This Is Philosophy of Religion: An Introduction, First Edition. Neil A. Manson.
© 2021 John Wiley & Sons, Inc. Published 2021 by John Wiley & Sons, Inc.

Absence-of-belief atheism is simply not having a belief in God. One way to lack belief in God is to be an agnostic. Agnosticism is the view that the question of whether or not God exists simply cannot be answered. (The word "agnosticism" is, again, a construction based on Greek: *non + knowledge + belief*. The word *gnosis* is Greek for "knowledge.") Agnostics do not take a stand on the existence of God. They stay on the fence – not because they lack the will to make up their minds, but because they think the evidence cannot justify forming a definite belief either way.

Another way to lack belief in God is simply to be unaware of the concept of God. There have been many people in human history who have been unaware of the concept of God. The idea of just one supreme being has not always been around. Even today, some people are raised in environments where they never encounter the idea of God – for example, because they are trapped in countries ruled by dictatorships such as North Korea. Because of their environment, believing in God just does not occur to them.

Positive atheism, however, is being acquainted with the notion of God and having a belief about God – namely, that God does not exist. People end up being positive atheists for all sorts of reasons, from bad personal experiences with churches and religious people to abstract arguments against the existence of God. Because the causes of positive atheism are so various and because this book is about the *philosophy* of religion, we will focus here on the arguments that positive atheists make against theism. Furthermore, because it gets tedious to write "positive atheist" over and over, the word "atheist" will be used hereafter to refer only to positive atheists, not to absence-of-belief atheists.

So what, exactly, are the reasons atheists give for thinking that God does not exist or for thinking that belief in God is irrational? Let us take a closer look.

5.2 Philosophical Underpinnings for Atheism

For many atheists, their atheism has grown out of their beliefs about epistemology. As we saw in Chapter 1, epistemology is the field of philosophy that concerns questions about knowledge, belief, justification, and rationality. Many atheists endorse some form of **evidentialism**[1] in epistemology. That is, they think that, for a belief to be reasonable, it must be backed up by evidence, and that it is wrong to believe something without adequate evidence. (We will look at epistemology and religious belief more carefully in Chapter 6.) How does this commitment to basing beliefs on evidence lead some people to atheism? Here are five ways.

---

[1] There is a lengthy discussion of evidentialism in this encyclopedia entry on religious epistemology: https://plato.stanford.edu/entries/religion-epistemology.

5.2.1 Lack of Empirical Evidence of God's Existence

If you have taken a class in logic, you were probably taught that there are many logical fallacies. Logical fallacies are just common patterns of mistaken reasoning. One of the most common logical fallacies is called <u>argument from ignorance</u>. The mistake is thinking that the absence of evidence for a proposition P is evidence that P is false. Arguing from ignorance is obviously not a valid form of inference. Most of you have no evidence that the mayor of your town does not hate you, but that is no reason to think that the mayor of your town hates you.

Yet there is a similar kind of reasoning that is not logically fallacious. If you have no evidence for P even after fairly and thoroughly looking for such evidence, and if you have good reason to think that some evidence for P would have been found if P were true, then you have evidence that P is false. For example, imagine that you are back in seventh grade and that you secretly like Shelby. You wonder whether Shelby likes you too. So you look carefully for evidence. You let it be known to mutual friends that you like Shelby. You send a friend request to Shelby on Facebook. You give Shelby a Secret Santa gift in December, with telltale signs that the gift came from you. In February you follow up with a little card on Valentine's Day. Despite all this, you hear nothing back from Shelby. There is a total lack of evidence that Shelby likes you, despite your repeated efforts to find that evidence. What can you conclude? You can conclude that probably Shelby does not like you. As the example shows, moving from the absence of evidence for P to the falsity of P can be a good inductive argument *if* you have looked carefully for evidence that P is true and *if* you would expect to find that evidence if P were true.

Many atheists hold that the situation with God is even worse than the situation with Shelby. Not only is there no concrete evidence that God likes them, but there is no concrete evidence that God even exists. They say that they have looked for empirical evidence of God but have not found any. (Remember that "empirical" means "verifiable by observation and experience.") They have looked for evidence of miracles but they think that in every instance the alleged miracle did not actually occur. They have prayed for things to happen but they regard their prayers as never having been answered. "Even when I pray for good, unselfish things such as that a sick person might recover or that a drought-stricken area gets rain," they say, "nothing really happens. Oh, sure, sometimes sick people get better and sometimes drought-stricken areas get rain – but never in a way that indicates my prayers made any difference. Healings and cases of drought relief do happen, but they happen with no pattern. They are completely random. That is not what you would expect if God were in control, but it is what you would expect if the only forces at work in the world were the blind forces of nature." That is how many atheists see things.

They expect certain observable consequences if God exists, but they do not see those consequences. So, for them, the concrete, observable evidence they would need to believe in God is just not there, and the lack of it points to God's nonexistence.

5.2.2 Lack of Good Philosophical Arguments for God's Existence

For atheists, all of the arguments for the existence of God – including the ones that were discussed in Chapters 3 and 4 – are failures. After looking at all the arguments, you may have found at least one of them pretty convincing. For example, you might have done some additional poking around after reading about the fine-tuning argument and concluded that it is a pretty strong argument. Cosmic fine-tuning for life, you might think, is pretty good evidence of God. Well, for atheists, none of the arguments for the existence of God are like that. Indeed, many atheists contend that the arguments for the existence of God are not just failures but that they are massively, sometimes laughably, bad. They rest on obvious confusions, implausible assumptions, or logical fallacies. (The ontological argument, in particular, comes in for a lot of abuse.) Without a good argument for the existence of God, they say, they have no reason to believe in God. For many atheists, the philosophical evidence for God is just not there.

5.2.3 Philosophical Arguments for God's Nonexistence

For atheists, there are a host of philosophical arguments for thinking that God does not exist. One category of argument was discussed indirectly in Chapter 2. For some atheists, the very concept of God is just not logically consistent. In other words, it is not logically possible that there exists something that is everything God is supposed to be. (See, for example, the books by William Rowe and Jordan Howard Sobel that are included in the bibliography at the end of Chapter 2.) Some people think that nothing could be omnipotent. Others think that nothing could be omniscient and impassible. And still others think that nothing could be omniscient, eternal, and free. Since we have already discussed these problems in Chapter 2, we will not go over them again. Yet there remains a philosophical argument against the existence of God that we have not discussed. It is the argument that, given all the evil and suffering in the world, there does not exist a being that is omniscient, omnipotent, and omnibenevolent (morally perfect). That argument is (strangely) not typically called the argument from evil for the nonexistence of God, but rather "the <u>problem of evil</u>." We will take a closer look at the problem of evil shortly.

5.2.4 Religious Diversity

<u>Religious diversity</u> (sometimes called "religious pluralism") is the fact that there are so many religions, and they are all so different. For many atheists, religious diversity is a powerful reason to reject all religions. For them, there is no reason to believe in God that is not an equally good reason to believe in one of the thousands of other deities that have been worshipped by large numbers of people. Atheists look at religious diversity in the same way as neutral observers look at top American college basketball programs like Kentucky, North Carolina, Duke, and Louisville. To the neutral observer, all the fans of the top programs seem to say the same good things about their own teams and the same bad things about all the other teams. In light of this equivalence, instead of thinking that one top program represents all that is true and good about amateur athletics and none of the rest do, the intelligent observer will conclude that actually none of them do.

Likewise, atheists will say that, when they ask Christians, for example, what evidence there is for thinking that God exists and that Christ was resurrected, they receive evidence that is symmetrical to the evidence offered by Muslims for thinking that Allah exists and that Allah revealed the Qur'an to the Prophet Muhammad. Likewise, they note, Hindus have all sorts of arguments for their beliefs. And so on, and so on, for each of the thousands of religions out there. All religions include claims of miracles allegedly performed by the deity or prophet in question. All of them point to <u>religious experiences</u> or revelations that their followers have had. All of them point to the morally exemplary behavior of members of their religion and to the great deeds done in the name of their religion. And so on and so on.

From the perspective of the atheist, all of these religions have equally good evidence for their truth. But that just means that they all have equally *bad* evidence for their truth. Since these religions cannot all be right, since they have symmetrical sets of evidence, and since we have no reason to believe that one of them must be right and all the rest wrong, the rational thing to believe is that none of them is right. From the perspective of the atheist, the only way for a Christian, Muslim, Hindu, or whoever to get around this problem is to adopt a different standard of evidence for their own religion than for competing religions. (Similarly, fans of North Carolina basketball are hard on Duke but easy on their own team, and vice versa.) It is a typical claim of atheists that, for example, Christians subject Islam to intense critical scrutiny but then completely abandon those standards when evaluating

Christianity itself. For atheists, that is blatantly unfair. They think that no standard of evidence, applied consistently, supports accepting one religion but rejecting the thousands of other religions with comparable bodies of evidence in their favor. For many atheists, that is a decisive reason to be an atheist. Soon we will take a closer look at this objection to theism from the existence of so many different religions. The objection is called "the **problem of religious diversity.**"[2]

5.2.5 Naturalistic Explanations of Religion

Almost every atheist agrees that there is some way to explain religious phenomena that relies solely on natural, physical, scientifically discoverable causes. That is, they endorse some naturalistic explanation of religion. (We will talk more about naturalism in Chapter 7. For now, just think of it as the view that only the natural world exists, so that there are no gods or spirits of any sort.) Specifically with regards to theism, atheists think they can account for why people believe in God in terms of psychology, anthropology, evolutionary theory, and other purely scientific modes of explanation. These explanations, they think, radically undermine belief in God. They compare explaining belief in God naturalistically to debunking a magician. If you see a skilled magician perform their tricks, you might think (though with considerable doubt) that maybe, just maybe they actually have supernatural powers. But once someone shows you exactly how the trick was performed – once someone has broken the spell, so to speak – you will recognize that there is nothing special about the magician and that you have no reason to believe that magic is real. Likewise, some atheists – people like the philosopher **Daniel Dennett**[3] – claim that they can explain belief in God naturalistically and thereby break the spell of religion. By doing so, they think, they remove any reason for theism.

Now that we have a sense of the philosophical bases for atheism, let us look more closely at their specifics. In this chapter we will look at the problem of evil and then the problem of religious diversity. In Chapter 7 we will discuss some of the most commonly provided naturalistic explanations of religion. In between, in Chapter 6, in the course of a broader discussion of epistemology and religious belief, we will look more carefully at evidentialism itself and ask whether it is a good epistemological position.

---

[2] In the literature, "religious diversity" and "religious pluralism" are often used synonymously. For the latter, see https://plato.stanford.edu/entries/religious-pluralism.

[3] https://www.britannica.com/biography/Daniel-C-Dennett.

5.3 The Logical Problem of Evil

The term "the problem of evil" is often used in philosophical contexts to refer to an argument. Where you see the term you may want to mentally substitute the term "the argument from the existence of evil to the nonexistence of God." Since that is such a mouthful, though, we will stick with "the problem of evil." So, what is this argument?

The argument starts with a basic fact: the world is full of evil people and awful events. Then it points to three characteristics of God: omniscience, omnipotence, and omnibenevolence. One version of the argument – the logical problem of evil – is a deductive argument for the nonexistence of God. According to it, it is not logically consistent to maintain that God – an omniscient, omnipotent, and omnibenevolent being – exists and yet there is evil in the world. Another version of the argument – the evidential problem of evil – is an inductive argument for the nonexistence of God. According to it, the existence, nature, and distribution of the evil we see in the world are powerful evidence against the existence of God. Proponents of the evidential argument from evil typically point to particular forms of evil, such as horrendous evils and gratuitous suffering, and claim to see no good reason why God would allow them. Due to limited space, in this chapter we will focus on the logical problem of evil.

The Logical Problem of Evil

(1) There is evil in the world.
(2) If God (an omniscient, omnipotent, and omnibenevolent being) does exist, there would be no evil in the world because: (a) if a being is omniscient, there is no evil it does not know about; (b) if a being is omnipotent, there is no evil it cannot prevent; and (c) if a being is omnibenevolent (wholly good), it would not permit any evil it knows about and can prevent.
So, (3) God does not exist.

This argument is valid. It is an instance of the argument form logicians call *modus tollens*. Here is the form: not-B; if A, then B; so, not-A. As we saw in Chapter 1, though, just because an argument is valid does not mean that the conclusion of it is true. All it means is that, if the premises are true, the conclusion must be true. But are these premises true? Let us take a look at them one by one.

5.3.1 Premise (1): The Nature and Scope of Evil

It seems hard to deny that there is evil in the world. War, slavery, genocide, catastrophes – humans have both brought about and suffered from these evils throughout history. Indeed, some of the people who have lamented the great deal of evil in the world most frequently and most vocally are theists. So it seems obvious that premise (1) of the logical problem of evil is true. But is it so obvious?

5.3.1.1 Evil as the Absence of Good

The early Christian theologian **St. Augustine**[4] proposed that evil is like a hole in the fabric of reality. For St. Augustine, there is no such thing as evil per se. Instead, some of God's creations just do not participate fully in goodness. They do not fully harmonize with the rest of God's creation. This is because absolute perfection is reserved for God alone. All of God's creations must somehow fall short of absolute perfection, otherwise they would not be distinct from God. Here is an analogy. We call the part of a bagel where there is no dough a hole, but there really are no such things as bagel holes. There are merely empty spaces where there could have been dough. (There actually is a cousin of the bagel called the bialy, which has no hole in the middle.) Likewise, St. Augustine thinks, humans label the limitation of goodness "evil," but there really is no such thing as evil. There is only incomplete goodness. For example, we call it an evil that everyone dies eventually. But, on Augustine's way of thinking, death is merely a limitation of a good thing – life – and if it were not for such limitations, we would not be distinct from God.

This is a fascinating proposal both morally and metaphysically; you may want to pursue it more deeply with your instructor. But the idea that evil is not real is pretty hard to swallow. Let us set aside this idea and assume for the sake of argument that there really is such a thing as evil. Is there more we can say about evil other than that it exists?

5.3.1.2 Moral Evil and Natural Evil

Well, it seems that not only does evil exist, but there is a lot of it. In order to get a handle on evil, it will be helpful to look at two basic categories of evil: moral evil and natural evil. Moral evils are evils that result from the free actions of humans (or other free beings). Murders, wars, betrayals are all examples of moral evil. Natural evils are evils that result from the workings of nature. Tsunamis, earthquakes, and epidemics are all examples of natural evil. Even within these categories, it seems there are innumerable instances of evil. To get a better sense of evil, it may help to focus on a particular time frame. Let us take the six-

---

[4] https://www.britannica.com/biography/Saint-Augustine.

month window from July 2017 through December 2017. What notable evils happened during that time?

In July, about 50 people trying to migrate to Spain from North Africa died at sea when their rubber raft capsized. In just one incident in an ongoing crisis affecting hundreds of thousands of ethnic Rohingya, one Rohingya refugee was killed and six were wounded by a mob in Myanmar, who attacked the victims with bricks. The terrorist group Boko Haram attacked an oil-drilling team in Nigeria, killing over 50 people. At least 14 people were killed in a gunfight in Mexico between rival drug gangs. A man in Pennsylvania confessed to abducting and murdering four young men; he buried the bodies on his farm. In August, Hurricane Harvey hit Houston, killing nearly 100 people and destroying thousands of homes. This natural disaster was accompanied by a phenomenon that is typical of natural disasters everywhere: an upsurge of human trafficking, including child sex trafficking. On the other side of the world, floods in India, Nepal, and Bangladesh killed hundreds and displaced millions. September saw Hurricane Maria devastate Puerto Rico. October began with the deadliest mass shooting in US history in Las Vegas. The Hollywood movie producer Harvey Weinstein was exposed as a serial sexual abuser, with the actress Salma Hayek testifying that he threatened to have her killed if she did not have sex with him. This story set off a wave of revelations of sexual harassment, abuse, and assault committed by a string of prominent men in US entertainment, media, and politics. A truck bomb was detonated in Mogadishu, Somalia, killing hundreds of people. In November, tens of thousands of people in Yemen died from disease or starvation as the government of Saudi Arabia refused to lift its blockade of Yemeni ports. An earthquake on the border between Iran and Iraq killed at least 500 people. Over 300 Sufis were gunned down while worshipping at their mosque in Sinai, Egypt. Finally, we get to December. A 10-year-old girl hanged herself as a result of bullying. A report was issued on prison camps in North Korea; a Holocaust survivor said that the conditions were at least as bad as those at Auschwitz. Lastly, wildfires in Southern California did incredible damage and caused an untold number of animals to die from burns and asphyxiation, including horses trapped in their stalls.

We will return to some of these incidents later in the chapter. For now, note a few things. First, the moral evils come in all forms, from torture and slavery as governmental policies (as in North Korea), to lifelong patterns of wrong action (as with Weinstein), to one-time acts of madness (as with the Las Vegas shooter). Second, the natural evils are not so clearly separable from the moral evils. For example, some blame the wildfires in Southern California on bad decisions by humans regarding land development, climate, and fire suppression. Yet there are natural disasters that clearly cannot be blamed on human activity – the earthquake in Iran and Iraq, for example. Finally, while it may be plausible in some cases to say that the victims of evil deserved it or were asking for it, clearly there are cases in which there is no plausible story in which the victims had it coming. It would seem that no one deserves to be shot just for being at a country music concert (which is what happened in Las Vegas). There seems to be no way at all in which a 10-year-old girl deserves to be bullied so badly that she commits suicide.

5.3.2 Premise (2): God's Knowledge of, Power over, and Desire to Eliminate Evil

Clearly there is a lot of evil in the world. So why does God not do something about it? The second premise of the argument is the claim that if God were all God is supposed to be, God *would* do something about it – namely, eliminate it, all of it. Here is the reasoning.

5.3.2.1 Omniscience

God is supposed to know everything there is to know. Now, as we saw in Chapter 2, there are some tricky issues concerning omniscience, for example, whether being omniscient includes knowing things before they happen. We can set aside those complications, however, when it comes to the problem of evil. Even if we were just to consider standard cases of knowledge at a given time, we see that God is supposed to know about every evil or bad occurrence either well before it happens or, at the very least, the moment before it happens. This is the justification for clause (a) of the second premise of the argument: "if a being is omniscient, there is no evil it does not know about."

For example, even if God did not know the intentions of the Las Vegas shooter before the shooter formed the intention to massacre people (perhaps knowing it ahead of time would have robbed the shooter of his free will), God certainly knew what was going on when the shooter purchased his guns and his ammunition. God knew as it was happening that the shooter was bringing weapons up to a hotel room and setting them up next to a window. God knew exactly what was happening right up to the moment when the bullets started flying. Similarly, God knew as it was ticking that a timer was ticking on the truck bomb in Mogadishu. God knew where the bomb was, where the truck was, and where all of the victims were. God certainly knew at least as much about the trajectories of Hurricane Harvey and Hurricane Maria as the meteorologists who were issuing dire warnings at the time. If humans saw the disasters coming, surely God saw them coming too. And God knew that flames were engulfing the barns in which so many horses in Southern California burned to death. If God is omniscient, then God knows everything it is logically possible for God to know about what is happening in the world. That includes knowing all of the horrible stuff.

5.3.2.2 Omnipotence

As with omniscience, so too with omnipotence. God is supposed to be able to make happen anything it is logically possible for God to make happen. Did God have the power to stop the terrible things mentioned earlier from happening? It seems so. God could have made the Las Vegas shooter die before he could carry out his evil scheme. If that is too dramatic, God could have made him trip on the rug and hit his head on a table, knocking himself out. God could have made the guns not fire. Likewise, God could have made the detonator on the truck bomb in Mogadishu fail. Regarding the hurricanes, surely God could have diverted them somewhere along the line, perhaps in a way none of us would even notice. Hurricanes form off the coast of northwest Africa in the eastern North Atlantic Ocean. No one pays any attention to what is going on in those waters until a hurricane gets reasonably big. Surely God could have prevented Hurricanes Harvey and Maria from forming, or have set them off on courses that would not have had them hit Houston and Puerto Rico directly. And so on. Such cases justify clause (b) of the second premise of the argument: "If a being is omnipotent, there is no evil it cannot prevent."

5.3.2.3 Omnibenevolence

What about God's perfect moral goodness? Does a being's omnibenevolence mean that it would not permit any evil that it knows about and can prevent? To answer that question, let us consider what we would say about a human who happened to have the specific items of knowledge and power mentioned earlier. Suppose a police officer knew what the Las Vegas shooter was in the middle of doing. This officer saw all the weapons and ammunition, saw everything being brought up to the hotel room, saw the equipment being assembled by the window, and saw the window being smashed open. Furthermore, suppose the officer had the ability to stop the attack. They could have shot the shooter, or perhaps just hit him with a taser. But now suppose the officer did nothing, and just let the Las Vegas shooter continue. How would we judge the officer morally?

However we would describe the officer – as cowardly, grossly negligent, or morally bankrupt – we would definitely *not* say that they behaved in an exemplary way morally. Their inaction in this case is not the behavior of a morally exemplary person. In normal cases, when you know something really bad is about to happen and you have the ability to prevent it, you prevent it. If you do not, you are not a very good person. And it seems the same goes for all the other cases in which God does not prevent evil. If you had the requisite knowledge and power to prevent any one of the evils mentioned earlier, but you did not, we would almost certainly judge you not to be a morally good person. What kind of person would just let a truck bomb go off, just let a fire burn down a stable and kill all the horses within it, just let a little 10-year-old girl get bullied terribly – especially if that person would not suffer any negative consequences from intervening? If you could stop any of those things, we think, you ought to stop them. And that is the justification for clause (c) of the second premise of the argument: "If a being is omnibenevolent, it would not permit any evil it knows about and can prevent."

So, when you put together the fact that there is great evil in the world with the claim that there would not be any evil in the world if God existed, you reach the conclusion that God does not exist. That is the logical problem of evil.

5.4 Responses to the Logical Problem of Evil

The logical problem of evil is a real problem for theists. Before we look at some of the standard responses theists make to it, however, it is important that we do what the atheists always insist we do when it comes to religion: apply a consistent standard.

5.4.1 A High Standard of Success for the Logical Problem of Evil

If atheists apply a particular standard when evaluating arguments for the existence of God, then, to be fair, they must permit theists to apply the same standard when theists evaluate arguments against the existence of God. If you go back to Chapter 3, you will see that one particular standard was articulated by David Hume in connection with a criticism he made of the design argument. Look back at the section on the identification problem. Hume claimed that the goal of people who run the design argument is not just to show that the designer of the world *might* be God. It is to show that the designer is *highly likely* to be God. If that is the standard, says Hume, then the design argument fails. The order and purpose we seem to see in the natural world are consistent with too many other possibilities for us to conclude that God is responsible for all of that apparent order. For example, Hume suggests that what we see in the natural world is just as consistent with the world having been designed by a committee of juvenile architects as by God. So the design argument fails because it does not nail down its conclusion.

Applying the same standard when it comes to the logical problem of evil, we see the atheist making a deductive argument from the existence of evil to the nonexistence of God. For that argument to succeed, it must nail down its conclusion. In order to be successful, a deductive argument must be valid and all of the premises must be true. The logical problem of evil is definitely valid, but are all the premises true? To cast reasonable doubt, the theist merely needs to tell a plausible story about how at least one of the premises is false. The plausible story does not need to be true. In other words, the theist does not need to provide a theodicy – a compelling story explaining why God would be expected to create a world with evil in it.

Compare the situation of the theist responding to the logical problem of evil with that of a defense attorney. One approach for successfully defending the client is to show that the evidence presented by the prosecution does *not* prove beyond a reasonable doubt that the client is guilty. To succeed, the defense attorney is not obligated to establish the client's innocence. The defense attorney merely needs to poke enough holes in the prosecution's case to show that it is inconclusive. Establishing the innocence of the client – for example, by proving conclusively that someone else committed the crime – would be great from the perspective of the defense attorney, but it is not necessary to winning the case.

As we will see, the focus of criticism is premise (2). The general strategy for rebutting the logical problem of evil is to provide some plausible stories about how God might exist but nonetheless permit evil. None of these stories actually needs to be the real reason God permits evil, just as it does not really need to be the case that the universe was designed by a committee of juvenile architects in order for that possibility to undermine the design argument. All the theist is aiming for here is to cast doubt on one of the premises. We need to keep that in mind when we evaluate the responses to the logical problem of evil.

5.4.2 Four Solutions to the Logical Problem of Evil

Given that the logical problem of evil is a very old problem for theists, as you might expect, a large number of solutions to it have been proposed over time. Following the twentieth-century philosopher **J. L. Mackie**,[5] we will group these solutions into four main categories. While perhaps not every solution to the logical problem of evil that has ever been proposed falls into one of these four groups, most do. Mackie thought none of the solutions worked. You can judge for yourself whether he was right.

---

[5] http://adb.anu.edu.au/biography/mackie-john-leslie-14214.

5.4.2.1 First Solution: Good Cannot Exist Without Evil

Perhaps the first thing you thought when you learned about the logical problem of evil is that it rests on a mistaken understanding of evil. Evil is not just an accidental characteristic of the universe, you might think. It is essential and ineliminable because, without it, there could be no good. You cannot have one without the other. Maybe the clearest expression of the notion that good cannot exist without evil comes from a concept in the Chinese religious tradition: **yin-yang**.[6] Just as you cannot have heat without cold or light without dark, you cannot have good without evil. The two are inextricably intertwined. Note the use of the word "cannot." As we saw in Chapter 1, words like "cannot" signal the presence of a modal proposition. In this case, the statement "Good does not exist without evil" is being advanced as necessarily true. You can read it either as "Necessarily, if there is good in the world, there is evil in the world" or "It is impossible that there is good in the world but that there is no evil in the world."

But is it necessarily true that, if there is good in the world, there is evil as well? As we saw earlier in this book, to show that a proposed truth is not necessarily true, you only need to come up with a counterexample to it. It seems that theists themselves must admit that there is a counterexample to the claim that good cannot exist without evil. Traditionally, theists insist that God created the entire world *ex nihilo* but that God was free not to have created the world at all. Creation was a free act, they say – an act of grace. Had God chosen otherwise, there would have been no "in the beginning," because there would have been no beginning, because there would not have been anything but God. In that scenario, the only thing in existence would be God. And, according to theists, God is perfectly, purely good. So, contrary to the suggestion that God could not prevent all evil because good cannot exist without evil, it seems that there is a way for God not to have brought any evil into the world. God could have not created a world at all.

This brings out an interesting contrast between monotheistic religions and many other religions that exist or have existed. Theisms are <u>monistic religions</u>. In monistic religions, there is only one fundamental spiritual being (Yahweh, God, Allah). But religions such as **Zoroastrianism**[7] and **Manichaeism**[8] are, or were, **dualistic religions**.[9] In those religions, there are two fundamental spiritual beings, and the existence of the world is the result of the opposition of those two beings. In Zoroastrianism, the good god was Ahura Mazda and the bad god was Angra Mainyu. They were locked in eternal struggle. If

---

[6] http://www.iep.utm.edu/yinyang.
[7] https://www.britannica.com/topic/Zoroastrianism.
[8] https://www.britannica.com/topic/Manichaeism.
[9] https://www.britannica.com/topic/dualism-religion.

your religion is dualistic, it does not face the logical problem of evil, because evil is just built into the foundation of all reality. But Judaism, Christianity, and Islam are not dualistic religions (though within those religious traditions there have been heretical dualistic sects such as Gnosticism in Christianity). Because theism is monistic and because theists say that God is perfectly good, they cannot subsequently assert that, as a matter necessity, good does not exist without evil.

Perhaps what the theist means when they respond to the logical problem of evil with "Good cannot exist without evil" is that if there were no evil, we would not notice or appreciate what is good. "Good cannot be appreciated without evil" is certainly a statement of fact regarding human psychology. If a child never experiences pain and is always provided with the very best of everything by their parents, they tend not to appreciate how good they have it. The child risks becoming "spoiled." Living in a world in which everything is good and nothing bad would be like growing up in an environment where everything is painted green. You would never recognize that everything was painted green.

Of course, everything would still *be* green. It is just that you would not notice. Likewise, in a world in which everything is perfectly good, everything would be perfectly good – it is just that no one would notice. But what is so bad about that? "Well," you might be thinking, "it is a very good thing that people recognize the existence of what is good." That is an important idea; we will address it below when we get to the third solution to the logical problem of evil. But it is not the same as the idea that good cannot exist without evil.

5.4.2.2 Second Solution: Evil Is Necessary as a Means to Good

If you happen to lift weights, you may be familiar with the slogan "No pain, no gain." The idea is that it is impossible to achieve the good of muscular development without the bad of physical pain. Likewise, some mothers claim that there is a necessary connection between the pain of labor and the joy of childbirth. Might this be why God permits evil – because there are certain goods that cannot be achieved without there being evils (pain, suffering, loss) along the way?

Alas for the theist, this solution is hard to maintain due to the fact that God is supposedly omnipotent. The second solution rests on the basic idea that there are chains of cause and effect, where some chains with good effects on the end involve evil links along the way. Since God is omnipotent, however, God controls what is linked to what. God sets the laws of cause and effect.

Take labor and childbirth, for example. It seems that God could have arranged things so that childbirth did not involve intense pain (and considerable risk) for the mother. Indeed, according to the book of Genesis, one of God's punishments for human sin was to make childbirth difficult and painful for women (Genesis 3:16). This implies that, before the Fall, childbirth was neither difficult nor painful. The theist may respond that humans brought this evil upon themselves because they disobeyed God of their own free will– we will look at the freewill solution to the logical problem of evil shortly. Or the theist may respond that the world would be a worse place if God miraculously made childbirth painless or gave people who wanted them huge biceps without lifting any weights – we will look at that sort of answer shortly too.

If we stick to the point of this proposed solution to the logical problem of evil, however, it seems that God cannot be excused for permitting evil on the grounds that evil is necessary as a means for good. This is simply because one of God's powers is deciding what causes are necessary for what effects. Being omnipotent, God *makes* the laws of cause and effect for this world. Therefore God cannot be constrained by the laws of cause and effect. For God, it is not true that evil is necessary as a means to good. Therefore the necessity of evil as a means to good is not a real solution to the logical problem of evil.

5.4.2.3 Third Solution: The World Is Better with Some Evil in It than if There Were No Evil in It

If you have ever broken up with someone you loved, you might have tried to console yourself by eating ice cream. Love is a great thing, but so is eating ice cream. If you lose one good thing, why not replace it with another? There is only one problem with this theory. The good of love and the pleasure of eating ice cream are on totally different levels. The two goods are not really comparable. No amount of ice cream consumption can equal the goodness of true love. (Do *not* try to prove this wrong.) Part of what makes true love so different in kind from eating ice cream is that true love requires another person, whereas ice cream is just stuff that you can buy at the grocery store. Entering into a relationship with another person inevitably involves risks – the risk that they never really loved you, the risk that they change their mind, the risk that their passion wanes, and the risk that they get sick, or even die. There is no such risk in the relationship between you and a pint of ice cream. And that is a big part of the reason why a pint of ice cream, though safer than true love, is not as good as true love. As the saying goes, it is better to have loved and lost than to have eaten a pint of ice cream.

This insight may help us to solve the logical problem of evil. What if there are different grades or levels of good? And what if some of the higher-grade goods logically require lower-grade evils? If that is the case, then, while it will be true that some goods can exist without evil, it will not be true that *every kind* of good can exist without evil. If we look again carefully at the evils listed earlier from the second half of 2017, maybe for each of them we can see a higher-level good for which the evil act or bad thing in question was necessary.

Take, for example, the fires in California. For all the damage done by those fires, they did provide an opportunity for one good thing: heroism. As with so many natural disasters, those fires were accompanied by stories of tremendous resilience and bravery. Or consider Hurricane Harvey. For all the tremendous damage it did, it also provided an opportunity for another good thing: generosity. Countless people raised funds and gave money to relief efforts, including elementary school students from around the world. Without those terrible natural disasters, there would never have been the opportunity for people to display those wonderful virtues.

We can represent this line of thinking with some diagrams. The first diagram represents one way God might have made the world. God might have created a world in which all any person, animal, or other sentient being ever experienced was great health, physical pleasure, and so on. In this possible world, there would no physical pain, suffering, or torment anywhere in created reality, no truck bombs, no hurricanes, no murders, and no sexual predators. Call this world "the perfect world." Or, better yet, call it "the 'perfect' world," because we want to leave the question open as to whether it really is as good as it seems.

The "Perfect" World

	Goods	Evils
First-order goods and evils	Pleasure, health, etc.	

Notice how there is nothing in the "Evils" box. Now, if it is true that the world is better with some evil in it than it could be if there were no evil in it, then we should think there is a possible world that is both more flawed than but also better than the "perfect" world. Call this "the flawed world."

The Flawed World

	Goods	Evils
Second-level goods and evils	Heroism, generosity, etc.	
First-level goods and evils	Pleasure, health, etc.	Pain, disaster, disease, etc.

Here there is something in the "Evils" box at the first level, but nothing in it at the second level. And what you get as a result of evil on the first level is a chance for good on the second level.

According to this line of thinking, the flawed world may be better overall than the "perfect" world, because the flawed world, for all its flaws, also contains goods of a higher level. If God is going to create anything at all, and if God's choice were only between the "perfect" world and the flawed world, we should expect God to have created the flawed world, not the perfect world. Therefore, the logical problem of evil fails as an argument against the existence of God. It is just not true that, if God exists, there would not be any evil in the world.

This is a pretty good start to an answer to the problem of evil, but as it stands it is not adequate. Critics will quickly point out that the world we see is not the flawed world, but rather something much worse. Notice that, in the flawed world, there are no second-level evils; there are no counterparts to generosity and heroism, for example. But clearly we do see second-level evils in the actual world – things like selfishness and cowardice. For example, in response to Hurricane Harvey, we not only saw heroism and generosity, but we also saw an upsurge in child sex trafficking. Events like Hurricane Harvey bring out not only the best in some of us, but also the worst in others of us. So, while it might be true that God would choose to create the flawed world rather than the "perfect" world, that still does not explain why God chose to create *this* world rather than the "perfect" world. To highlight this point, let us refer to the world we actually live in as "the deeply flawed world." Here is the diagram for it.

The Deeply Flawed World

	Goods	Evils
Second-level goods and evils	Heroism, generosity, etc.	Cowardice, selfishness, etc.
First-level goods and evils	Pleasure, health, etc.	Pain, disaster, disease, etc.

If this is the way things are, it is not so clear that it is better for God to create the deeply flawed world than the "perfect" world. Indeed, in some of your more unpleasant moods, you may think that, on the second level, there is way more stuff under the "Evils" column than under the "Goods" column – or, at the very least, that there is a rough parity between the second-level goods and evils. It is far from clear that our deeply flawed world is overall better than the "perfect" world – or even no world at all. (Perhaps this sort of gloomy reflection on evil explains a recurrent religious theme: God wiping out humanity and starting all over again.)

But the theist is not done yet. They will suggest a modification that saves this third solution to the logical problem of evil. What if there are goods that are of a kind or of a level beyond even the worst evils in existence? What if there is a kind of good unmatched by any evil? These would be transcendental, ultimate goods. They would be so much better in kind than even the worst evils that it might justify God in not preventing the lower-level evils – even though God knows about and has the power to prevent those evils. In that case, the diagram for our deeply flawed world was drawn wrongly. It ought to look like this.

The Modified Diagram of the Deeply Flawed World

	Goods	Evils
Third-level goods and evils	The transcendental, ultimate goods	
Second-level goods and evils	Heroism, generosity, etc.	Cowardice, selfishness, etc.
First-level goods and evils	Pleasure, health, etc.	Pain, disaster, disease, etc.

But what might these ultimate goods be? Several have been proposed: the development of souls, the building of character, the existence of beings capable of entering into a loving relationship with God, and many others. But we will focus on just one proposed ultimate good. It seems to be at the heart of all of the other proposed ultimate goods: free will. The fourth and final solution to the logical problem of evil is the idea that evil is necessary for the ultimate, transcendent good of there existing beings with free will who are morally responsible for their actions. Let us look at this proposed solution now.

5.4.2.4 Fourth Solution: Evil Is the Result of Human Free Will

Perhaps the most commonly offered explanation of why God allows evil is in terms of **free will**.[10] (Here "free will" is being understood in the incompatibilist's sense of the term, which we discussed in Chapter 2.) If humans are to have free will, it seems they must have a real choice between doing good and doing evil. If God always prevented moral evil, then no one would ever have made a real choice when they did something good, and so no one would ever have done anything good out of their own free will. And if no one ever did anything

---

[10] https://plato.stanford.edu/entries/freewill.

good out of their own free will – if all human actions were performed only in a sort of automatic, robotic, preprogrammed way – then those actions would not really be morally good. Yes, the actions would be good in a sense; they would have good effects. If someone were to hypnotize you to spend long hours working for charitable causes, you will do a lot of good. But you will not deserve to be praised for your actions, since you will have done them on account of having been hypnotized. On this line of thinking, the only way your actions can be morally praiseworthy is if you genuinely choose to do them. Genuine choice seems to require genuine freedom of the will.

Free will would also seem to account for the presence of natural evil. Without natural evil – without the threat of hurricanes, fires, earthquakes, floods, diseases, broken bones, and so on – humans would never have the opportunity to exercise their free will in any meaningful way. Without natural evil, the world would be a huge padded nursery. In a world in which people have a chance to exercise their power of choice in a morally significant way, people are going to have all sorts of obstacles to overcome – both natural obstacles and obstacles in the form of difficult people who abuse their power of choice.

In response to this idea, some atheists (Mackie, for example) will claim that our having free will puts a limit on God's power, so that there is a logical inconsistency between saying that God is omnipotent and that humans have free will. But, as we saw in our earlier discussion of free will (section 2.5 in Chapter 2, which deals with omnipotence), it may not be logically possible for God to *make* the world be such that you do a good action of your own free will. God could make you hit the person next to you. You could hit the person next to you of your own free will. But God could not make you hit the person next to you of your own free will, because that is not logically possible. Just as it is no diminution of God's power to say that God cannot make a round square or change the past, it is no diminution of God's power to say that God cannot control beings with free will.

A related response from some atheists is to say that our having free will is still consistent with there being no moral evil in the world, because God could have made us such that we always freely choose the good. It is certainly true that some free beings have excellent characters, good wills, and impeccable records of choosing the good. They seem to have little or no desire to harm anyone or anything. Nonetheless, those people have free will. Well, if *some* people are that way, why did God not just make *every* person that way? Why did God not just make all of us angelic by nature? It is a common theme in literature and film for the villain to shake their fist at the sky and ask "God, why did you make me this way?" Many atheists would ask the same question of God.

However, it is far from clear that this second response to the fourth solution makes sense. If God builds character traits into a person that guarantee that they will never do anything evil or bad, how does that person have free will?

Consider as an analogy a child who is raised by terrorists to be a killer themselves. How can we blame the child for ending up being a killer? Likewise, if a person is programmed by God to be saintly, it seems that the person does not deserve credit for behaving in a saintly way. Instead of the person's character being determined by God, it seems that the person's character must be of their own making if their actions are to be deemed morally praiseworthy or morally blameworthy.

Admittedly, the idea that someone is the originator of their own character is itself a difficult one. Whether you find this fourth solution to the logical problem of evil acceptable will depend on the stand you take regarding the concept of free will. Perhaps fortunately, however, limited space prevents us from looking in any great detail at the concept of free will. (That would take several more chapters.) What we can conclude is that the logical problem of evil can be answered *if* one adopts the appropriate views regarding the nature of free action. As we noted at the beginning of this section, atheists must meet a high standard when they advance the logical problem of evil. They must nail down the conclusion. Depending on what view of human freedom they adopt, it seems that theists have a way out. If that is so, then the logical problem of evil fails to prove that God does not exist.

5.5 The Problem of Religious Diversity

We have just seen that many atheists point to all the evil in the world as one of their reasons for denying that God exists. Another obvious fact about the world is that there are many different religions within it. How should a theist view the claims of their particular religion in light of this religious diversity? According to some atheists, no good position is available for theists regarding religious diversity. As they frame the problem, there are only two possible positions regarding religious diversity: either only one religion is true or no religion is true. The first one is highly problematic, so the second one is likely correct. Before we examine this line of thinking, let us first familiarize ourselves with some logical vocabulary.

5.5.1 Contradictory Versus Contrary Propositions

Contradictory propositions are ones such that, if one is true, then the other one must be false. For example, "Today is Tuesday" and "Today is not Tuesday" are contradictory propositions (assuming you are talking about the same "today" in both cases). Contradictory propositions come in pairs only; you cannot have a set of three or more propositions, all of which are contradictory to one another. Contrary propositions are different from contradictory ones. Contrary propositions are ones such that they cannot all be true, but they can all be false. And, unlike contradictory propositions, a set of more than two propositions can all be contrary to one another. For example, "All University of Mississippi students are from Natchez," "All University of Mississippi students are from Meridian," and "All University of Mississippi students are from Okolona" are contrary propositions. If one is true, the other two are false. But, because the three propositions are contaries rather than contradictories, another possibility is that all three of them are false.

5.5.2 Religious Doctrines as Sets of Propositions

As we saw at the end of Chapter 1, there is much more to a religion than just a set of doctrines. Even talking about a religion as being "true" seems to miss the point about much of religion. Religions include rituals, distinctive organizational structures, unique forms of religious experience, and many other things that cannot be expressed as simple true-or-false propositions. So it is quite an oversimplification to present a religion as just a list of propositions about doctrine. Nonetheless, doctrines are an important part of just about every religion. Furthermore, this clash of doctrines can give rise to conflict between religions. This conflict is not just a philosophical problem. It is a real-world problem, both now and in the past. Wars have been fought over differences of doctrine, for example, the Thirty Years War in Europe, which started 400 years ago.

So, even though we know there is more to religion than doctrines, let us suppose for the sake of argument that at the heart of each religion is a set of propositions, with each proposition being asserted as true by the followers of each religion. This set can be thought of as one large conjunctive proposition. (We discussed conjunctive propositions in Chapter 3 when we looked at the ontological argument.) Let us call one of these conjunctions a "core." So there will be core Christianity, core Buddhism, and so on.

Within each doctrinal core, there will be an independent clause about the central deity or deities that are said to exist (or, in the case of a religion like Buddhism, perhaps no deities). There will be an independent clause about the central human messenger (or messengers) of that religion. There will be an independent clause about how the central messenger relates to the deity. And there will be an independent clause about the primary, legitimate sources of the message given by the messenger. These items of belief are just for starters. Many other items will appear within most core conjunctions: ethical teachings, historical claims, legal rules, and eschatological claims, to name just a few. (Eschatology is the part of religious doctrine that concerns the afterlife and what the ultimate goal is of humans: getting to heaven, achieving nirvana, and so on.)

Let us take three monotheistic faiths as an example of the diversity of religions. We can sketch their different doctrines using a chart.

Monotheisms by Central Doctrines

	Judaism	Christianity	Islam
Name of prime deity	Yahweh/Jehovah	God the Father	Allah
Central messenger	Moses	Jesus Christ	Muhammad
Relationship between the messenger and the deity	The Chosen One; the designated leader of the Israelites	The Son of God; the second part of the Trinity	The Last Prophet of Allah
Primary source of information	The Torah and the Talmud	The Old and the New Testaments	The Koran and the Hadith

On this way of looking at things, core Judaism would be this: "There is only one god, Yahweh (or Jehovah); the Israelites are Yahweh's Chosen People; Moses was Yahweh's messenger to and designated leader of the Israelites; and you can find out what the message is by reading and listening to the Torah." Core Christianity would be this: "There is one god, God the Father; God sent his son Jesus to redeem the world; God the Father, Jesus Christ the Son, and the Holy Spirit are all members of the Holy Trinity – they are three persons in one; and you can find out what Jesus's message is by reading the New Testament." And core Islam would be this: "There is only one god, Allah; Muhammad is Allah's final prophet; and the message Allah gave Muhammad is contained within the Koran." (Remember, this is an extreme oversimplification of these rich and complicated religions.)

On the face of it, core Judaism, core Christianity, and core Islam are all contrary to one another. (We will ignore the possibility that, with proper reinterpretation, core Judaism can be absorbed within core Christianity and core Christianity can be absorbed within core Islam. We will ignore this possibility even though, historically, Christians claim to incorporate Judaism and Muslims claim to incorporate Christianity.) And if we add the core beliefs of the other major world religions to our list – core Hinduism, core Buddhism, core Taoism, and so on – it seems that we still have a set of contrary propositions. If that is right, then it seems that either just one of these religions is true or none of them are true. By the lights of atheists (and many others), it is implausible (at best) that one and only one religion is true. This is the problem of religious diversity.

Many atheists think the diversity of religions is a powerful reason in favor of their position, and even many theists think that religious diversity is a very significant problem for their religious belief system.

5.5.3 Four Responses to Religious Diversity

In response to the problem of religious diversity there are four basic options. (1) An exclusivist maintains two things: (a) only one religion's core doctrines are true, while the cores of all of the other religions are false; and (b) the failure of the adherents of those religions to hold to the right set of core beliefs excludes them (wholly or partially) from salvation. (We will use "salvation" here to mean a person's being saved somehow, either in this life or in the afterlife, from error, sin, and suffering.) So, for example, a Christian exclusivist is someone who says that Christianity is the only true religion, and that Jews, Muslims, Hindus, and Buddhists cannot achieve salvation. (2) An inclusivist maintains (a) but denies (b). So, for example, a Christian inclusivist is someone who says that Christianity is the only true religion, but that Jews, Muslims, Hindus, and Buddhists can achieve salvation if they meet the right conditions (if they lead good, moral lives, for example). (3) A pluralist denies (a). The pluralist says that the appearance of doctrinal conflict between the religions is illusory, because what we have called their "cores" are not actually propositions at all: although the individual components of a core seem to be true-or-false statements, they really are not. Instead of being true-or-false statements, they are simply means of leading people along the path to salvation. For the pluralist, more than one religion can help people achieve that goal. Finally, (4) an atheist denies (a) and goes further, saying that all religions are false. Atheists maintain that no religion has a core that is true. They also maintain that no religion provides a path to salvation if that means existence in an afterlife, simply because there is no afterlife. An atheist will say that the doctrinal cores believed by Jews, Christians, Muslims, and Hindus are all false. (Some atheists say to their religious friends, "I disbelieve all the same religions that you do, plus one more.") Let us look at the first three options one by one.

5.5.4 Religious Exclusivism

Consider this biblical verse. "I am the way; I am the truth and I am life; no one comes to the Father except by me" (John 14:6). It is hard to read this passage (and similar biblical passages) as anything but exclusivist. Jesus seems pretty clearly to be saying that the only path to salvation is through believing in him. Christianity is not the only religion to take this position about itself. In

Orthodox Judaism, it is taught that the Jews are God's chosen people – there is no other group that God chose as God's vehicle in this world. One of the Five Pillars of Islam, meanwhile, is the Shahada – the declaration that there is only one god, God, and that Muhammad is God's prophet. And it is not just the monotheistic religions that are exclusivist. There are Hindu exclusivists and Buddhist exclusivists too. Both historically and currently, exclusivism is a very common attitude for religious believers to take.

Philosophically, what can we say about exclusivism? There are two kinds of objections to exclusivism: social/political and theological.

5.5.4.1 The Social/Political Objection to Exclusivism

In modern democratic society, we are all taught to respect cultural and religious diversity. One way we do this is by granting that those whose beliefs differ from ours have just as much of a claim on the truth as we do. Furthermore, it is clear from everyday experience that there are people from a wide variety of faiths who are good citizens, who make tremendous contributions to their communities, and who live highly moral, ethical lives. If you were to say to one of these good citizens of a differing faith "On religion, you are totally wrong and I am right," you would seriously offend them. In our society, people who are exclusivists about their religion threaten all of us with discord. As history (both ancient and recent) clearly shows, when an exclusivist religion interacts with a contrary system, war and oppression often follow. If we allow that the religious exclusivists in our society may be right, we are setting ourselves up to experience tremendous social/political dysfunction. And that is the social/political objection to exclusivism.

Let us just assume for the sake of argument that the factual assertions behind this objection are true. Even so, is this a good reason to reject exclusivism? Not really. First, this reason for rejecting exclusivism rests, at least in part, on appealing to popularity. Appeal to popularity (or *argumentum ad populum* in Latin) is the logical fallacy of saying that proposition P is true because everybody (or almost everybody, or everybody who is worth caring about) believes that P. For example, Taylor Swift is one of the highest-paid and most popular recording artists in the world, but that does not automatically mean that her music is good. Likewise, respect for diversity is one of the most powerful and most repeated messages in modern society. The message is repeated in schools and universities, in news and entertainment, and in politics. It is a necessary message in our increasingly global society. But the centrality of that message is not a strong reason to think that exclusivism is false. Our current social/political preferences and our desire to live harmoniously seem to have no bearing on whether God exists (as Jews, Christians, and Muslims contend), whether there is no such thing as the self (as Buddhists contend), or whether people really are reincarnated (as Hindus contend). Indeed, a theme recurring throughout the history of religions is that religious people ought not to care what society ("the world") thinks.

There is a deeper problem with the social/political objection to exclusivism. It is not obvious that, in order to respect people whose fundamental ethical and religious beliefs differ from yours, you must regard their beliefs as being just as likely to be true as your own. First, it is condescending rather than respectful to say of someone with different fundamental beliefs, "Those beliefs are true for you." (Someone has probably responded to some argument or point you have made by saying something like "I respect your opinion." Did you think they were taking you seriously, or did you think they were just being dismissive?) True respect for others, it seems, involves treating them as rational agents capable of being wrong, as people who deserve a rational argument rather than a pat on the head.

Second, there are countless cases not involving religion in which intelligent, honest, well-meaning people disagree about something fundamental. If you are a political liberal, you probably know at least one intelligent, honest, well-meaning political conservative. If you think that *Moby-Dick* is the greatest novel in the English language, you probably know at least one highly literate person who thinks that *Moby-Dick* is incredibly boring and that Herman Melville spent way too much time describing whaling. By itself, the existence of such disagreement does not require that you give up your beliefs about politics, about literary quality, and so on. If it did, then for just about any important belief you hold, there would be an automatic reason to abandon it – namely, that some other intelligent person disbelieves it. Knowing that someone intelligent thinks that what you believe is false is not by itself a good reason to stop thinking it is true. And, if that is how it is with belief in general, why should it be any different for religious beliefs?

5.5.4.2 The Theological Objection to Exclusivism

The theological objection to exclusivism comes from the quite plausible idea that a good God would not want anyone to be unfairly excluded from salvation or to suffer unfairly for all eternity. As we saw when we discussed absence-of-belief atheism, there have been and still are people who have never even been exposed to the concept of God (much less to specific religions like Christianity or Islam). How could God deny them salvation when God never gave them a chance? There are also people who do amazingly good deeds for an entire lifetime. Are the Hindu gods really going to fault Mother Teresa (a woman who spent most of her life helping the poor, the dying, orphans, and lepers in the Indian city of Calcutta/Kolkata) because she was a Christian rather than a Hindu? A good deity would not do that. The seventeenth-century English philosopher **Edward Herbert**[11] expressed this thought beautifully in a statement written almost 400 years ago. If Christian exclusivists were correct, then

> the most innocent and commendable lives the heathens could lead would avail them nothing … How could I believe that a just God could take pleasure in the eternal reprobation of those to whom he never afforded any means of salvation, or endued with souls made after his own image; and whom he foresaw must be damned of absolute necessity, without the least hope or possibility of escaping it? I could not understand how they could call that God *most good and great*, who created men only to damn them, without their knowledge, and against their will.[12]

That is a very powerful objection to exclusivism. It is so powerful, in fact, that many intelligent theists try to avoid it by opting for some form of religious inclusivism.

5.5.5 Religious Inclusivism

Suppose you are, say, a Christian, but you do not think a good God would really deny a morally excellent person salvation just because that person believed in the wrong religion. If that is your attitude, what is the alternative to exclusivism?

5.5.5.1 Rahner's Christian Inclusivism

Religious inclusivists maintain that their religion is the one true religion, but that people of other faiths are still eligible for salvation. A good example of an inclusivist is the twentieth-century Catholic theologian **Karl Rahner**.[13] Christianity, he said, is the one true religion, the one intended for all people. But he also said that the truths of Christianity came into the world historically. They were revealed at specific historical moments and in specific places. For example, God revealed himself to the Jewish patriarchs Abraham, Isaac, and Jacob, rather than to other people in some other place. Jesus was born in Bethlehem, not the Bronx. This feature of the revelation of the truths of Christianity is reflected in numerous Christian doctrines and practices, for example, the baptism of children who die before they acquire reason. Christianity did not become a genuine option

---

[11] https://www.britannica.com/biography/Edward-Herbert-1st-Baron-Herbert-of-Cherbury.

[12] Herbert of Cherbury, "True Religion," in P. Helm (ed.), *Faith and Reason* (New York: Oxford University Press, 1999), p. 150.

[13] https://www.britannica.com/biography/Karl-Rahner.

for every single person in the world at the moment of Christ's resurrection: the Good News had not reached, say, Mongolia by then. Because of this, says Rahner, the status of those in cultures in which Christianity had or has not established a presence is similar to the status of those who lived before Christ walked the earth. Many of the people who have not accepted Christ's message because they have never been exposed to it are in the same category as people who did not accept Christ's message because they died before Jesus shared it.

For Rahner, then, the people who practice other religions, or no religion at all, are still eligible for salvation, even though Christianity is the one true religion. If Christianity is a real option for a person, then it is the only acceptable religion for that person, he says. But, if it is not a real option, then God's grace extends to those people nonetheless. In particular, he says, whenever people make moral decisions, grace is at work. And the religions to which they adhere can be "lawful" insofar as they promote a proper human relationship to God. All of this must be acknowledged, says Rahner, because everyone is shaped by their society and surroundings, even with regard to religious belief.

5.5.5.2 Objections to Inclusivism

Critics raise many objections against inclusivism. Here are two. First, inclusivism presupposes that the primary goal of a religion is to lead people to behave in a moral, ethical way. But not every religion sees itself that way. For example, it seems to be an essential element of Christian doctrine that more is required for salvation than ethical living. You cannot "earn" your way into heaven merely by acting ethically, many Christians say. You must also have the right set of beliefs. In particular, Lutheran and Reformed versions of Christianity promote the doctrine *sola fide* (Latin for "by faith alone"). There is some theological justification for such doctrines. If you think fallen, sinful humans are infinitely far from a perfect God, then it would be arbitrary of God to draw some ethical line and say, "Be better than this and you will be saved."

Second, inclusivism seems to rob religion of its importance. If a person can be saved without having any connection to, for example, the Christian church, and indeed while adhering to a contrary religion, what is the point of promoting and trying to convert people to Christianity? Saying that practicing Christianity makes one somewhat more likely to be saved is a pretty weak argument. Inclusivism of any sort, whether Jewish, Christian, Muslim, Hindu, or Buddhist, seems to make adhering to a particular faith pointless.

5.5.6 Religious Pluralism

Perhaps the problem with both exclusivism and inclusivism is the claim that just one religion is true. But how can anyone deny that except by agreeing with the atheists that all of them are false? Religious pluralists think they see a way: no single religion is true, not because they are all false, but because religious doctrines are not even meant to be interpreted as true-or-false statements. Ordinary language gives us many cases of statements that, on the surface, appear to be propositions – that appear to be true-or-false statements – but really are not.

5.5.6.1 Uses of Language that Seem to Be Statements of Fact but Are Not

Consider the schoolyard bully who approaches you and says, "You do not want to mess with me." On the surface, that seems to be a statement of fact. It is true if you do not want to mess with the bully, and it is false if you do want to mess with the bully. But, almost certainly, that is not what the bully means when he says, "You do not want to mess with me." Instead of asserting a proposition, he is issuing a command, "Do not mess with me." Commands are neither true nor false. If one of your parents tells you "Go to your room," you do not respond by saying "That's true!" or "No, that's false." Instead, you either do what they command or you do not.

Religious pluralists say that we should try to understand religious propositions in the same way. We should interpret them in terms of what they are being used to accomplish rather than in terms of their literal truth or falsity. For example, when a coach tells an athlete, "I want you to give 110%," the coach is not trying to state a fact (because it is impossible for anyone to give more than 100% of what they have to give). Instead, the coach is almost certainly just trying to motivate the athlete – to get the athlete psyched up. The statement "I want you to give 110%" is not meant to convey truth but rather to prompt action. If this is right, then statements of religious doctrine are not meant to convey truth, but to get people to do something. What exactly are they meant to do?

5.5.6.2 The True Goal of All Religions: Spiritual Growth and Reality Centeredness

Pluralists have various accounts of what religious doctrines and ideas are used to accomplish. Some say they are used to try to orient us toward the Real. Others say they are used to try to get us to live ethical or meaningful lives. Still others say they are used to promote spiritual growth. A good example of this last way of thinking comes from the leader of Tibetan Buddhism, the **Dalai Lama**.[14] Here is what he said in *The Bodhgaya Interviews*:

---

[14] https://www.britannica.com/topic/Dalai-Lama.

The variety of the different world religious philosophies is a very useful and beautiful thing. For certain people, the idea of God as creator and of everything depending on his will is beneficial and soothing, and so for that person such a doctrine is worthwhile. For someone else, the idea that there is no creator, that ultimately, one is oneself the creator – in that everything depends upon oneself – is more appropriate. For certain people, it may be a more effective method of spiritual growth, it may be more beneficial. For such persons, this idea is better and for the other type of person, the other idea is more suitable. You see, there is no conflict, no problem.[15]

On this way of thinking, religious doctrines and religious beliefs are really just like different workout playlists. For some people, a playlist of loud, harsh songs helps them to have a better workout. For other people, a playlist of more mellow songs optimizes their performance. No playlist is the "right" workout playlist. Which playlist is the right one for you just depends on your temperament.

In trying to identify the common goal of all religions, the twentieth-century philosopher **John Hick**[16] wrote about "the ultimate divine Reality," which he said was beyond any of the particular characterizations of divinity given by Jews, Christians, Muslims, Hindus, and so on. His view can be illustrated with the ancient fable of the elephant and the blind men. One of them feels its tail and says it is a rope, another feels its leg and says it is a wall, and so on. Likewise, Hick thinks, no particular religion represents the ultimate divine reality as it is in itself. But, all religions get at some aspect of the ultimate divine reality, and through each religion people can reorient themselves away from themselves – away from self-centeredness – and toward something bigger, higher, and more valuable. For Hick, religious "truth," such as it is, depends on a time and a culture. It is culturally relative. But those who can step outside of their own time, culture, and religious tradition will recognize that all religions have the same ultimate goal.

5.5.6.3 Objections to Religious Pluralism

What can we say about religious pluralism? Well, if you are the sort of person who wants everyone to live in a peaceful, tolerant world (and what sane person does not want that?), religious pluralism may sound really good to you.

---

[15] Dalai Lama, "Buddhism and Other Religions," in Michael Peterson, William Hasker, Bruce Reichenbach, and David Basinger (eds), *Philosophy of Religion: Selected Readings*, 5th edn (New York: Oxford University Press, 2014), p. 596.

[16] http://www.iep.utm.edu/hick.

Unfortunately, philosophical positions are not to be judged on how happy or hopeful they make us. Closer inspection reveals some very serious problems with religious pluralism.

Perhaps the biggest problem with it is the idea that, when religious believers make claims about their gods or their God and their doctrines, they are actually making claims about this thing – the ultimate divine Reality – without knowing it. This is pretty implausible. It implies that people such as Hick know better than religious believers themselves what they meant to say. Consider, for example, the author of the Gospel according to John. John began by saying this (John 1:1–3): "When all things began, the Word already was. The Word dwelt with God, and what God was, the Word was. The Word, then, was with God at the beginning, and through him all things came to be: no single thing was created without him." Whether that statement is true or false, it certainly seems to be a metaphysical assertion, an assertion about ultimate reality. According to people like Hick, John actually failed to make a metaphysical assertion. But it is quite implausible to deny that John was making a metaphysical assertion. John would have to be quite a dunce to not know how to say something about ultimate reality – certainly compared to Hick, who, by his own lights, *was* able to say something about ultimate reality.

In short, to deny that the author of the Gospel according to John is *really* making any claims about ultimate reality – even though that is precisely what John thought he was doing – is to insult the intellectual ability of John. It is fair for Hick (or anyone) to say that what John asserted is false, but, according to Hick, what John asserted is neither true nor false. And this is despite the fact that John thought it was true. That is a pretty condescending position to take about John's intellectual abilities. Hick thinks he himself can say true things about ultimate reality – for example, that our language cannot really describe it. Why will he not grant that John was capable of saying a false thing about ultimate reality – namely, that the Word has always been a part of it? To put this point a different way, why does Hick not regard himself and his theory of religion and of ultimate reality in the same way as he regards the teachings of Jesus Christ, Muhammad, the Buddha, Joseph Smith, and so on? If he is going to be fair, he should be saying of his own theory that it is neither true nor false. He should admit that it is just a way of getting people to do something – namely, to stop fighting over religion and to live in peace and harmony instead. If he were to admit that, we could applaud Hick for his noble gesture. But that would not be the same thing as agreeing that Hick's theory is true.

Another problem with pluralism is the idea that all religions seek to promote the same ultimate goal. Suppose that goal is, as Hick says, Reality-centeredness. What does it take for something to count as a means of achieving Reality-centeredness? Does taking LSD count? The twentieth-century writer **Aldous Huxley**[17] thought so. In that case, using LSD is just another means to Reality-centeredness. It is just another kind of religious practice. (This leads to a concrete problem in the United States now that marijuana use has been legalized in some states. There is a self-proclaimed "Church of Pot." Its members say that marijuana use is essential to their practice. Eventually, the government will have to decide whether to count such groups as religious groups.)

The problem with Hick's implicit definition of religion, then, is that any practice that is claimed to lead people to reality-centeredness will have to count as a religious practice. The criterion of religion at work in pluralism seems too loose. A related objection is that pluralists provide no reason for expecting all religions to do an equally good job of promoting reality-centeredness. There are many children's stories, and they all try to promote important life lessons, but that does not mean that they all do so equally well. Dr. Seuss's *Green Eggs and Ham* is not as good at imparting important life lessons as Aesop's fables. So why think that all religions promote reality-centeredness equally well? Maybe Christianity and Scientology both promote reality-centeredness, but Christianity does a better job than Scientology does.

Finally, pluralists end up having to say an extremely odd thing about religions like Buddhism. According to Buddhists, there is no such thing as the self. "No-self" is definitely part of core Buddhism. Whatever the official goal is of Buddhist practice, it is not to reorient selves from themselves to ultimate reality. For Buddhists, there is nothing to be reoriented toward ultimate reality in the first place. Does that mean that, for pluralists, Buddhism is not a religion? That seems very implausible, and it is certainly at odds with what most scholars of religion say about Buddhism.

Perhaps pluralists will instead maintain that, contrary to appearances, Buddhists do not *really* deny the reality of the self. Buddhists only *say* there is no self in order to get themselves and others to reorient themselves toward ultimate reality. On this view, Buddhists are sort of like drill sergeants who call their recruits "worthless" and "weak," or like the trainers in the 1970s therapy approach Erhard Seminars Training (EST). EST trainers would endlessly call the seminar participants "assholes" and "shits." The trainers probably did not call the participants those names because they really thought the participants were those things; they called them those names in order to get the participants to stop thinking only about themselves, to beat the egocentrism out of the participants. Is that how pluralists view the Buddhist doctrine of no-self? Again, that seems quite smug. The pluralists claim to know much better than the Buddhists themselves what Buddhism is all about.

---

[17] https://www.britannica.com/biography/Aldous-Huxley.

5.6 Concluding Thoughts on Arguments Concerning God's Existence

In Chapters 3 and 4 we looked at three arguments for thinking that God exists. In this chapter we have looked at two arguments for thinking that God does not exist. In each case, we saw that the arguments were not entirely conclusive. What if there just are no conclusive arguments either way? What should we do then? Should we all just be agnostics? Perhaps not. The assumption behind those offering these arguments (both for and against the existence of God) is that belief in God is a matter of reasons and of evidence. But what if it is not? What if, instead, it is a matter of pure choice? What if faith rather than reason is at the heart of belief in God? We will address that question in the next chapter.

Annotated Bibliography

Basinger, David (2002). *Religious Diversity: A Philosophical Assessment* (Burlington, VT: Ashgate).

After surveying all of the positions on religious diversity mentioned in this chapter, Basinger mounts a strong case for exclusivism.

Craig, William Lane and Walter Sinnott-Armstrong (2004). *God? A Debate Between a Christian and an Atheist* (New York: Oxford University Press).

The authors have published the contents of their public debates. The book gives an excellent sense of the main points of disagreement between theists and atheists.

Hick, John (1980). *God Has Many Names* (London: Macmillan).

In this accessible work, Hick argues for religious pluralism, contending that all of the major world religions seek the same goal and worship the same object.

Howard-Snyder, Daniel, ed. (1996). *The Evidential Argument from Evil* (Bloomington: Indiana University Press).

This collection of essays is a great starting point for students seeking an understanding of the other version of the problem of evil. Howard-Snyder's introduction gives a nice overview of the key issues in the debate.

Huxley, Aldous (2009 [1945]). *The Perennial Philosophy* (New York: HarperCollins).

Huxley defends religious pluralism with a truly encyclopedic knowledge of world religions, and in particular all the various forms of religious mysticism. He argues that all major religions share the same underlying principles, the same "perennial philosophy." The book is marvelous reading.

Martin, Michael and Ricki Monnier, eds (2003). *The Impossibility of God* (Amherst, NY: Prometheus Books).

This is a comprehensive collection of a wide variety of articles all arguing for the same conclusion: not only does God not exist, but it is impossible that God exists.

Meeker, Kevin and Philip Quinn, eds (2000). *The Philosophical Challenge of Religious Diversity* (New York: Oxford University Press).

> The title speaks for itself.

Plantinga, Alvin (1974). *God, Freedom, and Evil* (New York: Harper & Row).

> Still a classic, this book (and the essays that preceded it) set the terms of debate concerning the logical problem of evil. Plantinga's objections to the logical problem of evil were so compelling that they convinced many analytic philosophers to start talking about the evidential problem of evil instead.

Swinburne, Richard (1998). *Providence and the Problem of Evil* (Oxford: Clarendon Press).

> Swinburne lays out a comprehensive theodicy. These goods include not just the development of moral character, but the possibility of beauty. This is perhaps the most compelling modern account of why God allows evil.

van Inwagen, Peter (2006). *The Problem of Evil* (Oxford: Oxford University Press).

> This is another essential book on the topic. In the course of addressing the problem of evil, van Inwagen says much of value about the concept of God, about the free will solution to the problem of evil, and about the problem of "divine hiddenness" (the problem of why God does not make it more obvious to us that God exists).

6

EPISTEMOLOGY AND RELIGIOUS BELIEF

6.1 Theists and Atheists in a Stalemate

Let us take stock of what we have learned so far. First, is the concept of God logically consistent? We addressed that question in Chapter 2. As we saw, the answer is "maybe." Theists say it is; many atheists say it is not. Second, are there any good arguments for the existence of God? We looked at that question in Chapters 3 and 4. Again, the answer is "maybe." Many theists say there are; almost all atheists say there are not. Finally, are there any good arguments for the nonexistence of God? Yet again, the answer is "maybe." Most theists say there are not, almost all atheists say there are. So, based on our limited survey of some of the central positions and arguments in the philosophy of religion, it seems that theists and atheists have reached a stalemate.

When you play a game against an opponent and you find yourself in a tie or a draw time and again, you begin to suspect that something is wrong with the game itself. If you ever played tic-tac-toe as a child, you probably came to realize pretty soon that, if both you and your opponent followed the same basic strategy, you would never beat your opponent at tic-tac-toe and your opponent would never beat you. Perhaps arguing about the existence and nature of God is like playing tic-tac-toe. The rules of the game guarantee that any two competent opponents end up in a draw. If that is right, we might need to take a fresh look at the rules of the game when it comes to talking about God and religion. What rule or rules have guided us so far?

6.1.1 Faith, Reason, and Fideism

Up until now, the primary rule we have followed is this: Let logic, reason, and evidence be our guide when it comes to thinking about God and religion.

This Is Philosophy of Religion: An Introduction, First Edition. Neil A. Manson.
© 2021 John Wiley & Sons, Inc. Published 2021 by John Wiley & Sons, Inc.

Almost everything we have covered in this book so far has been expressed in terms of logical arguments and precise definitions. Maybe following this rule is a mistake. There is an idea we have not yet brought up: faith. Belief in God, many think, is primarily a matter of faith, not of reason. Many theists say that belief in God cannot be achieved simply by using logic and reason or observation and experience. God, they think, is beyond the reach of any of those human capacities. Belief in God is not a matter of reaching a conclusion based on a body of evidence. Instead, it is a matter of living life a certain way, of abandoning yourself to belief, of making a commitment despite all the doubt and uncertainty.

An extreme version of this approach is called fideism. ("Fideism" is from the Latin word *fides*, which means "faith," and from which we get the words "fidelity" and "infidel.") **Fideism**[1] is the view that belief in God is purely a matter of faith. Some fideists go so far as to say that, in order to be genuine and authentic, the act of believing in God must be *contrary* to reason in the mind of the believer. True belief requires taking a "leap of faith," in which one recognizes the absurdity of belief in God, but ignores that and believes anyway. The nineteenth-century Danish theologian **Søren Kierkegaard**[2] is a notable proponent of this approach. Fideism is a common reaction to the sort of analytical philosophical approach to God we have taken so far. If this way of thinking is right, then theists have no need to provide arguments for the existence of God. They do not need to show that the concept of God is logically consistent. They can just believe in God purely on faith.

6.1.2 Epistemology: Another Battleground in Philosophy of Religion

So have we gotten past the stalemate between theists and atheists? Not quite. Both atheists and a good number of theists are going to resist fideism mightily. Atheists will complain that allowing belief in God to be based solely on faith will open up a Pandora's box of other forms of irrationality, including superstition, magic, and the occult. Giving validation to those who believe solely on the basis of faith also permits the denial of accepted science. These forms of irrationality are not just cases of false belief. They are cases of false belief that threaten the rest of society. Many theists actually agree with atheists on this point. They think that it is immensely important for theism that science and reason support rather than oppose belief in God. They are not going to concede to anyone – not even to a fellow theist – that reason and evidence are not on God's side.

---

[1] https://plato.stanford.edu/entries/fideism.
[2] https://www.britannica.com/biography/Soren-Kierkegaard.

So now we have a new disagreement – a disagreement about what is and is not permissible when it comes to belief in general, and to belief in God in particular. To address this disagreement, we are going to have to look more carefully at some key ideas in epistemology. Epistemology, remember, is the theory of knowledge. It is the field of philosophy that concerns basic concepts such as knowledge, truth, belief, and rationality. One of the central concerns in epistemology is the justification of beliefs. (Note that there are many synonyms for "justification": grounds, reasons, basis, proof, evidence, warrant, and so on. We will just use "justification.")

According to a very natural understanding of beliefs, epistemic justification is a matter of fulfilling obligations on the part of the believer. We often speak of justification as a matter of duty, and of believing things without justification as a failure to fulfill one's duties. (Technically, this is called the <u>deontological conception of epistemic justification</u>.) For example, we say things such as "She should have known" or "He failed to do his due diligence." If justification is a matter of right and wrong, of what we should and should not believe, then a question immediately arises. Supposing that we have no evidence of God's existence, is it permissible nonetheless to believe in God on the basis of faith? Is belief on the basis of faith a violation of fundamental epistemic obligations? If it is, then the fideist is telling us to do something wrong. So, before we say that faith alone is an acceptable basis for belief in God, we are going to have to sort through some deeper epistemological issues. A good way to start is by looking at a classic account of the relationship between faith and reason.

6.2 The Classical View: Faith and Reason in Harmony

Historically, philosophers and theologians in the monotheistic traditions have given a great deal of thought to the role of faith in the life of the theist. The dominant view both in pre-Reformation (i.e. pre-Protestant) Christian theology and in Islamic theology fell between the extremes of pure faith and pure reason. In the medieval era, both Catholic theologians like **St. Thomas Aquinas**[3] and Islamic theologians like **Averroës**[4] held that there can be no conflict between the demands of faith on the one hand and the deliverances of reason on the other. Indeed, in *On the Harmony of Religion and Philosophy*, also translated as *The Decisive Treatise*, Averroës argued that Islamic faith *demands* that followers develop their rational capacities as best they can so that they can better engage in theology. For Averroës, the rational investigation of Allah by the human mind is not just possible; it is required.

---

[3] https://www.britannica.com/biography/Saint-Thomas-Aquinas.
[4] https://www.britannica.com/biography/Averroes.

6.2.1 Aquinas on Faith and Reason

The medieval Catholic theologian **St. Anselm**[5] described theology as "faith seeking understanding." This slogan encapsulates the standard Christian position on religious belief for the first 1,500 years of the church's existence. In chapters 3–8 of book 1 of *Summa Contra Gentiles*, St. Thomas Aquinas spelled out this position very clearly. Aquinas held that there were certain truths of the faith that could never be reached by human reason alone. Humans can come to know those truths only through the gift of divine revelation. An example of such a truth would be the triune nature of God, the fact that God is three persons in one. Other truths about God, however, can be known by reason and observation, unaided by divine revelation. For example, Aquinas thought that the cosmological argument was sound, so that reason and observation showed that there must exist a divine Creator of the universe. Yet, despite there being two sources of knowledge about God – reason and revelation – there is never a conflict between the two. And just because some important theological truths can be known by reason and observation alone does not mean that we should doubt all claims about God that cannot be established by reason and observation. Sometimes, said Aquinas, God reveals those truths to us, and that is how we know them.

Aquinas considers why God did not design humans so that they could know all, rather than just some, theological truths by reason and experience. Why did God make us so that we needed the aid of revelation? Why not make us so that we could access all of the truths about God through reason? Furthermore, why does God sometimes repeat in revelation what we can know about God from reason and experience? For example, why did God reveal to Moses and the Israelites that God created the world when they could have known it by following the cosmological argument? (Moses is supposedly the author of the first five books of the Bible, also called the **Pentateuch**.[6] The truth about creation as expressed at the very beginning of the book of Genesis was supposedly revealed by God to Moses directly on Mount Sinai.)

Aquinas had quite sensible, practical answers. Regarding the last two questions, he thought that God sometimes reveals what could be known by reason and experience for three reasons. First, most people are just not equipped to grasp the long trains of reasoning needed to reach certain theological truths. Many people are either not smart enough or not focused enough to do it. But just because they are not the smartest or the most focused people does not mean that God cares less about them than about theologians and philosophers. So, for the sake of ordinary people, God reveals to them what others can know from reason and experience.

---

[5] https://www.britannica.com/biography/Saint-Anselm-of-Canterbury.

[6] https://www.britannica.com/topic/Torah.

Second, theological reasoning takes a lot of time. Think how much time it took you to work through Chapter 4 on the design argument. Then consider that, after reading that chapter, you had only scratched the surface of the literature on that argument. More generally, doing theology at a high level takes years of training. Many people do not have enough time for that. They are too busy being electricians, teachers, social workers, and so on. But again, the world needs electricians, teachers, and social workers. For those not cloistered in a monastery studying theology night and day, God may provide by revelation what the scholars know by reason.

Third, human reason is prone to error. Even the smartest humans make mistakes. By reaffirming through revelation what could be known through reason, God is providing a kind of quality control. This reply ties in with Aquinas's answer to the first two questions as well. God made us with limited intellects. God's shrouding of some divine truths from our minds keeps us humble and gives us a better appreciation of God's fundamental majesty. It also makes us thirst for knowledge of God.

6.2.2 Rivals to the Classical View

The basic attitude of both Aquinas and Averroës regarding theology, philosophy, and belief in God is the same. Those who are capable of abstract, rational thought and who have the time and the means to do it ought to study philosophy and theology. This way they can come to know God to the extent that reason allows. Both of these theologians hold human reason in high regard. This does not mean that those without the needed talents for philosophy and theology are inferior to those who have those talents. God enables everyone to know God in one way or another. But reason is not to be disparaged, and applying reason to the careful study of God is a noble thing.

Aquinas's view of the connection between faith and reason was dominant in Christian thinking up until the Protestant Reformation. (Remember that, for much of the history of Christianity prior to the Protestant Reformation, Christian thinking just was Catholic thinking.) With the rise of Protestantism in Europe, however, the attitude of many Christian thinkers toward reason changed dramatically. The founder of European Protestantism, **Martin Luther**,[7] regularly derided reason if it was not firmly attached to faith. The unreliability of reason was thought to be one of the consequences of the Fall, and it was thought that our reason could be restored only by the grace of God. This strain of thought (usually in milder forms) can be found throughout the history of Protestantism and persists to this day. The influence of Protestantism

---

[7] https://www.britannica.com/biography/Martin-Luther.

on contemporary Christian thought has been immense. For many Christians nowadays, the badmouthing of reason and the elevation of pure faith comes as no shock. If they knew their history of theology, however, they would see that positions like Luther's are far from the only option for the theist.

For the purposes of this book, which is devoted to taking an analytical, logical approach to issues in the philosophy of religion, there is not much more to say about the idea that our reason itself has been corrupted and that belief in God must be contrary to reason. It is in the same category as theological voluntarism (discussed in Chapter 2). The positions are both argument stoppers. So let us look instead at another approach to religious belief. Proponents of this approach allow that there is a lack of conclusive evidence either for or against the existence of God, but maintain that there is still strong reason of a different sort to believe that God exists. Their central argument revolves around something called Pascal's wager.

6.3 Pascal's Wager: Faith in God as a Reasonable Risk

Blaise Pascal[8] was a seventeenth-century French mathematician, scientist, and philosopher. He is considered one of the founders of the modern mathematical theory of probability, and is also known for his unique approach to religious faith. To understand his approach, we first need to take a look at a larger question. How ought we to make decisions in cases in which there is significant uncertainty?

6.3.1 A Standard Case of Making Decisions Under Uncertainty: Gambling

Many decisions in life – actually, most of them – are made against a background of significant uncertainty. The field of study devoted to this feature of human existence is called **decision theory**.[9] The choices gamblers make about what bets to place give us clear, straightforward examples of such decisions. In Chapter 1 (section 1.2.1.3, which deals with *a priori* and *a posteriori* propositions), we considered the case of rolling two six-sided dice. As we saw there, the probability of rolling two dice and getting the sum of 7 is 6/36. Other probabilities can be calculated fairly easily. The probability of getting a 6 is 5/36, as is the probability of getting an 8. The probability of getting a 5 is 4/36, as is the

---

[8] https://www.britannica.com/biography/Blaise-Pascal.
[9] https://plato.stanford.edu/entries/decision-theory.

probability of getting a 9. And the probability of getting a 4 is 3/36, as is the probability of getting a 10.

You will want to know these probabilities if you ever play the casino game Craps. It is a game based on rolling two six-sided dice. Most of the bets are ones in which the shooter repeatedly rolls the two dice, hoping a certain number comes out before a 7. For example, in "place" bets, you get to choose between the numbers 4, 5, 6, 8, 9, and 10. If you put a place bet on the number 8, for example, and you roll an 8 before rolling a 7, you win. If a 7 comes out first, you lose. (All outcomes other than 7 or 8 are irrelevant, so if you rolled, say, an 11, you would get to roll again. You would keep rolling the dice until you got a 7 or an 8.) Of course, of all the numbers, 7 has the highest probability of being rolled, so you are always more likely to lose than to win a place bet. To compensate for this, the casino pays out on place bets at better than even money. A winning place bet on a 6 or an 8 pays 7–6, that is, if you place $6 on an 8 rolling out, and it does, you get your $6 back plus another $7. A winning place bet of $5 on a 5 or a 9 pays 7–5. And a winning place bet of $5 on a 4 or a 10 pays 9–5. Now that you have this information, imagine that you are forced to make a place bet in Craps. Which number should you choose?

6.3.1.1 How to Evaluate Decisions Made Under Uncertainty

Before answering this question, there are two very basic assumptions we can make about the behavior of bettors. First, they want to maximize their winnings and minimize their losses in the long run. If that is not what they are trying to accomplish in their wagers, they are gambling in a less than optimal way. Second, their betting behavior should be judged on the quality of the betting decisions they make, not on the outcomes of those decisions. This is a very important point but one that is easy to miss. Here is a thought experiment to illustrate this key concept. An evil criminal mastermind kidnaps you, ties a bomb to you, and then offers you a choice. The first option is that you roll two dice, and if anything but the number 12 comes up, the bomb explodes; if a 12 comes up, nothing happens. The second option is that you flip a coin, and if it comes out heads, the bomb explodes; if it comes out tails, nothing happens. You choose the first option. You roll the dice and out comes a 12. You survive. Should you congratulate yourself on the excellent decision you made?

No. You made a very, very bad decision. You opted to give yourself a 1-in-36 chance of surviving rather than a 1-in-2 chance of surviving. Even though you survived, it was not because you made a good decision. It was because you got quite lucky. You should not evaluate the quality of your decision based on how things turned out, but on the information available to you prior to when the chancy event (rolling the dice, flipping the coin, etc.) took place. (The professional poker player and trained psychologist **Annie Duke**[10] does a great job of explaining this mistake, which in poker slang is called "resulting.") And this is true, not just about gambles, but more generally about all decisions that are made under uncertainty. For example, intelligent football fans complain about "Monday morning quarterbacks" – people who look back at the game their team lost and blame the loss, in hindsight, on bad decisions by coaches or quarterbacks. In most cases, the criticisms are ill founded. The coaches and quarterbacks typically have the best information available at the time, and they make their decisions accordingly. It is just that, as with all sports, there is a lot of chance and luck built into the game. Sometimes, as they say, the ball just does not bounce your way. Monday morning quarterbacks overlook this because they have 20/20 hindsight. But, in the real world, no one has 20/20 foresight.

6.3.1.2 Expected Value as a Guide to Rational Decision Making

Let us get back to the question about place bets. If you go through the math, you will see that, when you make a $6 place bet on a 6 or on an 8, for every 11 times that you roll out a number that settles the bet, you will lose six times (for the 7) and win five times (for the 6 or for the 8). Since winning place bets on 6s and 8s pay 7–6, on average you will win $35 and lose $36 for every $66 you bet (1/66th of $1 is about 1.5 cents). If you make a $5 place bet on a 5 or a 9, the payout is 7–5. For every 10 times you get an outcome that settles the bet, you will lose six times and win four times. So, on average, you will win $28 and lose $30 for every $50 you bet (2/50th of $1 is 4 cents). And if you make a $5 place bet on a 4 or a 10, you will lose six times and win three times for every nine rolls that settle the bet. On average you will win $27 and lose $30 for every $45 you bet (3/45th of $1 is about 6.7 cents).

A term from probability theory applies here: "expected value." The <u>expected value</u> is just the expected return in the long run on a given wager or expenditure. The expected value of a place bet is calculated by figuring out the probability of winning and multiplying it by your profit if you win, then figuring out the probability of losing and multiplying it by your loss if you lose, and then adding those two figures together. The expected value of a place bet on a 6 or on an 8 is would be –1.5 cents for every dollar you bet. The expected value is –4 cents for every dollar you bet on a 5 or on a 9. And it is –6.7 cents for every dollar you bet on a 4 or on a 10. So, while the expected values of all of the place bets are negative, the least bad bets are 6 and 8.

If you are a rational gambler – a gambler who wants to maximize your winnings and minimize your losses – and if you were forced to make place bets, you

---

[10] http://annieduke.com.

should make them on 6s or 8s. And that is the right decision even if subsequently no 6s or 8s come up but lots of 4s, 5s, 9s, and 10s do. Again, this is because you should not evaluate the quality of the decision regarding a chancy event based on the results. Instead, you should evaluate the quality of the decision based on the information available to you prior to the outcome of the chancy event.

6.3.1.3 Low-Probability, High-(Dis)Value Events

Looking at decisions through the lens of expected value can be extended to a wide range of events, including decisions about events that have a low probability of occurrence. Indeed, calculating expected values for rare events is just what actuaries do for insurance companies. Take, for example, car insurance. The typical US car driver is calculated to get into one collision about every 18 years. Given the very low probability of getting into a collision on any given driving trip, you may think as a driver that you do not need to worry about this risk. However, the cost to you if you do get into a collision can be extremely high. There is not only the cost of fixing or replacing your car, but the cost of paying for the damage (including, perhaps, the medical damage) you have done to the people with whom you collided. Despite how unlikely it is that you get into a major accident, the consequences are so significant if you do that it makes sense to take action to guard against that risk. The action you should take (an action that is legally required in almost every US state) is to buy car insurance. You pay money to the insurance company and they issue a policy to you, promising to pay your bills if you get into a major accident.

Calculating expected values and using the results to guide your decisions is not limited, in principle, to some minimum probability or some maximum damage or reward. Theoretically, it could make a big difference to your decision whether the probability of something happening is one in a million, one in a billion, or one in a trillion. Likewise, it could make a big difference whether the value or the disvalue of an outcome is equivalent to a million dollars, a billion dollars, or a trillion dollars. (This is why an Australian company once bought up nearly all of the tickets in a major US lottery. The expected value of a ticket was positive – something that is very rare in lotteries.) And it could make a big difference to a public health or military decision whether the proposed action threatens to lead to the deaths of thousands of people, tens of thousands of people, hundreds of thousands of people, or millions of people. When making decisions about what to do in cases involving extremely low probabilities or extremely valuable or disvaluable outcomes, many of us are tempted to give up on calculations and to make our decisions on some other basis (emotions, hunches, "gut instinct"). But that would be a mistake.

For example, just because there is, on average, only one catastrophic asteroid strike on earth every 600,000 years does not mean we should ignore the risk. Indeed, some national governments are cooperating to create a defense system against such asteroids. Even when we are thinking about remote possibilities, astronomical rewards, and catastrophic risks, we still need to weigh our decisions carefully. In such cases, we still ought to calculate and compare expected values, and then pursue the course of action with the highest expected value (or lowest expected disvalue). That seems to be the most rational way of making decisions.

6.3.2 Belief in God as a Decision Made Under Uncertainty

According to Pascal, the decision whether or not to believe in God is very much a gamble, one involving extreme rewards and (possibly) extreme punishments. In section 3, passage 233, of his **Pensees**[11] he compares deciding whether to believe in God to betting on the outcome of a coin flip at the end of infinity. Does God exist? If we can ever come to know the answer, we will do so only after we are dead. But that does not mean that we cannot make a rational decision in spite of the immense uncertainty. For Pascal, the expected value of belief in God is infinitely positive, while the expected value of disbelief in God is negligible or infinitely negative. Thus, even if we can never know whether God exists – even if the evidence for and against God is totally inconclusive, so that theists and atheists are forever in a deadlock just based on reason and evidence – it is still rational to believe in God. It is better to believe in God than not in these circumstances in the same way that it is better to go with the coin flip than the dice roll in the evil criminal mastermind thought experiment. If Pascal is right, it would not matter that the evidence of God's existence is inconclusive. Believing in God would still be rational because it would be the right strategy.

6.3.2.1 The Expected Value of Belief and the Expected Value of Unbelief

Let us lay out Pascal's reasoning in more detail. He asks us to compare two expected values: the expected value of believing in God and the expected value of not believing in God. In both cases, the expected value is calculated by figuring out two values, then adding them together. In the case of believing in God, the first value is the probability of "winning" (that is, being right in thinking that God exists) multiplied by your "profit" if you are right. The second value is the probability of "losing" (that is, being wrong in believing that God exists)

---

[11] Pascal's *Pensees* can be accessed online at https://www.gutenberg.org/files/18269/18269-h/18269-h.htm#SECTION_III.

multiplied by your loss if you are wrong. In the case of not believing in God, the first value is the probability of "winning" (that is, being right in thinking that God does not exist) multiplied by your "profit" if you are right. The second value is the probability of "losing" (that is, being wrong in believing that God does not exist) multiplied by your loss if you are wrong.

For Pascal, if you believe in God and God does exist, then you get the reward of eternity in heaven. If you believe in God but God does not exist, then what have you lost? For Pascal, nothing. He even says that, regardless of whether God exists or not, you benefit from believing that God exists. So, for Pascal, believing in God is win–win.

> Now, what harm will befall you in taking this side? You will be faithful, honest, humble, grateful, generous, a sincere friend, truthful. Certainly you will not have those poisonous pleasures, glory and luxury; but will you not have others? I will tell you that you will thereby gain in this life, and that, at each step you take on this road, you will see so great certainty of gain, so much nothingness in what you risk, that you will at last recognise that you have wagered for something certain and infinite, for which you have given nothing. (section 3, ch. 233)

What is on the other side? If you believe that God does not exist and you are right, then you get something of value, presumably (an extra two hours or so on weekends for example). But, in the grand scheme of things, given that you only live a finite number of years, the value to you of rightly disbelieving in God is still small. But if you believe that God does not exist and you are wrong, then at best you miss out on heaven and at worst you spend eternity in hell.

So far, however, we have only part of the information that we need to complete our calculation of the two expected values (of believing in God and of not believing in God). What about the probability that God exists? Is it a 50% chance that God exists and a 50% chance that God does not exist? Is it 10% versus 90%? Is it 1% versus 99%? For Pascal, the answer does not matter. So long as there is some nonzero, noninfinitesimal chance that God exists, the expected value of believing in God is infinitely positive, while the expected value of disbelieving in God is infinitely negative.

> There is here an infinity of an infinitely happy life to gain, a chance of gain against a finite number of chances of loss, and what you stake is finite. It is all divided; wherever the infinite is and there is not an infinity of chances of loss against that of gain, there is no time to hesitate, you must give all. (section 3, ch. 233)

By "you must give all," Pascal means that you must believe that God exists. Believing in God is the right choice even if it turns out that God does not exist.

That is the conclusion of his argument – an argument that has come to be called **Pascal's wager**.[12]

Another way to look at Pascal's wager is through a 2 × 2 decision matrix. The rows indicate the two options regarding your belief in God: you believe or you disbelieve. The columns indicate the two options regarding the existence of God: God exists or God does not exist. And the boxes indicate the "wins" or "losses" in each case.

The Options in Pascal's Wager

	God exists (> 0% chance)	God does not exist (< 100% chance)
You believe that God exists	Infinite positive value (you go to heaven for all of eternity)	Mix of finite losses (e.g. of free time on weekends) and finite gains (e.g. of peace of mind)
You disbelieve in God	Either no positive value (you just do not go to heaven) or infinite negative value (you go to hell)	Mix of finite losses (e.g. of peace of mind) and finite gains (e.g. of free time on weekends)

If these are the right values, then what we get is an infinite expected value for believing in God and either a finite expected value or an infinite expected disvalue for disbelieving in God (depending on whether God punishes unbelievers in hell or merely extinguishes their existence without otherwise punishing them). If there is a 50% chance that God exists – well, 50% of infinity is infinity. So the expected value of belief in God is still infinitely positive even if there is only a 50% chance that God exists. If there is a 10% chance that God exists, then again, 10% of infinity is infinity. And so again, the expected value of belief in God is still infinitely positive even if there is only a 10% chance that God exists. And so on and so on, for every finite chance that God exists. Mathematically, Pascal thinks, it just does not matter what the probability is that God exists. So long as it is neither zero nor infinitesimal, the rational thing for you to do is believe in God.

If Pascal is right in his calculations, then we could sidestep entirely the question of whether there is adequate evidence for God's existence. So long as the probability of God's existence is not zero, it does not matter (for the sake of dictating the rationality of belief) just how probable it is that God exists. Religious faith is justified on the practical grounds of self-interest alone. (This is why Pascal's wager is sometimes described as a **pragmatic argument for the existence of God**.[13])

---

[12] https://plato.stanford.edu/entries/pascal-wager.
[13] https://plato.stanford.edu/entries/pragmatic-belief-god.

6.3.2.2 An Analogy to the Thinking Behind Pascal's Wager

Pascal's wager is an instance of an attractive argument form – a form that is used in all sorts of everyday contexts. The basic idea is "better safe than sorry." For example, when it comes to political decisions affecting the environment, many environmentalists urge us to follow the **precautionary principle**.[14] The precautionary principle says that, if the consequences of a policy decision are potentially catastrophic to the environment, then we ought to act to avoid the catastrophe, even if there is significant uncertainty about whether the wrong decision really will cause a catastrophe. This sort of reasoning is used to support, for example, a moratorium on the release of genetically modified organisms.

Consider the following precautionary argument against the use of nuclear weapons. It is based on the possibility of a nuclear winter. On this scenario, there would be a dramatic drop in global temperatures after any nuclear exchange due to the dust and ash raised up by multiple nuclear explosions.

> There are real uncertainties involved in the nuclear winter predictions. They are based on models of poorly-understood processes. Many of the complex scientific problems will take many years to resolve and some of the key uncertainties will remain unless there is a nuclear war. Science cannot provide certainty on this issue. However, one doesn't require certainty to take decisions about risks. With nuclear winter there would be no second chance. The potential costs are so enormous that it hardly matters for our argument whether the probability that the nuclear winter predictions are basically correct is 10 per cent, 50 per cent, or 90 per cent. The risk of a nuclear winter means that the present nuclear weapon arsenals are unacceptable.[15]

Similar arguments are given for taking immediate action to stop global warming. Even though we are unsure that the worst-case scenarios (e.g. complete melting of the polar ice caps) would occur, just the possibility of them is supposed to justify preventive measures. Another example concerns military thinking during the cold war between the United States and the Soviet Union. The United States contemplated a nuclear first strike against the Soviet Union in order to wipe out the enemy entirely – just to avoid the chance that the Soviets might destroy the United States later on when they became more powerful.

---

[14] This technical article spells out the many versions the precautionary principle can take: Neil A. Manson, "Formulating the Precautionary Principle," Environmental Ethics, 24:3 (2002), pp. 263–274, https://www.academia.edu/8104061/_Formulating_the_Precautionary_Principle_.

[15] Owen Greene, Ian Percival, and Irene Ridge, *Nuclear Winter: The Evidence and the Risks* (Cambridge: Polity Press, 1985), pp. 154–155.

Although the contexts are quite different, the reasoning across all of these cases is similar. When extreme outcomes are possible (either extremely valuable outcomes or extremely disvaluable outcomes), it seems that we can be rationally required to take action either to secure them or to avoid them, even if it is not very probable that those extreme outcomes will occur. We cannot just dismiss the outcomes as being improbable. We have to look at the value or disvalue of the outcomes if they do occur. In other words, we must think in terms of expected value.

6.3.3 Objections to Pascal's Wager

As you might imagine, Pascal's wager is controversial. Something seems wrong with the idea that you can justify your belief in God in the way Pascal describes. But what, precisely, is wrong with Pascal's reasoning? Here are three objections to it.

6.3.3.1 First Objection: It Rests on Scaremongering

One basic objection to Pascal's wager is that it relies on an all too common ploy: scaremongering (also known as fearmongering, alarmism, and being a Chicken Little). Look again at the quotation concerning a nuclear winter. The authors suggest that it is not very important to their argument what the actual probability is that the nuclear winter theory is correct. It is not relevant because the stakes are so high (global environmental devastation). A skeptic may look at that quotation and sense a trick being pulled. The people urging preventive measures regarding nuclear winter (or global warming or the Soviet Union) are not really sure what the probability is that their doomsaying is correct. But, instead of firming up their predictions, they just ratchet up the damage of the doom scenario. If they ratchet the doom up high enough, the probability that the doom scenario actually unfolds comes to seem irrelevant. In the case of Pascal's wager, the catastrophe is not just nuclear winter, the melting of the polar ice caps, or the utter destruction of the United States. No, it is something that, on the individual level, seems to be far worse: the loss of eternal bliss in heaven and possibly being condemned to eternity in hell.

This is a serious charge against those who support Pascal's wager as an argument for believing in God. And, of course, it is always wise to be on the lookout for scaremongering. But, as it stands, the allegation of scaremongering seems to beg the question. If you are 100% sure that a global nuclear war is impossible, or 100% sure that a nuclear winter would not result from a global nuclear confrontation, then you do not need to take precautions against a global nuclear war or against nuclear winter. But what if you are not so sure? What is wrong in that case with the argument from the possibility of nuclear winter for giving up atomic weapons?

Likewise, if God does not exist, or if God does exist but does not promise eternal reward in heaven and does not threaten eternal punishment in hell, then, yes, the supporters of Pascal's wager are engaged in a kind of scaremongering. Yet it is precisely these matters about which the audience for Pascal's wager is ignorant. Suppose you are one of those atheists who thinks that the very concept of God is not logically consistent, so that it is not even possible that God exists. In that case, you can be 100% certain that God does not exist and that you do not need to take out any sort of insurance policy against God's existence. But Pascal's wager is not addressed to you in that case. What if you are like most other nonbelievers in God? What if, while you do not believe in God, you worry that you might be wrong? What if you acknowledge that it is possible that God exists and that heaven and hell are real? What the critic of Pascal's wager needs is a reason for that sort of person not to be persuaded by Pascal's wager. Accusing Pascal of scaremongering is not much of an objection for someone who is not completely sure that there is no God, no heaven, and no hell.

6.3.3.2 Second Objection: Belief Is Not a Matter of Voluntary Control

Is it true that, for any proposition whatsoever, you can just decide to believe it? Clearly not, as the following thought experiment shows. Suppose a street hustler offers you $20 if you decide to believe that $2 + 2 = 7$. Feeling very confident of yourself, you take the $20. "That's great!" says the street hustler. "OK, I have another deal for you. You believe $2 + 2 = 7$, so clearly you believe $20 plus $20 equals $70. That means you would be *making* money if I gave you two $20 bills and you gave me less than $70 in return. So, rationally, if I give you two more $20 bills, you should be eager to give me $65 back. Let us make that exchange right now." And they force two $20 bills into your hand. Since street hustlers are menacing, you go along with them and hand back the two $20 bills they have just given you, the $20 they gave you for believing that $2 + 2 = 7$, and an additional $5. So now you have lost $5. What went wrong? Your mistake was claiming that you *really believed* that $2 + 2 = 7$. You did not really believe it because you cannot really believe it – not if you are sane. You can only pretend to believe it. When the street hustler asked you to put your money where your mouth is, you were exposed.

How about believing in God? Is it something that you can just decide to do? Many critics of Pascal have said it is not. Indeed, some theists think that your believing in God in order to maximize your expected value is like your believing that 2 + 2 = 7 in order to make $20: because it is an inauthentic belief based on selfish motives, you deserve to be punished for it. The critics say Pascal's wager falsely presupposes that a nonbeliever can just decide to believe in God. Belief does not work like that, they say. You cannot just decide to believe that you are rich, tall, and good-looking.

Yet Pascal was actually very astute psychologically. He was quite aware of this objection to his wager, and he avoided the suggestion that one could just flip a switch, start believing, and become a theist. Instead, Pascal thought of his wager as a tool for convincing nonbelievers to begin the process of coming to believe. In the same passage in which he presents the wager, Pascal gives voice to the inner thoughts of the doubter.

> "I confess it, I admit it. But, still, is there no means of seeing the faces of the cards?" – Yes, Scripture and the rest, etc. "Yes, but I have my hands tied and my mouth closed; I am forced to wager, and am not free. I am not released, and am so made that I cannot believe. What, then, would you have me do?"
>
> True. But at least learn your inability to believe, since reason brings you to this, and yet you cannot believe. Endeavour then to convince yourself, not by increase of proofs of God, but by the abatement of your passions. You would like to attain faith, and do not know the way; you would like to cure yourself of unbelief, and ask the remedy for it. Learn of those who have been bound like you, and who now stake all their possessions. These are people who know the way which you would follow, and who are cured of an ill of which you would be cured. Follow the way by which they began; by acting as if they believed, taking the holy water, having masses said, etc. Even this will naturally make you believe, and deaden your acuteness. (Section 3, ch. 233)

"Reason tells you you ought to believe in God," Pascal is saying to the non-believer: "It is your emotions that keep you from believing. Therefore, strive to become like those who already do believe. Read scripture, take the sacraments, go to church, and you will come to believe in God in time." The wager, he thought, would not by itself turn anyone from a nonbeliever in God into a believer in God. Instead, it would, he hoped, get some nonbelievers to start the process of changing their beliefs.

Let us review this objection to Pascal's wager. The objection is that belief in God is not a matter of voluntary control. In response to the objection, defenders of Pascal's wager draw a distinction between direct voluntary control and indirect voluntary control. If one could believe in God just by saying

"I now decide to believe in God," then belief in God would be a matter of direct voluntary control. But even though belief in God cannot be achieved so directly, it may still be possible to do things that will result in, or at least increase the chances of, your believing in God. You cannot just decide to believe in God, but you certainly can decide to join a church, read scripture, and associate with other believers. In that case, belief in God would be subject to indirect voluntary control even though it is not subject to direct voluntary control. So, Pascal's defenders say, this objection misses the mark.

6.3.3.3 Third Objection: Many Gods

Imagine you are the president of the United States during the cold war with the Soviet Union, and you have decided to make all your decisions in accordance with the precautionary principle. You listen to your advisers and you come to realize that a massive nuclear strike by the Soviet Union would wipe out most life in the United States. That is definitely an environmental catastrophe, so, according to the precautionary principle, you ought to do what is necessary to avoid that risk, even if you think that the probability that the Soviets launch such an attack is low. But then you get a briefing on the nuclear winter scenario. You come to see that wiping out the Soviet Union with nuclear weapons threatens to destroy the environment of the entire globe, including of the United States. That is also an environmental catastrophe, so, according to the precautionary principle, you ought to do what is necessary to avoid that risk too. But acting to remove the one risk creates the other risk, and vice versa. There is just no way to avoid the risk of environmental catastrophe.

This thought experiment illustrates a deep problem with Pascal's wager. Pascal writes as if the only religious options are believing in God or not believing in God. This is certainly not true, as proponents of the "many gods" objection insist. First, there are many options for religious belief besides monotheistic religions. It seems that a Hindu could run the same argument for being a Hindu, a Buddhist could run the same argument for being a Buddhist, and so on. Second, belief in God seems very hard to detach from worship within a more specific religious tradition. Within the monotheistic religions, there are many options: Judaism, Christianity, Islam, and newer religions like Mormonism. And within these traditions are further options: Reform, Conservative, and Orthodox for Judaism; Catholic, Protestant, and Eastern Orthodox for Christianity; Sunni, Shia, and Sufi for Islam; and so on. The splits go even deeper if you look at, for example, Protestant Christianity (of which there are dozens and dozens of forms). Which option for religious belief should the nonbeliever pick?

Maybe the religious inclusivists and the religious pluralists are right. Maybe, for the sake of achieving salvation, it does not matter which religion you follow, as long as you follow one of them and live a righteous life. But, as we have seen, religious inclusivism and religious pluralism face serious theoretical problems. What if one form of religious exclusivism is correct? Then Pascal's wager puts the nonbeliever in a quandary. Believing in God by practicing Roman Catholicism leads to an infinite reward if God exists and practicing Roman Catholicism is the only right way to worship God, but it also leads to an infinite punishment if the supreme being is really Allah and practicing a form of Sunni Islam is the only right way to worship Allah. Likewise, believing in Allah by practicing a form of Sunni Islam leads to an infinite reward if Allah exists and practicing a form of Sunni Islam is the only right way to worship Allah, but it also leads to an infinite punishment if the supreme being is really God and practicing Roman Catholicism is the only right way to worship God. And so on, for all the other religious options out there. Assuming that religious exclusivism is correct – that is, assuming there is only one true religion and salvation depends upon following it – it looks like Pascal's wager creates a new kind of stalemate for the nonbeliever, who would be paralyzed by all of the options for belief. For any religion, it looks like nonbelievers run the risk of being damned if they do not believe in it and also run the risk of being damned if they do believe in it. What should they do?

This, it seems, is the fundamental flaw with Pascal's wager. Pascal assumed there were only two choices: you do not believe in God or you do believe in God. In reality, there are far more than two choices because there is far more than just one way to believe in and worship a supreme being: there are "many gods." When Pascal's style of reasoning is applied to the choice from the full array of religious options, it leads to decisional paralysis. There is another way to put the same point. We saw earlier that Pascal said, "wherever the infinite is and there is not an infinity of chances of loss against that of gain, there is no time to hesitate, you must give all." In writing that, Pascal meant that belief in God does not present us with a host of ways of suffering an infinite loss. This seems to be false. Believing in God as, for example, a Southern Baptist risks leading to eternal punishment if, say, Sunni Islam is the exclusive religious truth.

When we started this chapter, we were looking for a way for the theist to escape from the deadlock with atheists. Pascal's wager does not give the theist that escape. It does not break the stalemate.

6.4 The Clifford–James Debate: Is Believing Without Sufficient Evidence Permissible?

We have just examined Pascal's argument that belief in God is rationally compelled by considerations of expected value. We have found that argument to be deficient. But perhaps a weaker position about belief in God can be defended. Perhaps it would be enough for the theist to establish that belief in God can be permissible despite the lack of any definitive evidence (either empirical or philosophical) that God exists. The theist would be saying, "Look, I know that I cannot prove that God exists. I do not have good evidence that God exists. Nonetheless, there is nothing wrong with my believing that God exists. My having faith that God exists is perfectly OK."

It should be no surprise at this point that there are philosophers on both sides of this particular issue. Two figures from the nineteenth century stand out for the opposite positions they took: the British mathematician **W. K. Clifford**[16] and the American psychologist **William James**.[17] Clifford's argument appeared in the essay "The Ethics of Belief," published in 1877 (shortly before he died prematurely of tuberculosis). James made his case in a lecture he delivered in 1896 entitled "The Will to Believe." In each case, let us first examine the structure of the argument.

6.4.1 The Core Argument of Clifford and the Core Argument of James

The arguments of both Clifford and James take the simple logical form of *modus ponens*. As we saw in Chapter 1, *modus ponens* is just this form: if A, then B; A; therefore, B. It is clearly a valid form of argument.

Clifford's Argument Against the Permissibility of Believing in God on Faith
(1) If believing things on faith alone is wrong in general, then believing in God on faith alone is wrong.
(2) Believing things on faith alone is wrong in general.
So, (3) Believing in God on faith alone is wrong.

In the case of Clifford, the first premise does not need much defending. It just says that, if a standard applies to belief in all cases, then it applies to belief in God in particular. Religious belief, Clifford thinks, does not deserve a special exception from the rules. The second premise is the one that requires defense. Clifford tries to establish the general principle that believing things on faith is wrong by appealing to a lot of particular cases. These are not cases of belief in God or in other supernatural beings. Instead they are mundane, everyday cases.

---

[16] https://www.britannica.com/biography/William-Kingdon-Clifford.
[17] https://www.britannica.com/biography/William-James.

The argument of James, meanwhile, employs *modus ponens* twice.

James's Argument for the Permissibility of Believing in God on Faith
(1) If there are some matters other than belief in God such that believing them on faith alone is not wrong, then believing things on faith alone is not wrong in general.
(2) If believing things on faith alone is not wrong in general, then (unless a reason is given for thinking belief in God is a special exception) believing in God on faith alone is not wrong.
(3) There are some matters other than belief in God such that believing them on faith alone is not wrong.
So, (4) Believing things on faith alone is not wrong in general.
So, (5) Believing in God on faith alone is not wrong (unless there is a reason for thinking belief in God is a special exception).

The first premise is clearly true. If you can find particular cases such that believing a proposition on faith is not only not wrong, but is clearly permissible, then the general claim "It is always wrong to believe anything on faith" is clearly false. Similarly, as with Clifford, there is not much debate over the second premise. If it is not impermissible in general to believe things on faith – if there are cases where belief on faith is permissible – then it is not impermissible to believe in God on faith (unless there is some reason for thinking belief in God is a special case). In James's argument, it is the third premise that requires defense. In support of the third premise, James tries to provide what philosophers sometimes call "companions in guilt." Just like Clifford, James gives mundane, everyday cases of believing in things on faith. He hopes that, by getting us to reflect on those cases, we will all come to agree that the act of believing is permissible in those cases.

So, the disagreement between Clifford and James boils down to a disagreement about the array of everyday cases in which people believe things on faith. What are these cases? Well, being creatures of their time, both Clifford and James gave examples that may not be very relatable to students today. Both brought up sailing ships! Clifford's central example of the wrongness of believing things on faith was the owner of a run-down sailing ship scheduled to take emigrants on a long journey overseas. In the course of making his counterarguments, James gave the example of taking a risk by joining an expedition to the North Pole.

In addition to reviewing their somewhat out-of-date examples, we will look at some more relatable cases of believing things on faith. Then we will see if we can discern the general features of those cases. This will help us to see what it is that Clifford thinks makes belief in God on faith wrong and what it is that James thinks makes belief in God on faith permissible.

6.4.2 Wrongly Believing Things on Faith

At first glance, Clifford has chosen the more difficult position to defend. We are taught to respect and honor faith. Faith is supposed to be a good thing. What, then, is wrong with believing things on faith? And, if it is wrong to believe on the basis of faith, what does that mean for belief in God?

6.4.2.1 Clifford's Principle

All of Clifford's examples are meant to illustrate and bolster his general claim, a claim that has come to be called <u>Clifford's Principle</u>: "it is wrong always, everywhere, and for anyone, to believe anything upon insufficient evidence."[18] In what sense of "wrong" does he think such belief is wrong? For Clifford, the wrongness is moral wrongness (so Clifford is working with a deontological conception of epistemic justification). Believing in a proposition without sufficient evidence is a violation of social obligations. Belief on faith threatens the health and welfare of others. Clifford's example is of a shipowner sending a ship out to sea without checking whether it is truly seaworthy. The shipowner just believes that the ship is safe without any actual evidence. By believing in something without backing up that belief with evidence, the shipowner does something wrong: he risks the lives of all of the passengers. If the ship sinks, their deaths are on his hands. (In the US legal system, he would be guilty of what is called "criminal negligence.") And, even if the ship makes it to port safely, the shipowner still did something wrong. Remember, as we saw earlier in this chapter, you should not judge the quality of a decision by its results but by the information available to you prior to chance coming into play. By that standard, a successful trip does not absolve the shipowner of guilt; it just makes him (and his passengers) lucky.

6.4.2.2 Violations of Clifford's Principle: Other Examples

There are many examples of beliefs that, when held without any evidence, pose a danger to other individuals or to the general public. Suppose there is a college student (call this student X to protect their identity) who foresees in the very near future hooking up and having unprotected sex with a partner X does not know terribly well. X thinks, "I wonder – do I have any sexually transmitted diseases?" Let us suppose that X has some evidence that STDs

---

[18] William Clifford, "The Ethics of Belief," in Peterson et al. (eds), *Philosophy of Religion: Selected Readings*, p. 107.

may be a possibility in their case. X may have a history of unprotected sex, or X may have come to know that a prior sexual partner now has an STD. But let us suppose that X also has some evidence against having any STDs. X has no obvious symptoms, and the last time they went to the doctor, the doctor did not raise any concerns. Overall, the evidence is inconclusive each way. What should X do?

There is evidence that X can obtain to answer this question. X can get tested for STDs. But getting tested costs money. Furthermore, it takes time to go to the doctor and it takes additional time to get the results. If X delays hooking up until after taking and getting the results of an STD test, the opportunity for a hook-up will pass X by. So X thinks, "Well, I do not have any evidence that I *do* have an STD. Besides, thinking that I might have an STD is really stressing me out. So I will just block it out. I am just going to believe that I do not have any STDs. That will make me feel better about myself." Breathing a sigh of relief, X hooks up and has unprotected sex with a partner, never telling that partner the hidden story.

Did X do something morally wrong? Most definitely. Were the partner to find out, they would probably be extremely angry with X, whether or not X transmitted an STD to them. X put someone else's health at risk. X had no right to do that. It does not matter if things turned out OK in the end. It was still wrong of X to believe what they believed. Just as you should not judge the quality of a decision by its outcome, you should not judge the moral rightness or wrongness of X holding the belief "I am free of STDs" by whether or not that belief turned out to be true. Instead, you should judge the moral rightness or wrongness of X holding that belief from the evidence available to X at the time. X had inadequate evidence for the belief, so X was wrong to believe it. X should have refrained from holding that belief. And that would mean refraining from having unprotected sex until solid evidence of a lack of STDs comes in.

Other examples of irresponsibly held beliefs are easily multiplied. How would you have liked it if, as a child, your parents had selected your baby-sitter by just randomly hiring someone off of the streets? Suppose they had done no background checks, obtained no referrals. Suppose they had never even met your babysitter before. Sure, things might have worked out. Even if not everyone is great with children, few people are outrightly cruel, evil, or horrible to children. Still, we would all agree that your parents did something morally wrong. And they did something morally wrong because they believed something on insufficient evidence. Rather than checking out the potential babysitters, they took it on faith that the person they had randomly selected would be a decent babysitter. Even if the person they selected turned out to be a great babysitter, they still did something wrong.

6.4.2.3 Application of Clifford's Principle to Belief in God

Interestingly, Clifford never mentioned religious beliefs in particular in his essay. He did not talk about God. However, it is clear by his words and his examples that religious belief is the target. He wrote that belief

> is desecrated when given to unproved and unquestioned statements, for the solace and private pleasure of the believer; to add a tinsel of splendour to the plain straight road of our life and display a bright mirage beyond it; or even to drown the common sorrows of our kind by a self-deception.[19]

In saying those things, he was repeating some of the most common allegations against religious belief (allegations we will hear again in Chapter 7). Atheists such as Sigmund Freud and Karl Marx depicted religious belief as a comforting myth, an "illusion" (Freud's term) that serves as a kind of painkiller ("the opiate of the masses," in Marx's famous phrase) for the lifelong hardships that confront the average person. It is quite clear in the context that Clifford thinks the same about religious belief as they do.

Clifford emphasizes that the wrongness of believing without sufficient evidence is a consequence of a basic fact of human psychology: belief almost always leads to action. Those who really believe that vaccinating children causes autism are not going to just keep that belief to themselves. They are almost certainly going to avoid vaccinating their own children, and they are likely to push for laws and public policies that enable them and people like them to forego vaccinating children. What results? Public health crises like the measles outbreak in California in 2015. Analogously, according to many atheists, belief in God can lead to all sorts of harmful actions: corporally punishing children because God commands us to and forgoing medically necessary blood transfusions because of a supposed scriptural prohibition on blood transfusions, to give just two of many oft-given examples. The belief in God, Clifford thinks, does not just sit there inert in your brain. It guides your actions. Given the potential effects on everyone else of those actions, you owe it to everyone to make sure that every belief of yours is based on good evidence.

6.4.3 Permissibly Believing Things on Faith

Before learning about Clifford's arguments, you may have expected James to win an easy victory. But now, it seems, Clifford's position is strong. What did James say in reply to Clifford?

---

[19] Clifford, "The Ethics of Belief," p. 105.

6.4.3.1 Statement of James's Position

Clifford gave some compelling examples where believing on faith leads to or risks harm to others. But James replied that, in certain circumstances, believing on faith is permissible simply because it is required. Faith is required for the achievement of all sorts of everyday good things: friendship, love, marriage, career success, and so on. Because faith is required, it cannot, as a general matter, always be wrong to believe on faith. Here James appeals to a slogan that is oftentimes invoked in philosophy: "<u>ought</u>" implies "<u>can</u>." When we say that someone ought to have done something, we are saying implicitly that the person could have done that thing. If it is true that you ought to have saved a drowning child, then implicitly you could have saved that drowning child. Conversely, suppose you cannot lift up a large automobile by yourself. In that case, it cannot be that you ought to have lifted up the large automobile by yourself that was crushing a child to death.

Likewise, James thought that there are many everyday cases – what he calls <u>genuine options</u> – in which belief in a certain proposition is momentous, forced, and live. For example, suppose you have dated a person named Robin for several months. Now consider the proposition "Robin is a suitable marriage partner for me." The proposition is momentous in the sense that whether or not you believe it will likely change your life forever. The proposition is forced in the sense that you cannot remain neutral. Neutrality amounts to disbelief. (You: "Do you love me?" Robin: "It is not that I do love you, and it is not that I do not love you. I am waiting for more evidence." Pretty clearly, Robin does not love you. In this case, choosing not to decide is, in fact, making a choice.) And the proposition is live in the sense that it is a realistic possibility for you. It is not a proposition so remote that you cannot even think of believing it. These genuine options are propositions that cannot be decided on purely intellectual grounds. They require input from our passional natures. They require a leap of faith.

In such cases, there is only so much evidence gathering you can do. At a certain point you will have to make a commitment. If Clifford's principle is correct, you are obliged in such situations never to believe, never to commit yourself to the truth of the proposition. But this would deprive you of the potential benefits of believing. That has got to be wrong, James thought. "A rule of thinking which would absolutely prevent me from acknowledging certain kinds of truth if those kinds of truth were really there, would be an irrational rule,"[20] he said in his address. Since Clifford's principle is wrong, believing on

---

[20] William James, "The Will to Believe," in Peterson et al. (eds), *Philosophy of Religion: Selected Readings*, p. 114.

faith is not necessarily wrong. Therefore, unless a good reason is given for thinking that belief in God is an exception, James thinks, believing in God on faith is not necessarily wrong.

6.4.3.2 Other Examples of Permissibly Believing Something on Faith

James thinks that there are many cases such that, if we want to achieve a clear good, we cannot help but believe on faith. In those cases, it cannot be wrong to believe in something on insufficient evidence. We just saw marriage as an example. You can get a lot of information about a potential spouse prior to marrying them, but you never really know until you are actually married how that person will be for you. At some point, you have to dive in. This is why marriage is so often described as "taking the plunge." And, if you never take the plunge, you will miss out on what many people regard as one of life's great goods.

When this author was 14, he went around Annapolis, Maryland, with a group of other teenaged boys, jumping off of bridges into Spa Creek and the Severn River. We were warned beforehand that beneath the waters there might be pylons we could not see. If we dived in and hit one of them, we could end up paralyzed. But we had no way of knowing where the pylons were without jumping into the water. The only way to find out was to dive in. So, if we wanted to experience the great pleasure of jumping off a high bridge into the cool waters below us, we had to take the plunge. It was that, or never dive off any bridges. This author jumped. He did not end up paralyzed, by the way, although he did break his wrist and he still has a scar on his left leg.

There are many other examples of faith being necessary for the achievement of an everyday good. Aspiring athletes, aspiring actors, aspiring anyones all need to start with a basic belief: "I can do this." But how can they know that ahead of time? How do very successful people know that they will be successful prior to striving for success? In almost all cases, they do not. Instead, the belief in themselves comes first. It is a precondition for success. As James put it, there are certain cases where "faith in the fact helps to make that fact."[21] Career success is definitely one of those cases. That is why, when highly successful people look back on their lives, they oftentimes say something like "I always believed in myself."

Yes, sometimes such beliefs will turn out to be false. Only a small fraction of American high school athletes end up playing their sport professionally. The sports landscape is littered with the crushed egos of young athletes who believed in themselves. The same is true of countless other occupations: art,

---

[21] James, "The Will to Believe," p. 113.

music, acting, politics, and even academia. Given this harsh reality, it is easy to resign yourself to failure. Homer Simpson (from *The Simpsons*) articulated what seems to be the more realistic position. "No matter how good you are at something, there are about a million people better than you." While that sentiment is true in many cases, it is not merely sad; it is self-defeating. Yet Clifford's principle seems to urge us toward that sort of negative thinking. If Clifford's principle prevailed and all people were realistic rather than aspirational about their abilities and prospects, society would be full of single, frustrated Bart Simpsons. (Bart replied to Homer "Got it! Can't win, don't try.")

The world would clearly be a worse place if no one anywhere ever believed anything upon insufficient evidence. And that is why many philosophers have concluded that, despite the rousing language of Clifford, James won the debate.

6.5 Concluding Thoughts on Faith and Reason

We have surveyed a variety of positions theists can take regarding the relationship between faith and reason. The classical picture of theologians like Aquinas was that both faith and reason made valuable contributions to a proper belief in God. Many theists today still hold to this classical picture, and it is not obviously wrong. But it is hard to maintain for theists who concede that there is no good empirical evidence of the existence of God and there are no good philosophical arguments for the existence of God. Theists who do make this concession may think that faith in God is nonetheless justified on the sorts of grounds Pascal gave. But, as we saw, there are quite serious objections to Pascal's wager. For theists who see little empirical or philosophical evidence of God's existence, the best option, it seems, is to defend a position like that of James. If belief in God is like other "aspirational" beliefs that most people regard as perfectly acceptable to have, then believing in God on faith alone also seems to be quite permissible.

And yet … in this chapter, the entire discussion of faith and reason presumed something. It presumed that theists and atheists were in a stalemate when it comes to evidence for and against the existence of God. Many atheists think they have one more card to play. They think they can explain, in a perfectly natural and scientific way, why it is that people would believe in God even if God did not exist. That, in turn, means, that belief in God is irrational. And it is irrational, these atheists think, even if there is no proof that God does not exist. We will examine this line of thought in the next chapter.

Annotated Bibliography

Plantinga, Alvin (2000). *Warranted Christian Belief* (New York: Oxford University Press).

Though not covered in this chapter, the position called **reformed epistemology**[22] is laid out in full by Plantinga in this dense but rewarding book.

Plantinga, Alvin and Nicholas Wolterstorff, eds (1983). *Faith and Rationality: Reason and Belief in God* (Notre Dame, IN: University of Notre Dame Press).

This is one of the classic collections of papers on the epistemology of religion. It has essays by some of the key figures in analytic philosophy of religion, including Alvin Plantinga, George Mavrodes, Nicholas Wolterstorff, and William Alston.

Rota, Michael (2016). *Taking Pascal's Wager: Faith, Evidence, and the Abundant Life* (Downers Grove, IL: InterVarsity Press).

Rota gives a modern defense of Pascal's classic argument in this accessible book. Unusually for a philosophy book, it includes some biographies, specifically, lengthy biographical sketches of three historical figures who took the "leap of faith" and committed themselves to God.

Swinburne, Richard (2005). *Faith and Reason*, 2nd edn (New York: Oxford University Press).

The third in his trilogy of books on the philosophy of religion, in this volume Swinburne examines what the title indicates, the relationship between reason and faith when it comes to belief in the existence of God.

---

[22] https://plato.stanford.edu/entries/religion-epistemology/#RefoEpis.

7

NATURALISTIC EXPLANATIONS OF RELIGION

If you have made it through the book so far, you may very well be impressed by all of the deep questions that come up in connection with God and religion. But what if you started the book neither believing in God nor belonging to any religion? You may think that everything we have discussed so far is academic at best and useless at worst. "These religions are all hogwash anyway," you may be thinking. "I did not need to read this book to know that." If this reflects your attitude toward religion, there is still a very important question about religion that ought to interest you. If religion is just a big mistake, why are so many people religious? What explains why so many people, both in the past and in the present, believe in God, gods, spirits, souls, angels, heaven, hell, miracles, karma, and so on? If none of those things exist, why do so many people believe that they exist?

It turns out that these questions, too, are ones that philosophers have addressed. In this chapter, we will survey some of the most influential theorists of religion. For these thinkers, religion is such a widespread and influential human phenomenon that it cannot be dismissed as stupid and antiquated. It is their duty, they think, to come up with a theory that explains why religious phenomena exist and why religions have the features that they do. We will see what they have to say. And if you are religious yourself, you will want to know who these theorists are and what they think of you. You ought to know your enemies.

7.1 What a Naturalistic Explanation Is

How should we explain the account in the book of Genesis of a worldwide flood (Genesis 6:1–8:22)? One way is to say that it actually happened – that God exists and caused a worldwide deluge that lasted 40 days and that Noah

This Is Philosophy of Religion: An Introduction, First Edition. Neil A. Manson.
© 2021 John Wiley & Sons, Inc. Published 2021 by John Wiley & Sons, Inc.

survived. While possible (in a very broad sense), this explanation strikes even most theists as deeply implausible. It simply does not fit with the data we have from numerous scientific fields like geology, paleontology, and biology. Furthermore, while some theists feel that they have to interpret all their sacred texts literally, most approach scripture on the assumption that significant parts of it are not meant to be taken literally. So explaining the flood story by saying that God really did cause a worldwide flood is not only implausible but, for most theists, unnecessary.

Another way to "explain" the flood story in the book of Genesis would be to dismiss it as just another strange myth. But that answer fails to account for the existence of similar flood stories throughout the ancient world. There was a flood story in the epic of Gilgamesh. There were flood stories in Greek and Roman mythology. Flatly dismissing the flood story as a complete fabrication does not explain this coincidence. But what could the flood story be if it were not just pure myth?

A scientific picture is emerging that, though controversial, seems to offer a plausible history of the flood story as having arisen from distortion of reports of a real occurrence. In other words, there really was a catastrophic flood – just not as catastrophic as that claimed in the book of Genesis. Archaeological and geological evidence indicates that, about 7,500 years ago, what is now the Black Sea in eastern Europe was a dry basin inhabited by humans. Rising waters brought about by the end of the Ice Age led to a natural dam at what is now the Bosporus Straits being broken. A vast area was flooded in the course of a few weeks. The ruins of whole villages have been found beneath the Black Sea. This cataclysm was likely preserved in ancient Near Eastern myths, and stories of it probably spread globally. It is reasonable to think that the flood story found its way into many religious texts, including the book of Genesis.

Supposing this account were true, it is a satisfying explanation of the existence of the flood story. It ties together many different facts in the way good scientific explanations are supposed to do. The explanation involves no mysterious forces or supernatural powers. At no point does it involve saying that there actually was miraculous interference by God in the course of nature. The explanation confines itself to scientifically and historically verifiable claims. It is much easier for most people to accept than the religious explanation that there was a worldwide flood caused by God. This explanation also shows a measure of respect for the religious traditions of which the flood story is an element. Although the explanation does not involve God, it also takes the flood story as something worth investigating scientifically. In seeking its origin, those advancing this explanation honor the flood story and the religious traditions of which it is a part. They treat the story with a bit more respect than those who simply dismiss it as an ancient tale told by illiterate shepherds.

Could all of religion be likewise explained in a scientific manner? Such is the hope of many philosophical naturalists. **Naturalism**[1] is the view that only natural entities exist. The metaphysical aspect of naturalism is the claim that there are no gods, ghosts, or supernatural entities of any sort. The epistemological aspect of naturalism is the claim that the best way (perhaps the only way) to obtain knowledge of the world is through the methods of science. By definition, all naturalists are atheists. Note, however, that this does not mean all atheists are naturalists. For example, some Buddhists deny that any gods exist. Therefore they count as atheists. But they also say that the material world is an illusion. So they are not naturalists either. Still, most atheists endorse naturalism, and even many theists adopt naturalism as their working assumption for scientific purposes. A naturalistic explanation of religion, then, is any explanation of religion that presupposes the truth of naturalism.

Many naturalists claim that all of the phenomena of religion can be accounted for solely in terms of natural forces. These phenomena include the contents of religious texts, the character of religious and mystical experiences, religious rituals, religious doctrines, church structures, and the effect of religion in history, politics, and economics. For many naturalists, religion is a predictable consequence of known or knowable natural causes. Why people believe in gods, spirits, and souls is no more of a mystery than why children sometimes make imaginary friends, why mobs form, why people believe in good luck and jinxes, and why every culture has burial rituals.

These naturalists acknowledge the real occurrence of (most) religious phenomena, but they explain those phenomena without assuming that any supernatural objects or forces actually exist. To take Christianity as an example, naturalists think that the contents of the Bible, the experiences people have when they claim to feel God's presence, and the rapid spread of Christianity in the Roman era can all be explained in purely natural terms. There is a long history of naturalistic explanations of religion drawing from the traditional social sciences: anthropology, sociology, economics, and psychology. The favored naturalistic explanations of religion nowadays involve parts of these classic approaches, but add new theoretical elements: evolutionary biology, evolutionary psychology, and neuroscience.

Collectively, these explanations seem to provide powerful support for naturalism. First, they promise to make naturalism intellectually satisfying by resolving what the biologist **E. O. Wilson**[2] calls "the enduring paradox of religion" – namely, "that so much of its substance is demonstrably false, yet

---

[1] https://plato.stanford.edu/entries/naturalism.
[2] https://www.britannica.com/biography/Edward-O-Wilson.
[3] E. O. Wilson, *Sociobiology: The New Synthesis* (Cambridge, MA: Belknap Press, 1975), p. 561.

it remains a driving force in all societies."[3] For the naturalist, the existence, prevalence, and power of religion is a puzzle demanding a solution. These explanations promise to solve that puzzle.

Second, if naturalists really can explain all of the phenomena of religion naturalistically (that is, without assuming that gods, angels, demons, souls, spirits, reincarnation, karma, or miracles really exist), they will have done more than just show how naturalism is consistent with all of the observed facts. They will have shown, in addition, that the naturalistic worldview is superior to any religious worldview. That is, in fact, the way many atheists view their favored naturalistic theory of religion. They see it as a tool in a struggle against religion.

Naturalistic theories of religion, then, are not just of scientific interest. Their religious and philosophical implications are profound. Therefore, these theories demand close attention. Our examination of them begins by surveying three classic approaches and three modern ones. We will see both how they differ and what they have in common. Our survey ends with an evaluation of the philosophical and religious implications of the naturalistic theories of religion. We will explore what they mean both for atheists and for theists.

Before we proceed, it is worth noting that the division of theories into clear categories is a bit artificial. Not many naturalists restrict their explanation of religion to just one approach. But for almost every naturalist, one approach takes precedence over the others. Due to limitations of space, the survey will be wide-ranging and thematic. For more detailed presentations of these theories, you should look at some of the suggested readings at the end of this chapter.

7.2 Three Classic Approaches to Explaining Religion Naturalistically

7.2.1 Anthropomorphic Projection Theories

Almost 350 years ago philosophers as diverse as **Thomas Hobbes**,[4] the author of *Leviathan*,[5] and **Baruch Spinoza**,[6] the author of *Ethics*,[7] asserted

---

[4] https://www.britannica.com/biography/Thomas-Hobbes.

[5] Hobbes's *Leviathan* can be accessed at http://earlymoderntexts.com/authors/hobbes.

[6] https://www.britannica.com/biography/Benedict-de-Spinoza.

[7] Spinoza's *Ethics* can be accessed at http://earlymoderntexts.com/assets/pdfs/spinoza 1665.pdf.

that religion results from an all too human tendency to try to explain too much. In the course of trying to explain natural occurrences such as plagues, floods, famines, and so on, our ancient ancestors mistakenly projected human qualities out into a supernatural world of their own creation. This led to religion.

There are four basic elements to these anthropomorphic projection theories. (A) Primitive humans were hyperactive explainers. (B) Primitive humans were biased toward purposive explanations, that is, toward explaining things in terms of goals and purposes. (C) Primitive humans projected their own psychological states onto the gods they created. (D) Through the power of culture, modern humans inherited the religious beliefs of their primitive ancestors.

7.2.1.1 (A) Hyperactive Explaining

"It is peculiar to the nature of man, to be inquisitive into the causes of the events they see," said Hobbes at the beginning of chapter 12 of *Leviathan*, a chapter entitled "Of Religion." He said we humans are unique among animals in being very active explainers. Indeed, we are hyperactive explainers. We are reluctant to accept that some things happen by chance or without a purpose. Now imagine that you were a member of a tribe that existed, say, 8,000 years ago. Scientific methods had not yet been developed. How would you expect your fellow tribe members to respond if a bolt of lightning killed a fellow tribe member, if a child was born on the same day that an elder died, or if a disease skipped over your village but ravaged a neighboring village? You would expect them to look for an explanation. It is human nature to do so.

7.2.1.2 (B) Purposive Explanation

Because our primitive ancestors lacked scientific methods and scientific forms of explanation, they turned to the form of explanation that was best suited to their emerging social world: purposive explanation. A purposive explanation (also called an intentional or personal explanation) involves purposes: desire, need, jealousy, anger, and so on. We explain things in terms of purposes every day. For example, if you see deep scratches along the side of your new car, and you know that you have not been in an accident, you are going to think someone is really angry at you. Likewise, when they saw something they did not understand, our primitive ancestors assumed that there existed a person of just the right kind to explain that thing. They did that because purposive explanations were the only kind of explanations they knew how to give. If someone got struck by lightning, our ancient ancestors reasoned, then someone must have wanted that person to get struck by lightning.

7.2.1.3 (C) Projection

If a person has the power to cause lightning to strike, then obviously you must take care not to become the target of that person. In order to avoid things like lightning strikes, our ancestors needed to figure out the purposes of these mysterious, powerful beings. Since they could not communicate with these nonexistent beings, humans projected their own purposes onto the gods. Projection is the psychological phenomenon of attributing to someone else one's own thoughts and feelings. So, for example, if you hate your boss, you might remark to your coworker that it seems everyone hates your boss.

Through projection, primitive humans naturally regarded the supernatural beings they dreamed up as being just like the natural beings with which they were most familiar: themselves. The gods loved and hated, felt jealousy and pride, lusted and loathed. This led to a curious behavior by our primitive ancestors. Spinoza wrote in the appendix to part I of *Ethics*:

> Among so many of Nature's blessings they were bound to discover quite a number of disasters, such as storms, earthquakes, diseases, and so forth, and they maintained that these occurred because the gods were angry at the wrongs done to them by men, or the faults committed in the course of their worship.

To placate the gods, one had to provided them with food or to show gestures of submission, just as one would feed a guest or bow to a king to keep the king happy. This fear of the gods and desire to please them explains religious rituals, practices of abasement and worship, sacrificial offerings, and so on.

7.2.1.4 (D) Cultural Transmission

The belief in gods persists to this day because, once religious belief entered the human mind, it got passed down from generation to generation. Religion is subject to cultural transmission – through children's stories, myths, art, education, and so on. Even "advanced" religions such as Christianity can be explained in terms of the same fundamental patterns displayed in "primitive" religions, with the difference between "primitive" and "advanced" being that the big, established religions have had more time, resources, and need to tidy up their stories than "primitive" religions.

7.2.2 Sociological Theories

Over 150 years ago, the philosopher and economist **Karl Marx**[8] advanced a theory of religion in **numerous writings**[9] within his larger theory of politics,

---

[8] https://www.britannica.com/biography/Karl-Marx.

[9] All of Marx's writings, as well of the writings of many other Marxists, are available at https://www.marxists.org/archive/marx/index.htm.

economics, and society. For Marx, religion emerges from powerful social forces. Religion is primarily a group phenomenon, not an individual one. There are four basic elements to this theory. (E) The religion of a society is a product of its social, political, and economic structures. (F) The religious beliefs and practices of individuals in a society reflect the social, political, and economic dynamics of that society. (G) Religion serves a dual function with respect to social control: the powerful use it to oppress the weak, while the oppressed comfort themselves with it rather than revolt against their oppressors. (H) As a society moves toward justice and equality, religion becomes increasingly unnecessary; when society becomes perfectly just socially, religion will disappear.

7.2.2.1 (E) The Sociological Thesis

Sociology is the study of societies and social structures as natural objects that are capable of being investigated scientifically. Sociologists study human societies with the same mindset that primatologists study bands of gorillas and entomologists study ant colonies. According to the sociological thesis, religious beliefs and practices are just further aspects of human societies, and the best way to understand religion is in terms of the functions it fulfills in the complex machinery of social life. For example, in his book *The Rise of Christianity: A Sociologist Reconsiders History* the sociologist Rodney Stark explains the flourishing of Christianity in the late Roman Empire in terms of advantageous social structures and networks. Because of their emphasis on community and caring, early Christian groups were able to withstand epidemic diseases much better than non-Christian groups, says Stark. He thinks that Christianity's rise can be explained in terms of the social functions it performed: promoting literacy, strengthening family bonds, surviving disasters, and so on. More generally, sociologists of religion seek to explain all the major facets of religion in terms of religion's effect on society.

7.2.2.2 (F) The Reflection Thesis

For proponents of the sociological approach, religion is a primitive form of psychological and sociological speculation. Figuring out other people is incredibly difficult. Understanding society is even harder. Because they did not have the tools of science, primitive humans tried to understand themselves and their societies as best they could – through myth and through reflection on their gods. According to the reflection thesis, if you want to understand how the people of a society think of themselves and of the world, study their religion, because their religion is a hidden reflection of the underlying structures and dynamics of their society.

This was the view of **Ludwig Feuerbach**,[10] an early nineteenth-century philosopher and anthropologist whose work influenced Marx profoundly. In chapter 1 of *The Essence of Christianity*[11] he wrote:

> Religion is man's earliest and also indirect form of self-knowledge. His own nature is in the first instance contemplated by him as that of another being. ... The divine being is nothing else than the human being, or, rather, the human nature purified.

Marx likewise claimed in *Capital*[12] that religion holds up a cracked mirror to society: "The religious world is but the reflex of the real world." "Religion is the self-consciousness and self-esteem of man who has either not yet found himself or has already lost himself again," and it is "an inverted world-consciousness," he said in *Economic and Philosophic Manuscripts of 1844*.[13] Like Feuerbach and Marx before them, advocates of the sociological approach today see religion as reflecting society. They think that closely studying religion will reveal hidden social structures and dynamics.

7.2.2.3 (G) The Oppression Thesis

Religion arises, Marx claimed, because society is divided into classes. Ancient Roman society was divided into the **patricians**[14] and the **plebeians**.[15] Late medieval society in Europe was divided into **landlords and peasants**.[16] **Capitalism**[17] is the free-market economic system that arose during the Industrial Revolution and is the economic system of most of the world today. Under capitalism, the main classes are the **bourgeoisie**[18] (the people who own and manage the businesses) and the **proletariat**[19] (the people who work for the owners and the managers in exchange for wages). In each case, says Marx, we can identify

---

[10] https://www.britannica.com/biography/Ludwig-Feuerbach.

[11] Feuerbach's *The Essence of Christianity* can be accessed at https://www.marxists.org/reference/archive/feuerbach/works/essence.

[12] Marx's *Capital* can be accessed at https://www.marxists.org/archive/marx/works/1867-c1/ch01.htm.

[13] Marx's *Economic and Philosophic Manuscripts of 1844* can be accessed at https://www.marxists.org/archive/marx/works/download/pdf/Econs-1844.pdf.

[14] https://www.britannica.com/topic/patrician.

[15] https://www.britannica.com/topic/plebeian.

[16] https://www.britannica.com/topic/history-of-Europe/Landlords-and-peasants.

[17] https://www.britannica.com/topic/capitalism.

[18] https://www.britannica.com/topic/bourgeoisie.

[19] https://www.britannica.com/topic/proletariat.

one class as the oppressors and the other as the oppressed. According to the oppression thesis, religion plays a crucial role in both the oppression of the weak and the response of the weak to their oppression.

For Marx, the poor, weak, and oppressed need relief from their suffering, so they create a fantasy world beyond this one where their pain is soothed. That is why they believe in heaven. In *Economic and Philosophic Manuscripts of 1844* he said:

> Religious suffering is, at one and the same time, the expression of real suffering and a protest against real suffering. Religion is the sigh of the oppressed creature, the heart of a heartless world, and the soul of soulless conditions. It is the opium of the people.

The rich, powerful oppressors, meanwhile, use religion to justify their oppression and to keep themselves in power.

In each society, the oppressors create an ideology – a set of ideas that works to impose social control, often at an unconscious level. Examples of ideologies include the caste system in India and **the doctrine that kings rule by divine right**.[20] These ideologies perpetuate oppression by convincing the oppressed that divine powers established and approve of the oppressive social structures. Even seemingly harmless elements of religious ethics can play a role in an oppressive ideology. For example, Marx alleges that the common religious demand to engage in charity gives an advantage to the ruling classes. You cannot give what you do not have, and the oppressed have virtually nothing to give. Only the ruling classes have the excess resources needed to be charitable. By being charitable, the ruling classes signal their power to everyone else. The religious demand to give to the poor therefore privileges the wealthy and keeps the poor down. The emphasis on charity also provides an inbuilt justification for never addressing the root cause of poverty that makes charity necessary – namely, unjust social structures.

7.2.2.4 (H) The Secularization Thesis

The oppression thesis suggests a related idea. If oppressive social structures cause religion, then there would be no need for religion if oppressive social structures are eliminated. As social structures become less oppressive – as the relationships between humans become ever more just and equitable – religious belief will become less common. So social progress leads to secularization – the societal trend away from religious belief and toward nonbelief.

---

[20] https://www.britannica.com/topic/divine-right-of-kings.

According to the <u>secularization thesis</u>, once society is reshaped on a fair and equitable basis, religion will disappear. "The religious reflex of the real world can, in any case, only then finally vanish, when the practical relations of every-day life offer to man none but perfectly intelligible and reasonable relations with regard to his fellowmen and to Nature," said Marx in *Capital*.[21] Belief in the secularization thesis is widespread, and for good reason. Secularization is a very real phenomenon in much of the Western world, with regular church attendance declining steadily in Europe and the United States over the past century.

7.2.3 Freudian Psychological Theories

Almost 100 years ago, the pioneering psychologist **Sigmund Freud**[22] set out his theory of religion in popular books such as *The Future of an Illusion* and *Civilization and Its Discontents*. His theory incorporated elements of both the anthropomorphic projection and sociological approaches, but Freud added a quite new ingredient to the naturalistic broth: the idea that religion results from unconscious mental processes common to all humans. Deep-seated psychological forces – forces that shape our minds from birth – push us to believe in God or in gods. There are four basic elements to this theory. (I) Unconscious mental mechanisms powerfully affect our beliefs and our actions. (J) Some of these unconscious mental mechanisms are not aimed at producing true beliefs. (K) The psychological development of a person from infancy to adulthood progresses through age-appropriate stages, yet humans tend to go back to some age-inappropriate stage in the face of frustration of their desires. (L) Religion results from the unconscious mental process of wish fulfillment, a process that is aimed at anxiety reduction rather than truth. Religious belief involves a person's going back to an infantile psychological state in which they receive total love and protection from their parents.

7.2.3.1 (I) Unconscious Mental Processes

Freud's most important contribution to psychology was his identification of universal, innate mental mechanisms that operate in us at a hidden level. We are not consciously aware of these mechanisms when they are working. These unconscious mental processes have an enormous effect on what we believe and how we act. Yet they never make themselves known to us unless we undergo

---

[21] Marx's *Capital* can be accessed at https://www.marxists.org/archive/marx/works/1867-c1/ch01.htm.
[22] https://www.britannica.com/biography/Sigmund-Freud.

special procedures such as psychotherapy. Nowadays belief in unconscious mental processes is so widespread that their existence is taken for granted. Indeed, most of us have explained someone else's behavior in terms of unconscious "defense mechanisms" such as projection and repression. Yet the idea of unconscious mental processes the nature of which can be revealed by careful investigation really blossomed only with Freud.

7.2.3.2 (J) Mental Processes Not Aimed at the Truth

Some mental processes typically aim to produce true beliefs. Take memory as an example. When you try to remember something – say, where your cell phone is – the goal is to retrieve the truth. Freud claimed that a crucial feature of many unconscious mental processes is that they aim to produce something other than true belief. For example, extremely painful experiences such as combat stress are blocked in conscious thought. The result is "repressed" memories which can be unlocked only by psychotherapy. In cases like these, the unconscious mental process is not aimed at providing a person with the truth. It is quite the opposite. Some unconscious mental processes are aimed precisely at avoiding, burying, or redirecting the truth.

7.2.3.3 (K) Psychological Development

Newborns lack the full array of mental tools possessed by adult humans. Freud thought that the passage from infancy to adulthood proceeds unevenly and through stages. For example, in very young children the stages are oral, anal, and genital. Likewise, our bodily development occurs in distinct biological stages: infancy, adolescence, adulthood, and senescence. Importantly for Freud, psychological progression never completely erases earlier stages, so that regression – going back to an earlier, age-inappropriate stage – remains possible. Frustration of one's basic desires – for love, sex, status, or revenge – can cause so much psychic strain that one copes by regressing. For example, the businessperson caught cheating and surrounded by officials ready to make an arrest may collapse on the floor and mutter "I want my mommy."

7.2.3.4 (L) Religion as Wish Fulfillment

Freud identified wish fulfillment as one of many mental processes not aimed at the truth. Wish fulfillment is an unconscious mental process that is aimed at reducing anxiety by presenting as probable or actual states of affairs that in reality are very unlikely, if not impossible. For example, buyers of lottery tickets get relief from the stress of their lives by thinking ahead to the goods that they will buy when they win the lottery. They are engaged in wish fulfilment, or "wishful thinking," when they imagine what they will do with all that money. The intensity of their belief is out of all proportion to the probability that it may come true.

Belief in God, said Freud, arises from a combination of wish fulfillment and regression to an age-inappropriate psychological stage. As they grow out of infancy and toward adulthood, people become aware of the harsh realities of life. In response, they seek what Freud called a "father figure" – a being possessing precisely the features of a small child's idealized picture of a parent. To the helpless infant, parents are all-powerful, all-knowing, loving, just, and mysterious. The sense of security and certainty an infant feels when their parents dote on them is overwhelmingly good. The loss of that sense of security is painful. In the face of anxiety, adults unconsciously seek to regain the feeling that they had as very small children. They thus create objects to fill the role that their demystified parents no longer play. Freud claimed that this is how belief in God arises. For Freud, it is no accident at all that God is referred to as "our father." Unconsciously, our minds crave something to fulfill that role.

7.3 Two Evolutionary Approaches to Explaining Religion

As with all of the classic approaches, evolutionary approaches to religion find the source of religion in the human realm. Religion arises from our minds and our societies. Much more so than the classic approaches, however, the view of the mind and of society underlying the evolutionary approaches derives from a scientifically rich and well-supported biological theory: Darwin's theory of evolution by natural selection. From its beginnings 150 years ago, evolutionary theory has been used to answer basic questions about humans such as where we came from, why we walk on two feet and have opposable thumbs, and how we are related to other animals. In the last half-century, however, evolutionary theory has increasingly been applied to human mental and social structures themselves.

7.3.1 Explaining Religion Through Evolutionary Psychology

According to proponents of **evolutionary psychology**,[23] human thought – both conscious and unconscious – is the product of evolutionary forces. It arose in a certain sort of environment. It has various odd features that are best explained in terms of their usefulness to our ancestors. For example, craving sweets leads

---

[23] https://www.britannica.com/science/evolutionary-psychology.

to obesity nowadays, but in the low-calorie environment of the Stone Age, that urge for high-calorie food helped keep our ancestors alive. Likewise, though we now see them as logical fallacies, belief-forming processes like hasty generalization and stereotyping were adaptive for our primitive ancestors. A feature is adaptive if it contributes to the survival and reproduction of the organisms that have the feature. Nowadays, when one person dies after eating a mushroom, we can employ scientific tests to determine what exactly in the mushroom caused the death. Long ago, however, believing that all mushrooms were poisonous was close to the optimal strategy, even if the belief was false. Those who believed that all mushrooms were poisonous were more likely to survive and reproduce than those who risked death by employing a trial-and-error strategy. According to proponents of evolutionary psychology, the tendency to form useful but mistaken beliefs was a heritable trait that became hardwired into our brains. These error-prone belief-forming processes helped create religion.

The evolutionary psychology approach to religion consists of four basic elements. (M) The human mind is best viewed, not as a unified whole, but as a collection of modules that evolved to perform specific tasks. These modules can be adaptive without producing true beliefs. (N) Several of our mental modules are devoted to detecting and responding to other agents, so our minds are predisposed to see agency, intention, and purpose everywhere. (O) Mental modules equip all humans with recipes for belief, including beliefs about the agents we detect. These templates strongly constrain possible religious beliefs. Despite the seeming diversity of religions, all religions share underlying similarities because of the constraints imposed by the templates these modules provide. (P) Religion is a by-product of a mental architecture that evolved to navigate the natural and social worlds inhabited by our primitive ancestors. Although the specific mental processes that produced religion were all adaptive in the environments in which they arose, they can and often do lead to false beliefs, including religious ones.

7.3.1.1 (M) Mental Modules: Adaptive, Not Truth Seeking

Just as the software package of a computer contains a host of subprograms and applications, say cognitive psychologists, the human mind is composed of a patchwork of subprograms. These mental modules are brain subsystems devoted to specific tasks like remembering faces, assessing risks, and classifying objects as people, animals, plants, or tools. **Cognitive psychology**[24] is the study of these mental modules. They can be adaptive (that is, advantageous to

---

[24] https://www.britannica.com/science/cognitive-psychology.

their bearers) even if they predictably fail in certain situations. The psychologist **Daniel Kahneman**[25] and his coauthor Amos Tversky famously called the rules underlying these modules "heuristics." Heuristics are decision-making short-cuts that work most of the time but that fail in specific, identifiable circum-stances. (Kahneman discussed many of these heuristics in his best-selling book *Thinking, Fast and Slow*.[26]) Their key insight was that decision making in the real world takes place in a demanding environment. Factors such as ease, speed, and the necessity of avoiding calamities often work against the rational ideal of generating only true beliefs. Take hasty generalization as an example. While ideally it should be avoided, out in the real world making snap judgments may be the optimal strategy. Rather than spend time and risk death by testing out an array of mushrooms, a person might conclude that all mushrooms are poison-ous after just one or two bad experiences with them.

7.3.1.2 (N) Agency Detection

In cognitive psychology, an *agent* is any being that moves of its own volition and for its own purposes. Agents include animals as well as humans. Agents were among both the most threatening and most desirable objects in the envi-ronment of our primitive ancestors. For example, a mastodon could kill you, but it could also feed your tribe for a month if you killed it. So, if you were in the Stone Age and there were mastodons around, it was imperative that you knew how to detect the signs of their presence. As a result, evolution put a lot of pressure on early humans to develop sophisticated methods of agency detection. For example, we inherited from our ancestors various mechanisms for discerning whether the noise intruding on our night-time campfire is a per-son, a predatory animal, or just the wind. These mechanisms produce a high percentage of false positives (mistakenly thinking that there is an agent around when in fact there is not) so as to avoid false negatives (mistakenly thinking that there is not an agent around when there is). This makes sense from an evo-lutionary perspective since the cost of a false negative is so high. If you fail to detect just one prowling tiger, you die. But this tendency results in humans rou-tinely attributing agency when it is just not there. Thus belief in gods and spirits can be explained in part as arising from what the psychologist Justin Barrett has called a hyperactive agency detection device – a mental module geared toward attributing agency at the drop of a pin.

---

[25] https://www.britannica.com/biography/Daniel-Kahneman.
[26] Jim Holt's review of Kahneman's *Thinking, Fast and Slow* gives a good overview of the themes of the book: "Two Brains Running," http://www.nytimes.com/2011/11/27/books/review/thinking-fast-and-slow-by-daniel-kahneman-book-review.html.

7.3.1.3 (O) Universal Templates for Religious Belief

Possession of the mental modules studied by cognitive psychologists, including the mental modules devoted to agency detection, is not limited to particular humans at particular times. It is universal. We are all born with these patterns of thinking etched into our brains. If religion is produced by these universal templates for religious belief, we should expect all religions to show signs of coming from the same recipe. Proponents of the evolutionary psychology approach point to a host of universal features of religious belief. They correlate each feature with an appropriate mental module. For example, in almost all religions, the supernatural beings worshipped are not abstract, impersonal entities like the Force from the *Star Wars* films. They are agents such as God, Shiva, and Zeus. They are the sorts of beings you can pray to, talk with, and be on the lookout for. This is no accident. Because of hyperactive agency detection, "agent-like concepts of gods and spirits are *natural*," says the anthropologist Pascal Boyer in his book *Religion Explained: The Evolutionary Origins of Religious Thought*. Likewise, says Boyer, it is a universal feature of religion that the gods we worship are social beings who are motivated to interact with us and who possess strategic information such as what the next move of our enemies will be in battle or whether a drought will end soon. This feature of religion comes from the array of social interaction modules with which all normal humans are equipped.

7.3.1.4 (P) Religion as a Byproduct of Our Underlying Evolved Psychology

Putting these three strands together, proponents of the evolutionary psychology approach say they can explain religion as a product of our own minds. Our minds evolved to help our ancestors survive a world in which other agents were a central concern. Religion is universal because the basic structure of the human mind is universal. Our inbuilt mental modules, which evolved to make inferences about agents, actually create the gods and spirits religious people worship, pray to, and contemplate. Given how our minds work, then, it is no surprise that religion arose among us. But that is no reason to think that religious beliefs are true, any more than the "naturalness" of fallacious belief-forming processes like hasty generalization makes the beliefs produced by those mechanisms true.

7.3.2 Sociobiological Explanations of Religion

A quite different strand of explanation, but one that still falls under the evolutionary umbrella, was first articulated by the evolutionary biologist E. O. Wilson, who wrote the controversial classic *Sociobiology: The New Synthesis*. According to Wilson, <u>sociobiology</u> is an approach that views social behaviors – from the activities of a beehive or an ant mound to the organization of human society – as resulting from evolution by natural selection. The right sorts of social behaviors confer advantages on the groups that practice them. For example, an individual bee is not too big a threat, but when bees swarm to protect the hive they create a defensive force that is one of the most powerful in the animal world. These advantages can be selected for by nature. Cooperative behavior among animals gets rewarded by evolution in the long run. In the final chapter of his book, Wilson turns the lens of sociobiology onto humanity itself. (All of the quotations that follow are from that chapter.) Regarding religion, Wilson speculates that the rise and spread of various religious and ethical systems can be explained in the same sort of way we explain the behavior of other social animals. "A form of group selection operates in the competition between sects. Those that gain adherents survive; those that cannot, fail. Consequently, religions, like other human institutions, evolve so as to further the welfare of their practitioners."[27]

In what ways does religion promote group survival? Some religions have doctrines that encourage group defense or high rates of reproduction. These religions, Wilson thinks, survive better and come to have more adherents. For example, why is it that, over the last century and a half, the population of Mormons in the world has grown tremendously but there are only a handful of Shakers left? For Wilson, the reason is obvious: Mormons encourage large families while Shakers demand celibacy. Likewise, the explanation for the belief within some religious communities that martyrs go directly to heaven is that those with the belief are more willing to fight and die for their social group than those without it. Thus societies that transmit the belief that martyrs go directly to Heaven will have an advantage in combat. "God wills it, but the summed Darwinian fitness of the tribe was the ultimate if unrecognized beneficiary."[28]

Sociobiological explanations involve two ideas that are controversial among Darwinians. Together they lead to a third idea which is the core of the sociobiological approach to religion. (Q) Traits that are not adaptive for an individual organism may nonetheless bring an advantage to the group of which the individual is a member. So it makes sense to talk about natural selection at the level of the social group. (R) Evolutionary explanations can invoke a unit of selection other than the gene: the *meme*. Memes are ideas and cultural practices that can be treated as heritable traits. They are passed on from one generation to the next and they spread from one culture

---

[27] Wilson, *Sociobiology*, p. 561.
[28] Wilson, *Sociobiology*, p. 561.

to another by imitation. (S) The origin, spread, and current distribution of religious beliefs and practices can be explained in terms of the way in which religious memes contribute to the survival and reproduction of the human social groups that hold them.

7.3.2.1 (Q) Group Selection

Most people conceive of natural selection – "the survival of the fittest" – as operating on individual organisms. But in principle natural selection can operate at other levels of organization, so long as an appropriate **unit of selection**[29] is identified. Consider **kin selection**.[30] A behavior that decreases the chances of an individual spreading all of its own genes can nonetheless be selected for if it increases the chances that the genes of its close relatives (*kin*) are spread. This is because kin share many genes. This explains why worker bees sacrifice their lives for the sake of the hive. The worker bees are the queen's offspring, so they all share genes. By defending the hive, the "self-sacrificing" bees are actually helping to spread some of their own genes.

This example suggests that some seemingly altruistic behaviors (donating most of one's money to charity or risking one's life to save others) – behaviors that, intuitively, seem inexplicable in Darwinian terms – may actually be explained in terms of benefit at a nonindividual, group level. Sociobiological explanations involve what is called **group selection**.[31] Although the idea of group selection was largely rejected in the middle of the twentieth century, group selectionist explanations are more common in evolutionary biology nowadays. Sociobiologists think that moral behaviors such as altruism can be explained, in part, in terms of group selection.

7.3.2.2 (R) Memes

Not only do evolutionary explanations extend beyond individual organisms, but they are not restricted to tangible, physical items. The most commonly discussed unit of selection in evolutionary biology is the gene. It clearly has a physical bearer in the DNA molecule. But maybe we can treat more abstract items as fundamental units of selection. The philosopher of biology **Peter Godfrey-Smith**,[32] who wrote *Darwinian Populations*

---

[29] https://plato.stanford.edu/entries/selection-units.
[30] https://www.britannica.com/topic/kin-selection.
[31] https://www.britannica.com/science/group-selection.
[32] This is the author's website: https://petergodfreysmith.com.

and *Natural Selection*, coined the term "Darwinian population" to mean "a population – a collection of particular things – that has the capacity to undergo evolution," with the members of the population featuring "variation in individual character, which affects reproductive output, and which is heritable."[33] On that broad definition, we can talk of the evolution of things like languages, even though languages consist of nonphysical, abstract items like words.

Some evolutionary explanations of religion work with this broad conception of natural selection, with the units of selection being religious <u>memes</u> – cultural elements that can be considered as passed on by imitation rather than genes. A good example of a meme is ... the idea of a meme. The term "meme" was coined by Richard Dawkins in the mid-1970s. Its use slowly spread in the 1980s and 1990s. With the rise of the internet, everyone talks about memes nowadays. Marriage rites, ethical rules, and theological claims about the nature of God are all memes. Thus everything about religion could, potentially, be explained in terms of evolution by natural selection.

7.3.2.3 (S) Advantages to the Group of Religious Memes

Combining group selection with the idea of memes suggests exploring what the benefits are to the group of particular religious memes. E. O. Wilson thinks he can explain a lot about religion in this way: "It is useful to hypothesize that cultural details are for the most part adaptive in a Darwinian sense, even though some may operate indirectly through enhanced group survival." This leads him to suggest a host of connections between religious memes and societal benefits; "Human rituals ... not only label but reaffirm and rejuvenate the moral values of the community";[34] "[religious] ceremonies can offer information on the strength and wealth of tribes and families"; "Shibboleths, special costumes, and sacred dancing and music" bring about "religious experience," making the individual "ready to reassert allegiance to his tribe and family, perform charities, consecrate his life, leave for the hunt, join the battle, die for God and country."[35] Once we look at religion from the point of view of the social group, say sociobiologists, many otherwise puzzling features of religion are readily explained.

---

[33] Peter Godfrey-Smith, *Darwinian Populations and Natural Selection* (New York: Oxford University Press, 2009), p. 6.

[34] Wilson, *Sociobiology*, p. 560.

[35] Wilson, *Sociobiology*, p. 561.

7.3.3 How the Evolutionary Theories Draw from the Classic Theories

Many proponents of evolutionary theories of religion say that those theories mark a clean break from the classic theories. They see in their favored approach the potential for breakthroughs unachievable by the older approaches. Evolutionary theories of religion, they think, are radically new and different. However, our survey of the evolutionary approaches shows that, thematically at least, they bear a strong resemblance to the classic ones. If Hobbes, Spinoza, Feuerbach, Marx, and Freud were alive today, they would see many of their ideas about religion reflected in the new evolutionary theories.

As an example, let us look at a particular feature of monotheistic religions to compare the evolutionary explanation of it with the classic explanation. All believers in God are supposed to think God is all-knowing (omniscient) and all-powerful (omnipotent). Why is this so? Why is God not thought to be limited in power or knowledge? The psychologist Justin Barrett points to research findings from childhood psychology. In his article "Religious Belief as an Evolutionary Accident," he writes:

> belief in the divine attributes of a supergod such as those in Abrahamic traditions receives special support from cognitive structures. Specifically, super-knowledge, super-perception, super-power (especially to create natural things), and immortality all benefit from the operation of mental tools in childhood development.[36]

Regarding omniscience, he says:

> In the enormous area of research concerning children's developing Theory of Mind, data strongly support the position that before around five years of age (and sometimes later) children assume that everyone's beliefs about the world are infallible. That is, if a three-year-old child knows that he has a coin in his pocket, he assumes that his mother, too, will know that he has a coin in his pocket.[37]

---

[36] Justin Barrett, "Religious Belief as an Evolutionary Accident," in Jeffrey Schloss and Michael Murray (eds), *The Believing Primate: Scientific, Philosophical, and Theological Reflections on the Origin of Religion* (New York: Oxford University Press, 2009), p. 90.

[37] Barrett, "Religious Belief as an Evolutionary Accident," p. 90.

Likewise, Barrett explains the attribution to God of omnipotence as arising from "children's tendency to treat adults as god-like by overestimating their strength and power."[38]

Let us compare Barrett's theory to Freud's. Freud set out the basics of his view of religion in *Civilization and Its Discontents*. For Freud, God is the believer's substitute for the god-like parents who are lost to maturation as the developing believer moves from infancy into childhood, then adolescence, and finally adulthood. Because it is incomprehensible and too harsh for us, experience with the world of adults (with what is nowadays called "the real world") leads some of us to regress to a childish stage: "The origin of the religious attitude can be traced back in clear outlines as far as the feeling of infantile helplessness."[39] He writes that religion is

> the system of doctrines and promises which ... assures him that a careful Providence will watch over his life and compensate him in a future existence for any frustrations he suffers here. The common man cannot imagine this Providence otherwise than in the figure of an enormously exalted father.[40]

For Freud, belief in God (I) arises from unconscious mental processes that are (K) present in our earliest stages of psychological development and that (J) do not lead to the truth but (L) replicate the child's idealized conception of the parent. All four elements (I), (J), (K), and (L) are present in Barrett's theory. The basic move is the same for both theorists. The central difference is that Barrett has the benefit of much better scientific evidence for his claims than Freud had for his.

Other parallels are easy to find. The idea that (M) the mind contains mental modules that are adaptive but are not truth seeking matches Freud's idea that (I) there are unconscious mental processes that (J) are not aimed at the truth. The idea that (N) we are hard-wired to overdetect agency matches the idea of Hobbes and Spinoza that humans are (A) hyperactive explainers who (B) are disposed toward purposive explanations. The idea that (R) religious memes spread across populations and through time, and (S) can bring advantages to the societies possessing them, matches the ideas that (D) religions are culturally transmitted and (E) can be explained in terms of the social functions they fulfill.

More generally, evolutionary theories of religion that focus on individual psychology fuse themes from the anthropomorphic projection theory of

---

[38] Barrett, "Religious Belief as an Evolutionary Accident," p. 92.

[39] Sigmund Freud, *Civilization and Its Discontents* (New York: W. W. Norton, 1989), pp. 20–21.

[40] Freud, *Civilization and Its Discontents*, p. 22.

Hobbes and Spinoza with themes from the psychological theory of Freud, while sociobiological theories of religion are very similar in terms of their basic themes to the sociological theory of Marx. These connections suggest that we take with a grain of salt any claim that evolutionary theories of religion represent something totally new. The scientific evidence behind the evolutionary theories is new and powerful. The newer evolutionary theories refine the classic theories in many important respects. Nonetheless, the basic modes of explanation are quite similar.

7.4 Neuroscience and Religious Experience

There is one last approach to explaining religion naturalistically that deserves mention. It does not fit under the categories we have already covered, but is increasingly influential. This new approach specifically addresses the phenomenon known as **religious experience**[41] – any experience where it appears to the subject that they are directly aware of some sort of divine or religiously significant reality. For example, **St. Teresa of Ávila**,[42] a Carmelite nun from sixteenth-century Spain, reported the following:

> I was at prayer on the festival of the glorious Saint Peter when I saw Christ at my side – or, to put it better, I was conscious of Him, for neither with the eyes of the body nor with those of the soul did I see anything. I thought He was quite close to me and I saw that it was He Who, as I thought, was speaking to me. Being completely ignorant that visions of this kind could occur, I was at first very much afraid, and did nothing but weep, though, as soon as He addressed a single word to me to reassure me, I became quiet again, as I had been before, and was quite happy and free from fear. All the time Jesus Christ seemed to be beside me, but, as this was not an imaginary vision, I could not discern in what form: what I felt very clearly was that all the time He was at my right hand, and a witness of everything that I was doing, and that, whenever I became slightly recollected or was not greatly distracted, I could not but be aware of His nearness to me.[43]

Similar testimonials are common throughout the world's religious traditions. The experiencers claim to have been directly aware of some religiously significant person or state of being. Because religious experiences

---

[41] https://plato.stanford.edu/entries/religious-experience.
[42] https://www.britannica.com/biography/Saint-Teresa-of-Avila.
[43] *The Life of Teresa of Jesus*, trans. and ed. Allison E. Peers (New York: Sheed & Ward, 1960), repr. in Peterson et al. (eds), *Philosophy of Religion: Selected Readings*, pp. 41–42.

are private, it seems they cannot serve as evidence to anyone but the experiencer. But to the experiencer, such experiences are typically profound and life altering.

Philosophers ask numerous questions about religious experiences. What is their nature? Are they best classified as perceptions or as something else? Is human language adequate to capture their meaning? Do they justify those who have them in any particular religious beliefs? Given that religious experiences happen across diverse religions, how can such experiences favor one religion over another? Although these are all excellent questions, we do not have the space to address them in this book. Instead, we will look at what modern naturalists say about the phenomenon of religious experience.

7.4.1 Neurotheology

Since the 1960s, there has been an explosion of scientific investigation of the mechanics of the human brain, from the nuts and bolts of neurons and synapses all the way up to brain regions like the hippocampus or the parietal lobe. This new field of study has been enabled by technologies like functional magnetic resonance imaging (fMRI). These technologies enable neuroscientists to track what is going on inside the brain during thinking. They are even able to investigate conscious thinking, with the subjects reporting to investigators what they are thinking as their brains are being scanned. In light of the discoveries enabled by these technologies, a new kind of naturalistic explanation of religious experience has emerged. It has been labeled by its practitioners (half-jokingly, it seems) as "neurotheology." Neurotheology is an interdisciplinary field of inquiry that tries to connect modern brain science with the phenomena of religion, particularly with religious experience.

The basic idea is that religious experience is best explained, not in terms of a subject having direct contact with the divine, but in terms of the subject's brain being in an unusual (but scientifically explicable) physical state. If the human brain is put into unusual conditions – for example, by being deprived of oxygen during controlled-breathing exercises, or by being exposed to magnets – it will do unusual things. One of those unusal things is to create religious experiences in subjects. If that is correct, then the fact that people have religious experiences indicates, not a supernatural realm of gods and spirits, or a true reality in which there is no division between self and world, but merely that a brain is under some sort of unusual strain. (This in itself is not a totally new idea. Nearly 100 years ago, in his book *Religion and Science*, the philosopher **Ber-**

---

44 https://www.britannica.com/biography/Bertrand-Russell.

trand Russell[44] quipped that "from a scientific point of view, we can make no distinction between the man who eats little and sees heaven and the man who drinks much and sees snakes."[45])

To get the flavor of such explanations, look at the newspaper article "Tracing the Synapses of Our Spirituality,"[46] in which Shankar Vedantam sets out the view that certain forms of religious experience – experiences during meditation, religious conversion, and so on – can be explained in terms of "neural networks, neurotransmitters, and brain chemistry." Two experiments get special mention in the article. In one, brain scans taken of Tibetan Buddhist monks while they meditated showed that the monks had significantly decreased activity in the parietal lobe of the brain. The parietal lobe is the part of the brain responsible for spatial orientation. The suggestion of many neurotheologians is that it is thus merely the brain that is responsible for the monks being in their "oneness with the universe" state of mind. And this is not restricted to the meditative states of Buddhist monks in particular. Neurotheologians say the same basic explanation applies to religious experience in general. The noted neurotheologian Andrew Newberg was quoted in the article as saying just this about the loss of the sense of self, which is such a common feature of religious experience:

> When people have spiritual experiences they feel they become one with the universe and lose their sense of self. We think that may be because of what is happening in that [brain] area; if you block that [brain] area you lose that boundary between the self and the rest of the world. In doing so you ultimately wind up in a universal state.

In the other experiment cited in the article, subjects were made to wear a magnetized helmet. When the magnets were on high, a high percentage of the test subjects reported "feeling a presence" they could not see, with many subjects weeping. Other subjects talked about demons and spirits. The results of these sorts of experiments led the reporter to suggest that "the flash of wisdom that came over Siddhartha Gautama – the Buddha – [could] have been nothing more than his parietal lobe quieting down." The researcher in the magnetized helmet experiment said his research shows "religion is a property of the brain, only the brain and has little to do with what's out there." Of course, that is an overstatement; as we have seen, there is a great deal more to religion than

---

[45] Bertrand Russell, *Religion and Science* (Oxford: Oxford University Press, 1961), p. 188.
[46] Shankar Vedantam, "Tracing the Synapses of Our Spirituality," *Washington Post*, June 17, 2001, https://www.washingtonpost.com/archive/politics/2001/06/17/tracing-the-synapses-of-our-spirituality/ee8a4fe0-d09a-4382-bf5d-2a32d262b576.

just religious experience. Yet, if the neurotheologians are right, even the most intimate aspects of religious life – namely, personal spiritual feelings – can be accounted for naturalistically.

7.5 Evaluating the Naturalistic Explanations of Religion

Now that we have a grasp of the diverse approaches to explaining religion that naturalists take, we are in a position to evaluate those approaches. In trying to do that, however, we immediately confront a difficulty. Naturalists and religious people are in separate camps. They disagree, not just about the existence of supernatural entities, but about a whole host of philosophical matters. They disagree about what the proper standards are for rational belief. They disagree about what the foundations of morality are. They even disagree about how to define "natural." The divisions are so great that there may be few criteria both sides share for evaluating the naturalistic explanations of religion. Rather than spending time trying to find enough common ground between these camps to give a neutral assessment, let us break the task of evaluating the naturalistic explanations of religion into two parts. First we will evaluate the naturalistic explanations of religion from a naturalistic perspective. Then we will evaluate the naturalistic explanations of religion from a religious perspective. Readers can decide for themselves how to balance those evaluations.

7.5.1 Naturalistic Explanations of Religion from a Naturalistic Perspective

Naturalists have a rich and scientifically informed array of options for understanding what they encounter in religion. For them, the prospects for fully explaining religion look good. Certainly there are important issues to be settled. For example, there is much debate among evolutionary theorists of religion about whether religion is adaptive. Furthermore, evolutionary theorists have yet to say much about atheistic religions (religions in which no gods are worshipped). Atheistic religions form a large category, one that includes Buddhism, Confucianism, Daoism, Jainism, and some forms of Hinduism. Despite the work that still needs to be done in important areas like these, however, it appears that naturalists have developed a solid approach to explaining religion, and all that remains is to extend that approach by doing more and better science. Digging deeper, however, we see considerable infighting among the naturalists. These divisions suggest that the various approaches to explaining religion naturalistically are incompatible as they now stand and cannot be merged into a unified scientific theory of religion. This, in turn, means that naturalists have much work to do in developing the theoretical tools to explain religion in a consistent, coherent way.

7.5.1.1 First Division: Naturalists Who Are Opposed to Evolutionary Explanations of Religion

The most fundamental split is between those who embrace the use of evolutionary biology and psychology and those who avoid it. In the social sciences – the academic fields of anthropology, sociology, economics, and psychology, as well as intersecting fields like religious studies, ethnic studies, and gender/sexuality studies – there is great resistance to understanding human phenomena primarily through the lens of evolutionary biology. Evolutionary theories of cultural phenomena like religion are seen as threatening to reintroduce what is seen by many social scientists as a dangerous and discredited idea: *human nature*. Some evolutionary theorists – most notably the cognitive scientist Steven Pinker – proudly endorse the idea of human nature, so long as that idea is cleansed of its religious elements and grounded in modern evolutionary biology. But, as Pinker himself documents, many social scientists do not like his sort of position.

Some advocates of evolutionary approaches to religion are sensitive to the problem. David Sloan Wilson (no relation to E. O. Wilson), a biologist and the author of *Darwin's Cathedral*, acknowledges that "the scientific study of religion has traditionally been the province of anthropologists, sociologists, and psychologists. As a newcomer, any modern evolutionary approach to religion must prove itself against these older traditions."[47] Wilson spends chapter 2 of *Darwin's Cathedral* trying to reconcile his new approach with the older ones, in particular with Rodney Stark's sociological approach. But Stark is not in a mood for reconciliation. He writes at the start of *Discovering God*: "This entire body of recent work [on the origins of religion from biologists and evolutionary psychologists] is remarkably inferior because so few authors could restrain their militant atheism. Contempt is not a scholarly virtue."[48] Overall, it seems that, in order for there to be a single, unified, best naturalistic theory of religion, the naturalists opposed to taking an evolutionary approach to religion must reconcile themselves with (or surrender themselves to) those in favor of it.

---

[47] David Sloan Wilson, *Darwin's Cathedral: Evolution, Religion, and the Nature of Society* (Chicago: University of Chicago Press, 2002), p. 47.
[48] Rodney Stark, *Discovering God: The Origins of the Great Religions and the Evolution of Belief* (New York: HarperOne, 2007), p. 1.

7.5.1.2 Second Division: Evolutionary Psychologists Who Are Opposed to Sociobiology

Another division lies within evolutionary approaches, between evolutionary psychology and sociobiology. As noted earlier, the sociobiological approach rests on two controversial notions: group selection and memes. As we saw in Section 7.3.2.2 on memes, we can talk about the evolution of the elements within a Darwinian population if that population has members featuring variation in individual character, with that variation affecting reproductive output and also being heritable. But just because the language of evolution fits a population does not mean that the elements of the population are natural items or even really exist. Godfrey-Smith spends all of chapter 2 of *Darwinian Populations and Natural Selection* on precisely this issue.

For example, ghost stories vary in their individual character. Those variations affect how many times a particular ghost story is told, and each retelling of that ghost story inherits important features of the original. We find it tempting in cases like this to talk about the evolution of ghost stories. But just because we talk that way does not mean that we really think ghost stories are natural, physical things, or that ghosts are real. For an evolutionary explanation to be naturalistic, it is not enough that it be evolutionary. The units of selection must be natural entities or be realized by natural entities, in the same way that genes are coded in DNA, which is just a chemical. The processes by which they are selected must also be natural – neither gods nor humans can steer things. All of this is just to say that it is crucial to add the modifier "by natural selection" to "Darwin's theory of evolution." Without it, we lose what makes Darwin's theory special.

Some evolutionary theorists are sticklers on this point. Pinker writes in "The False Allure of Group Selection":

> No one "owns" the concept of natural selection, nor can anyone police the use of the term. But its explanatory power, it seems to me, is so distinctive and important that it should not be diluted by metaphorical, poetic, fuzzy, or allusive extensions that only serve to obscure how profound the genuine version of the mechanism really is.[49]

He goes on to argue at length that the idea of "group selection" is one of those illegitimate extensions of natural selection. Memes too have come under attack. In his final analysis of them, Godfrey-Smith says that memes (which he sometimes calls "cultural variants" and which Boyer calls "units of culture") constitute

---

[49] Steven Pinker, "The False Allure of Group Selection," *Edge*, June 18, 2012, http://edge.org/conversation/the-false-allure-of-group-selection.

a very marginal Darwinian population: "The world is full of phenomena that look Darwinian but will not fit this narrow set of requirements [for being a Darwinian population] … Surely the way the world fills up with laptops looks very much like the way it fills up with rabbits."[50] We can label ideas, learned behaviors, and even artifacts as memes, but it does not mean that memes really are subject to natural selection.

Settling this point is crucial for naturalistic explainers of religion. Without group selection and without memes, the sociobiological theory of religion cannot get off the ground. This leaves the evolutionary psychology theory of religion as the lone evolutionary approach. That approach is well suited to explaining "individualist" aspects of religion (e.g. conceptions of God and prayer) but poorly suited to explaining "groupish" aspects of religion (e.g. the structure of religious organizations, religious customs, and the growth and spread of particular religions). It is the groupish aspects that sociological theories try to explain. Yet, as Pinker insists, the methodology and theoretical commitments of the traditional social sciences are so frequently at odds with those of the evolutionary psychologists that neutral observers would rightly wonder how the two approaches to explaining religion could both be right.

7.5.2 Naturalistic Explanations of Religion from a Religious Perspective

While naturalists will see the naturalistic theories of religion as promising, religious believers will likely see them as threatening. But should they? To see whether they should, let us consider an analogy. Suppose Alexis and Belinda are good friends who often talk about politics. Alexis is a political conservative and Belinda is a political liberal. One day the two of them have an angry debate about health-care policy. It ends without either having changed their mind. Coincidentally, the next day Belinda reads Thomas Frank's *What's the Matter with Kansas? How Conservatives Won the Heart of America*, a book that is touted as "unraveling the great political mystery of our day: Why do so many Americans vote against their economic and social interests?" Inspired by Frank's book, Belinda develops a theory that explains to her own satisfaction why Alexis mistakenly endorses political conservatism. According to Belinda, maladaptive memes have been transmitted from conservatives to Alexis – more precisely, to Alexis's brain. Should Alexis be worried?

One thing Alexis might worry about is whether Belinda is right. In that case, she could ask Belinda to explain her theory further and to borrow her copy

---

[50] Pascal Boyer, *Religion Explained: The Evolutionary Origins of Religious Thought* (New York: Basic Books, 2001), p. 162.

of Frank's book. Suppose Belinda complies. Alexis then spends time reading Frank's book, as well as some material explaining memes. At the end of all of that reading, Alexis concludes that Belinda is wrong – that it is just not true that she, Alexis, holds her conservative beliefs irrationally and does so because conservatives have transmitted maladaptive memes to her brain. Are Alexis's worries over? No. Now she has a new worry. What could prompt Belinda to develop such a demeaning theory about Alexis? True friends do not need theories of one another; they get along naturally. Alexis begins to worry that Belinda no longer sees her as worth talking with, at least when it comes to politics. The state of dialogue must have become really bad from Belinda's perspective for her to develop such an unfriendly theory about Alexis. What will Belinda do to Alexis next? Shun her? Ostracize her? Stop following her on social media? These are real worries for Alexis.

This example suggests two things. First, naturalists explaining religion naturalistically is a particular instance of a common phenomenon. It happens all the time that believers in a theory extend that theory so that it explains why some people stubbornly refuse to believe it. Christians have theories about why people who are not Christians do not accept the Christian message, such as "Their minds are clouded by sin." Marxists have theories about why people reject Marxism, for example, "They suffer from **false consciousness**."[51] (Perhaps it is just human nature to explain away your opposition.) Second, the example suggests that religious believers should divide the question. First, do the naturalistic theories of religion show the religious believer that their own beliefs are irrational? Second, what do the naturalistic theories of religion signal about the standing of religious believers with naturalists and within the wider society? Are they a sign that bad things are on the way? The second question will be addressed at the end of this chapter. As for the first question, there are two reasons religious believers can give for thinking that the naturalistic explanations of religion do not show that their religious beliefs are irrational.

7.5.2.1 The First Reason: Naturalistic Explanations Misrepresent Religion

For any theory of any phenomena to count as a success, it must be true to the facts and sensitive to the complexities of the phenomena explained. Naturalistic theories of religion must explain religion as it really is. They must not rest on false, distorted, or simplistic claims about religious phenomena. Yet religious believers can claim – with some justification – that their beliefs and behaviors have been "explained" only by having been misrepresented.

---

[51] https://www.britannica.com/topic/false-consciousness.

For example, several naturalists offer *costly signaling* theories of specific religious behaviors, whereby charitable giving, altruism, and sacrifice signal high reproductive fitness to potential mates. As part of his sociobiological explanation of religion, E. O. Wilson says that "the famous potlatch ceremonies of the Northwest Coast Indians enable individuals to advertise their wealth by the amount of goods they give away."[52] He is suggesting a basic explanation for all religiously demanded charity. Marx had a similar idea. Yet that explanation presupposes that charitable giving is public. Not all religions teach that charitable giving should be public.

Christians will respond that making charity public is neither what Jesus taught nor what Christians typically do. "When you do an act of charity, do not let your left hand know what your right hand is doing; your good deed must be secret, and your Father who sees what is done in secret will reward you" (Matthew 6:3–4). Some Christian churches have gone out of their way to make giving anonymous: by eliminating collection plates and using a bucket that parishioners approach individually during communion, or by setting donation through electronic debit. Many ministers scrupulously shield themselves from the knowledge of who donated how much. They make sure that all such information is handled separately by the church treasurers. In an ideal scenario, anonymous Christian charity signals nothing about the giver, so costly signaling does not apply. And, given that anonymous charity removes from the giver all of the benefits of advertising, Christianity would seem to discourage charitable giving within the Christian community as a whole. This means that, on costly signaling theories, we should expect less, not more, overall charitable giving in Christian communities than in communities that encourage public displays of charity. But that is the opposite of what the social science tells us about actual Christian charitable giving. Thus costly signaling theories simply do not fit the Christian practice of anonymous charitable giving. At least, this is something Christians can plausibly claim.

There are many other examples of naturalistic theorists of religion that misrepresent the religions they claim to explain. Of the golden rule – "Do unto others as you would have them do unto you" (Luke 6:31) – David Sloan Wilson says that group selectionists "are predicting that a religion instructs believers to behave for the benefit of their group, which is supported by the Ten Commandments and the Golden Rule."[53] But does the golden rule really mean "Do unto others *in your group* as you would have them do unto you"? Christians can plausibly say that it does not. (Notice how naturalists seeking to explain religion inevitably get involved in the treacherous task of scriptural interpretation.) Treating Jesus as promoting the in-group version of the golden rule is

---

[52] Wilson, *Sociobiology*, p. 561.
[53] D. S. Wilson, *Darwin's Cathedral*, pp. 96–97.

even more implausible given the story of the Good Samaritan (Luke 10:25–37). "And who is my neighbor?" asks a lawyer. "Not just your fellow Jews," says Jesus, "but everyone – even the despised Samaritans." So Christians can claim, plausibly, that the golden rule has been explained only by misrepresenting it.

Again, consider Jesus's teaching that aggrieved parties ought to "turn the other cheek" (Matthew 5:38–42): "Do not set yourself against the man who wrongs you. If someone slaps you on the right cheek, turn, and offer him your left. If a man sues you for your shirt, let him have your coat as well." Do Christians really believe that? David Sloan Wilson does not think so. He interprets this passage as regulating in-group conduct only, at least in his analysis of the catechism John Calvin produced for the citizens of Geneva. But at least some Christians (e.g. monks) can plausibly reply that they really do believe it. They do not just refuse to retaliate when harmed. Sometimes they open themselves up to even more harm, and they behave in this way toward anyone who harms them, not just Christians who harm them. If some Christians really do behave in that way, what possible selectionist explanation could there be for that? "None, which is why no one believes and behaves in that way"? "None, but anyone who behaves in that way is crazy"? If those are the answers, Christians can reply – plausibly – that some Christians in their right minds, both now and in the past, do believe this and behave in such a way. So, for Christians, the naturalists just have not explained those beliefs and behaviors.

The point is general. Religious believers of all stripes should worry that their belief system is rendered irrational by the naturalistic explanations of religion only if those explanations accurately represent their belief systems. It seems there are many cases where religious believers can plausibly reply that, by their own lights, this condition has not been met.

7.5.2.2 The Second Reason: They Presuppose Naturalism Is True

It is pretty obvious that religious people and naturalists differ mightily on the interpretation of everyday religious phenomena like praying, reading scripture, or putting money in the collection plate. What is the source of this difference? In *Warranted Christian Belief*, the philosopher **Alvin Plantinga**[54] suggests that disagreement about naturalism itself explains the difference. He argues that naturalism is a powerful, comprehensive, totalizing worldview, just as Christianity is, and that it colors everything the naturalist thinks and sees, just as Christianity colors everything the Christian thinks and sees. In that case, Plantinga argues, Christians should not be too worried that naturalists can explain

---

[54] Here is a brief profile of Alvin Plantinga: https://www.nd.edu/features/plantinga.

the beliefs and behaviors of Christians naturalistically. After all, naturalists are operating with a worldview that, by the lights of the Christian, is just false. Plantinga's point can be generalized so that it applies to a wider range of religious believers than just Christians.

The underlying picture of rationality Plantinga works with is one in which humans are equipped with cognitive powers or faculties – faculties like reason, memory, self-awareness, and so on. Beliefs are the outputs of these faculties. To have what Plantinga calls "warrant," a belief must be produced by faculties geared toward the production of true belief and operating in the right sort of environment. To use Plantinga's terminology, the faculties must be performing their "proper function." They must be doing what they are supposed to do. Are the faculties that produce Christian belief functioning properly? According to naturalists, no. They say Christian belief, like all religious belief, is produced by faculties that are either operating in the wrong environment (see G above) or are not geared toward the production of true beliefs (see J and M above). Therefore, the beliefs produced by these faculties are irrational, according to naturalists.

But on Plantinga's picture, God created us so that we have an inbuilt ability to know God. This faculty is called the _sensus divinitatis_ – Latin for the "divine sense." If Christianity is true, then our faculties _are_ performing properly when they produce Christian belief. What needs to be explained, for Plantinga, is why people do _not_ believe in God. The answer, he suggests, is that our cognitive faculties have come to malfunction as a result of sin. What this illustrates, says Plantinga, is that naturalistic theories of religion show that Christian belief is irrational only if naturalism is true and Christianity is false. But whether or not naturalism is true and Christianity is false is precisely what naturalists and Christians disagree about. So that naturalists can "explain" Christian belief should not bother Christians unless Christians are given independent reasons to think naturalism is true.

How about the naturalistic explanations of religion themselves? Do they, just by themselves, give Christians reason for thinking that naturalism is true? Plantinga addresses an argument from the philosopher Philip Quinn that they do. Quinn said that, since naturalistic theories of religion show that the belief in God would arise in humans even if God does not exist, the hypothesis that God really does exist is "explanatorily idle." The hypothesis that God exists is unnecessary. Plantinga responds that Christian theism is not put forward as a hypothesis that explains why people believe in God, so Quinn is faulting Christians for failing to do something that they do not think they have to do.

These are difficult but important points, so let us illustrate them with two examples. The first is drawn from the history of science. Prior to **Isaac Newton**,[55] the motion of bodies was explained through a theory developed

---

[55] https://www.britannica.com/biography/Isaac-Newton.

by the ancient philosopher **Aristotle**.[56] For Aristotle, any moving body – for example, an arrow shot by an archer – moves because a force (*impetus*) has been imparted to it. The body keeps moving until all the impetus is used up. For Aristotle, that was why things like arrows slow down and eventually stop. They run out of impetus. (This is actually how most people think of "momentum," although the ordinary person's sense of that term is quite different than the physicist's.) On this view, the natural state for any body is rest, so if a body is not moving, no explanation is needed of why it is not moving. But, if a body is moving, an explanation is needed for both how it began to move and why it continues to move.

Newton said that Aristotle was wrong. According to Newton's first law of motion, it is uniform ("inertial") motion, not being at rest, that is natural. Being at rest – having zero velocity – is only one form of inertial motion. If a body is moving at a certain speed in a certain direction, it is natural that it continue to move at that very same speed in that very same direction, so long as no forces are acting upon it. This is why the space probes Voyager 1 and 2 are still moving beyond the solar system despite not being propelled for decades.

Now suppose defenders of Aristotle were to argue as follows: "On our theory there is a force that accounts for why an object keeps moving. The force is called 'impetus,' and there is nothing like it in Newton's theory. On Newton's theory, that an object that was moving continues to move is *completely unexplained*. It is just a brute fact that moving objects continue to move. So Aristotle's theory is better than Newton's. Aristotle's theory explains something Newton's theory does not: why things keep moving. Aristotle wins, Newton loses!"

This is a bad argument. It is true that Newton's theory cannot "explain" the fact that objects keep moving. But that is because inertial motion is simply presupposed by Newton's theory. The first law of motion just is one of the starting points (*axioms*) of Newton's theory. It is used to explain other phenomena, but it is not itself explained. If we want to judge Newton's theory, we need to see how well it helps us explain everything else. On that criterion, Newton had great justification for believing in his first law of motion. It helped him to explain all sorts of things that Aristotle's impetus theory could not – things like why Voyager 1 and 2 are still going.

The second example is religious. It connects back to our prior discussion of religious experience. Many Buddhist monks claim that, when they meditate, they feel one with the universe. As we saw, neuroscientists have used various imaging technologies to see what is going on in the brains of these monks. They find that these experiences correlate with decreased activity in

---

[56] https://www.britannica.com/biography/Aristotle.

the parietal lobe of the brain. Suppose a naturalist tells a Buddhist monk that science explains why meditating Buddhist monks think they are one with the universe, and that this shows Buddhism is irrational. Should the Buddhist monk worry?

Well, by the lights of the Buddhist, there just is no self that is distinct from the rest of reality. "No self" is one of the core beliefs of the Buddhist. It helps Buddhists explain many other things, for example suffering. The nonexistence of the self and the oneness of everything is a starting point for Buddhism. It is one of the central insights through which all else is explained, just as the first law of motion is axiomatic in Newton's theory. The naturalist is saying that naturalism has the advantage over Buddhism because naturalism explains why the Buddhist believes what, for the Buddhist, is their starting point! When the naturalist says that naturalism explains why the Buddhist believes they are one with the universe, the Buddhist can retort that Buddhism explains why the naturalist believes they are separate from the universe. (Somehow this seems like a very Buddhist insight.)

These examples indicate that who is winning depends on how we keep score. What appears to naturalists as something demanding an explanation appears to some Christians as not needing any explanation. What, by the lights of the naturalist, is a victory for the naturalist is, by the lights of the Christian, a draw between the naturalist and the Christian. So, by the lights of the Christian, says Plantinga, the naturalist has failed to show that Christian belief is irrational. And, as the example of Buddhist meditation indicates, this strategy can be generalized to religions other than Christianity.

7.5.2.3 The Social Implications of Naturalistic Theories for Religious Believers

Let us end this chapter with some thoughts about the social implications for religious believers of the naturalistic explanations of religion. For many naturalists, there is no longer any point in debating religious believers regarding the truth of their beliefs. All that remains is to analyze their stubborn resistance, in the same way as Belinda analyzed Alexis's stubborn adherence to conservatism. The naturalistic theories provide a way for naturalists to do that, and there is nothing religious believers can do to stop them. Naturalists are free to flesh out their worldview as they see fit. When naturalists move from explaining the beliefs of religious believers to classifying religious believers as pathological, however, things get worrisome.

An emerging pattern among some naturalists is to talk publicly about religion as a meme infecting the minds of the religious. For example, Kathleen Taylor, a neuroscience writer with a background in philosophy and the author of *The Brain Supremacy*, suggests that religious fundamentalism may soon be classified as a treatable mental illness: "Someone who has for example become radicalised to a cult ideology – we might stop seeing that as a personal choice that they have chosen as a result of pure free will and may start treating it as some kind of mental disturbance," she says. "In many ways it could be a very positive thing because there are no doubt beliefs in our society that do a heck of a lot of damage,"[57] for example, the belief that corporal punishment of children is divinely sanctioned. Notice the meme talk. It is the meme – the belief that "Whoever spares the rod hates their children, but those who love their children are careful to discipline them" (Proverbs 13:24) – that is doing the damage. It is not the person holding the belief who is to blame. The belief that God supports corporal punishment is one of many religious memes that the philosopher **Daniel Dennett**[58] [58] David Dennett, *Darwin's Dangerous Idea: Evolution and the Meanings of Life* (New York: Penguin, 1995), p. 516. thinks should be eliminated. In his book *Darwin's Dangerous Idea*, he writes that religious believers

> who will not accommodate, who will not temper, who insist on keeping only the purest and wildest strain of their heritage alive, we will be obliged, reluctantly, to cage or disarm, and we will do our best to disable the memes they fight for.[59]

The language of memes cleverly detaches the believer from the belief, but, unlike real viruses, memes (if they exist at all) do not just float in the air. They reside in human brains and bodies, and there is no way to disable religious memes without, as Dennett admits, caging or disarming religious believers. For religious believers, that is something to worry about.

Annotated Bibliography

Boyer, Pascal (2001). *Religion Explained: The Evolutionary Origins of Religious Thought* (New York: Basic Books).
    This is a comprehensive and fascinating treatment of religion from the perspective of evolutionary psychology. Boyer begins the book with an extensive discussion

---

[57] Quoted by Meredith Bennett-Smith, "Kathleen Taylor, Neuroscientist, Says Religious Fundamentalism Could Be Treated as a Mental Illness," http://www.huffingtonpost.com/2013/05/31/kathleen-taylor-religious-fundamentalism-mental-illness_n_3365896.html.
[58] https://www.britannica.com/biography/Daniel-C-Dennett.
[59] David Dennett, *Darwin's Dangerous Idea: Evolution and the Meanings of Life* (New York: Penguin, 1995), p. 516.

of older naturalistic theories of religion, including all of the approaches discussed in this chapter.

Dennett, Daniel (2007). *Breaking the Spell: Religion as a Natural Phenomenon* (New York: Penguin Books).

A philosopher specializing in biology and psychology, Dennett attempts to give a comprehensive evolutionary explanation of religion. The idea of memes plays a crucial role in his theory.

Freud, Sigmund (1989 [1930]). *Civilization and Its Discontents* (New York: W. W. Norton).

Freud spends the first two chapters of this book giving his psychological theory of religion and of religious experience. For a fuller treatment of religion, see his *The Future of an Illusion* (New York: W. W. Norton, 1989), originally published in 1927.

Newberg, Andrew (2018). *Neurotheology: How Science Can Enlighten Us About Spirituality* (New York: Columbia University Press).

This is the most up-to-date statement of his position from perhaps the world's leading researcher on the brain science behind religion and religious experience.

Plantinga, Alvin (2000). *Warranted Christian Belief* (New York: Oxford University Press).

In this difficult but rewarding book, Plantinga rebuts "the Freud–Marx complaint" – the argument that naturalistic explanations of religion show Christian belief is unwarranted.

Schloss, Jeffrey and Michael J. Murray, eds (2009). *The Believing Primate: Scientific, Philosophical, and Theological Reflections on the Origin of Religion* (New York: Oxford University Press).

This collection of essays gives the reader a great sense of where things stand with evolutionary approaches to religion.

Thrower, James (1999). *Religion: The Classical Theories* (Edinburgh: Edinburgh University Press).

This textbook does exactly what it promises, giving a comprehensive survey of the classic approaches to explaining religion naturalistically.

Wilson, David Sloan (2002). *Darwin's Cathedral: Evolution, Religion, and the Nature of Society* (Chicago: University of Chicago Press).

This is probably the best book-length example of an attempted sociobiological explanation of religion.

Wilson, Edward O. (1975). *Sociobiology: The New Synthesis* (Cambridge, MA: Belknap Press).

In the final chapter, "Man: From Sociobiology to Sociology," Wilson lays out his theory of religion and ritual. Over 40 years after its first publication, it is still provocative.

POSTSCRIPT: BUDDHISM AND THE ENDURING MYSTERY OF RELIGION

We have covered a great variety of viewpoints on religion in this book. In the course of our survey, we delved into almost every major branch of philosophy, including logic, metaphysics, epistemology, and ethics. We have also touched on ideas from a host of scientific fields, including physics, evolutionary biology, psychology, sociology, and neuroscience. It seems that we have looked at religion from every conceivable angle and we have gone as far as we can go. Even if we do not have answers to all the questions we have raised, can we at least say that now, after completing a course in the philosophy of religion, we have a good grasp of the main philosophical problems concerning religion?

Perhaps not. It seems we have ignored the most important thing about religion: its spiritual effects. You probably know at least one person (possibly you yourself) who has been completely transformed as a result of "getting religion." Religious belief can be the most powerful force in a person's life, far more powerful than the tugs of family, career, prestige, and romantic love. How does religion have this effect? What is the trick? We have said very little about this utterly crucial matter. Is there anything to say? Perhaps the effect of religion on the human spirit is the enduring mystery of religion.

If religion has a code to crack, this author has no idea how to crack it. What he will do is deepen the mystery by showing that the profound spiritual transformation religion can effect can happen in the absence of belief in God. To see how, let us look at a classic of Mahayana Buddhism, *The Way of the Bodhisattva* (*Bodhicharyāvatāra* in Sanskrit). It is a 10-chapter poem by the eighth-century Buddhist monk **Shantideva**.[1]

Originally delivered as a sermon to his fellow monks at Nalanda Monastery, this work articulates the essentials of Buddhist belief and practice. On almost

This Is Philosophy of Religion: An Introduction, First Edition. Neil Manson.
© 2021 John Wiley & Sons, Inc. Published 2021 by John Wiley & Sons, Inc.

every major point of philosophy, Buddhism departs from the theistic religions, which have been the primary focus of this book. Nonetheless *The Way of the Bodhisattva* is a spiritual treasure that has affected millions of people in a profound way. As the Dalai Lama himself said to one of the translators, "If I have any understanding of compassion and the practice of the bodhisattva path, it is entirely on the basis of this text that I possess it."

Before we look at the spiritual aspects of Buddhism, we need to grasp the metaphysical differences between Buddhism and the theistic religions. To do that, let us remember some of the key elements of the latter. According to all the theistic religions, there is one supreme being, God. Unlike every other being, God exists necessarily. God exists by God's own nature, not by having been created by some other being or force. For everything else, God is the ground of being, that is, every other being besides God is contingent and dependent, while only God is necessary and independent. Each contingent, dependent being traces its existence back to an act of creation *ex nihilo* by God. According to scripture, this act of creation occurred at a specific point in time, and so the universe is not eternal. Yet God stands outside of the universe; unlike everything else we experience, God is not confined to the sequence of cause-and-effect relationships we observe around us in the physical world.

Buddhists hold to a radically different view, as Shantideva makes clear. To understand Shantideva on these points, we need to remember that, in India in the eighth century, Hinduism was prevalent, but not Judaism or Christianity. (Islam was making inroads, but did not become a dominant force in India until many centuries later.) In Hinduism, as in theism, there is an ultimate source for all of reality: Brahma. But, unlike the God of Judaism, Christianity, and Islam, Brahma is impersonal (though Brahma is sometimes conceptualized as a personal power, Ishvara). For Buddhists, there simply is no such ultimate source of reality. Indeed, for Buddhists, nothing whatsoever exists necessarily and of its own nature: all things are contingent and dependent. As a consequence, nothing is "real" in the sense of being a truly enduring thing (a "substance," to use the language of classical Western metaphysics). Everything whatsoever is impermanent: the earth, the skies, even the gods. This impermanence extends to the self, so that ultimately, there is no self and thus nothing that might survive death. Recognizing the nonreality of all things is the key to enlightenment and to an

---

[1] Shantideva, *The Way of the Bodhisattva: A Translation of the Bodhicharyavatara*, rev. edn, trans. Padmakara Translation Group, with a Foreword by the Dalai Lama (Boulder, CO: Shambhala, 2006). References in the text to particular passages in *The Way of the Bodhisattva* are given by chapter number, followed by verse number. Also, here is a link to an informative encyclopedia article about Shantideva: https://plato.stanford.edu/entries/shantideva.

attitude of universal compassion and responsibility (*bodhichitta*). The result of enlightenment is Nirvana - a transcendent state of being free from the endless rounds of suffering built into worldly existence (*samsara*). This basic assertion of Buddhist metaphysics is stated in a famous verse from chapter 9 ("Wisdom"):

> When something and its nonexistence
> Both are absent from before the mind,
> No other option does the latter have:
> It comes to perfect rest, from concepts free. (9.34)

In the course of supporting this fundamental Buddhist view, Shantideva provides arguments to disprove Hindu doctrines regarding Brahma. For our purposes, these arguments apply just as well to God.

There are two passages where Shantideva argues against the existence of an ultimate cause of all things. The first is in chapter 6 ("Patience"), where he tries to make the point that anger is never an appropriate response to any harm done to you, because the actions of a harmful being are always the result of prior causes rather than originating from the being itself. When a being does something harmful, there is no one to blame and no one to get angry at. This essential ethical tenet of Buddhism derives from the metaphysical principle that *every event whatsoever* is the result of antecedent causes. In order to support this metaphysical rule, Shantideva must reject the idea that there is even one exception to it. And that leads him to criticize the idea of a first cause (what he here calls "the primal substance" and "the self").

> The primal substance, as they say,
> And that which has been called the self,
> Do not arise designedly,
> And do not think, "I will become."
>
> For that which is not born does not exist,
> So what could want to come to be?
> And permanently drawn toward its object,
> It can never cease from being so.
>
> Indeed! This self, if permanent,
> Is certainly inert like space itself.
> And should it meet with other factors,
> How could they affect it, since it is unchanging?
>
> If, when conditions act on it, it stays just as it was before,
> What influence have those conditions had?
> They say that these are agents of the self,
> But what connection could there be between them?

> All things, then, depend on other things,
> And these likewise depend; they are not independent.
> Knowing this, we will not be annoyed
> At things that are like magical appearances. (6.27–31)

Note the similarity of these arguments to the ones we saw in earlier chapters of this book, where we discussed the logical consistency problem for theism and the idea that God is a necessary being. Shantideva takes the side of the atheist here. He says that self-creation makes no sense and that being truly permanent makes a being both impervious to outside influence and incapable of acting. Permanence comes at the cost of causal irrelevance, so even if a "primal substance" does exist, it has absolutely no connection to the world and no effect on it.

Shantideva provides related arguments in the chapter "Wisdom." Here is what he says about Brahma/Ishvara:

> If Ishvara is held to be the cause of beings,
> You must now define for us his nature.
> If, by this, you simply mean the elements,
> No need to tire ourselves disputing names!
>
> Yet earth and other elements are many,
> Impermanent, inert, without divinity.
> Trampled underfoot, they are impure,
> And thus they cannot be a God Omnipotent.
>
> The Deity cannot be space – inert and unproductive.
> He cannot be the self, for this we have refuted.
> He's inconceivable, they say – then likewise his creatorship.
> Is there any point, therefore, to such a claim?
>
> What is it that he wishes to create?
> Has he made the self and all the elements?
> But are not self and elements and he himself eternal?
> And consciousness, we know, rises from its object.
>
> Pain and pleasure have, from all time, sprung from karma,
> So tell us, what has his Divinity produced?
> And if there's no beginning in the cause,
> How can there be beginnings in its fruits?
>
> Why are creatures not created constantly,
> For Ishvara relies on nothing but himself?
> And if there's nothing that he has not made,
> What remains on which he might depend?

If Ishvara *depends*, the cause of all
Is but the meeting of conditions and not Ishvara.
When these obtain, he cannot but create;
When these are absent, he is powerless to make.

If Almighty God does not intend,
But yet creates, another thing has forced him.
If he wishes to create, he's swayed by his desire.
So even though Creator, what of his omnipotence? (9.118–125)

These are complex, compressed arguments. It would take a separate course in Buddhist philosophy to understand them fully. Yet the gist of the passage is clear: the idea of a necessary, independent, self-existent creator of all reality is full of paradoxes and logical inconsistencies. Whatever the right metaphysical view is, theism is the wrong one, according to Buddhists.

But how can something be a religion if belief in God is rejected? What do Buddhists say about what we should believe and how we should live our lives if they do not believe in God? To answer these questions, it will be helpful to compare Buddhism to a particular version of theism, so let us stick with the familiar: Christian theism. In Christian theism, God created the world, in part, as an abode for humans. The world God created for us was perfect because God is perfect – perfectly good as well as perfectly powerful. Because God gifted us with free will, however, we humans had the capacity to disobey God, which we did and still do. Our sinfulness introduced evil into the world and separated us from God. Without salvation, after death sinful humans will suffer eternal torment in hell. Escape from this terrible fate comes only from entering into the right relationship with God. This relationship requires a complete spiritual transformation, a reorientation away from serving oneself and toward serving God through serving others. This spiritual act requires God's grace, through which the sins of even the most wicked humans can be washed away. The reward for this spiritual transformation is an eternity in heaven. And this reward was made possible by God's providing us with the greatest gift imaginable – his Son, Jesus Christ, who sacrificed his life for us and who, prior to being resurrected, descended into hell itself to bring about universal salvation.

Many elements of this picture are missing from Buddhism. The universe was not created for us. It was not created at all. It just is, eternally, as is the cycle of death and rebirth (reincarnation). Furthermore, neither the universe nor the realms of rebirth (including the hells) are ultimately real. For Buddhists, nothing in the universe is a true substance and no aspect of it is substantial. Free will in the libertarian sense is also nonexistent; all events are the result of antecedent causes. But suffering nonetheless occurs, and after death those who fail to embrace bodhichitta risk being reborn in the lower realms. Buddhists and Christians share a belief in hell, at least; in *The Way of the Bodhisattva*, the many realms of hell are vividly described.

Yet there is a way to escape this grim reality. It is to follow the path first laid out by Siddhartha Gautama, the Buddha. It is here, with the steps along the way to spiritual transformation, rather than with the metaphysical views, that we begin to see deep similarities between the Christian and the Buddhist messages. Shantideva's description of the Bodhisattva discipline bears a striking resemblance to what we find in Christian literature.

The salvific message is described as exceedingly rare and precious, as we see in chapter 1 ("The Excellence of Bodhichitta") and in later chapters such as chapter 3 ("Taking Hold of Bodhichitta"). Against all odds, we can be saved from sin.

> Just as on a dark night black with clouds,
> The sudden lightning glares and all is clearly shown,
> Likewise rarely, through the Buddha's power,
> Virtuous thoughts rise, brief and transient, in the world. (1.5)

> For I am like a blind man who has found
> A precious gem inside a heap of dust.
> For so it is, by some strange chance,
> That bodhichitta has been born in me. (3.28)

The transformative change brought about by bodhichitta is described as overwhelming and instantaneous, not at all dissimilar to the Christian notion of being born again.

> Should bodhichitta come to birth
> In those who suffer, chained in prisons of samsara,
> In that instant they are called the children of the Blissful One,
> Revered by all the world, by gods and humankind.

> For like the supreme substance of the alchemists,
> It takes our impure flesh and makes of it
> The body of a Buddha, jewel beyond all price.
> Such is bodhichitta. Let us grasp it firmly! (1.9–10)

> As though they pass through perils guarded by a hero,
> Even those weighed down with dreadful wickedness
> Will instantly be freed through having bodhichitta.
> Why do those who fear their sins not have recourse to it? (1.13)

Pursuit of this path requires total commitment. Everything must be abandoned for the sake of the goal, for the alternative is to slip back into the endless suffering of the cycle of death and rebirth.

> My body, thus, and all my goods besides,
> And all my merits gained and to be gained,
> I give them all and do not count the cost,
> To bring about the benefit of beings.
>
> Nirvana is attained by giving all,
> Nirvana is the object of my striving;
> And all must be surrendered in a single instant,
> Therefore it is best to give it all to others. (3.11–12)

Those who seek Nirvana are aided by Bodhisattvas, enlightened beings who have reached a state whereby they can escape samsara, but whose love and compassion are so great that they remain within it in order to help other beings. (Think of them as the Buddhist equivalent of saints.) As we see in this passage from chapter 6 ("Patience"), we can repay the Bodhisattvas only by doing as they do, that is, surrendering every selfish concern for the sake of others.

> By helping beings we repay the ones
> Who sacrifice their lives for us and plunge into the hell of Unrelenting
>   Pain.
> Should beings therefore do great harm to me,
> I'll strive to bring them only benefit.
>
> For those who have become my lords,
> At times, took care not even of their bodies.
> Why should I, a fool, behave with such conceit?
> Why should I *not* become the slave of others? (6.120–121)

These passages give just a hint of what becomes obvious after reading *The Way of the Bodhisattva*: Buddhism provides a route to self-abnegation and to universal love and compassion just as much as any theistic religion does. If the most important thing to know about religion is that it can bring about profound spiritual transformation, then read *The Way of the Bodhisattva* and see that such transformation can happen in the absence of belief in God.

As we see when we examine the case of Buddhism, profound spiritual transformation can take place without any belief in God. That religion, whether theistic or not, can bring about profound spiritual transformation is clear. But *how* it does so is a mystery we must leave for others

GLOSSARY

A posteriori: applied to a proposition, it means that it is knowable only through observation and experience.

A priori: applied to a proposition, it means that it is knowable independently of experience.

Absence-of-belief atheism: the lack of belief in God due to not having a concept of God.

Adaptive: applied to biological characteristics, it means that the feature contributes to the survival and reproduction of the organisms that have it.

Agnosticism: the position that God's existence can be neither affirmed nor denied because the question of whether or not God exists cannot be answered.

Analogical version of the design argument: the version of the design argument that is based on making an analogy between natural objects and systems (e.g. organisms) on the one hand and human artifacts on the other.

Antecedent: the "if" clause in a conditional statement, it specifies a sufficient condition for the consequent: so, in "If God does not exist, then everything is permitted," the proposition "God does not exist" is the antecedent.

Anthropomorphic projection theories: theories of religion that assert that religion results from a natural human tendency to try to explain things in terms of the human-like goals and purposes of invisible agents.

Anthropic principle: the idea that, when we are trying to understand the significance of the fine tuning of the cosmic parameters for life, we should remain aware of an observational selection effect: if the universe were not just right for life, we would not exist to observe it.

Anthropocentrism: the intellectual mistake of overrating the importance of human beings in the total picture of reality.

This Is Philosophy of Religion: An Introduction, First Edition. Neil A. Manson.
© 2021 John Wiley & Sons, Inc. Published 2021 by John Wiley & Sons, Inc.

Appeal to popularity: the logical fallacy of saying that a proposition, P, is true because many or most people believe that P.

Argument: a set of propositions in which one, the conclusion, is supported by the others, the premises.

Argument for incompatibility: the argument for the conclusion that, if God has foreknowledge, then humans do not have free will.

Argument from ignorance: the logical fallacy of thinking that the absence of evidence for the truth of a proposition, P, is evidence that P is false.

Aseity: applied to God, it means complete independence from any other being, including the impossibility of being either created or destroyed.

Atemporal: existing outside of time (as opposed to sempiternal – existing within time but at all times).

Atheism: the belief that God does not exist.

Bayesian inference: an inference made using Bayes's theorem, a formula in the mathematical theory of probability that shows how we ought to change our degree of belief in a proposition, P, in the light of new evidence for or against P.

Brute fact: a fact for which there is no explanation whatsoever; it just is what it is, and that is that.

Clifford's principle: the claim that it is wrong always, everywhere, and for anyone to believe anything on the basis of insufficient evidence.

Compatibilism: the position regarding free will according to which an action is done freely if it is the action the person wanted to do.

Conceptual analysis: the exploration and clarification of the most basic components of thought.

Conclusion: in an argument, it is the proposition being argued for.

Conditional probability: the probability of a proposition, X, being true, given the truth of some other proposition, Y; it is symbolized as $P(X/Y)$.

Conditional statement: a proposition of the form "if [antecedent], then [consequent]"; for example, "If God does not exist, then everything is permitted" is a conditional proposition.

Consequent: the "then" clause in a conditional statement, it specifies a necessary condition for the antecedent; so, in "If God does not exist, then everything is permitted," the proposition "Everything is permitted" is the consequent.

Consistency: the relationship that holds within a set of propositions where it is possible that all of them are true.

Contingency: a proposition that is neither a necessity nor an impossibility.

Contingent being: a being that does not exist but could have existed, or that does exist but could have not existed.

Contradictory propositions: propositions such that if one is true then the other one must be false.

Contrary propositions: propositions such that they cannot both be true but they can both be false.

Cosmic parameters: the basic features of the universe as a whole such as its age, mass, curvature, average temperature, density, and rate of expansion subsequent to the Big Bang.

Cosmological argument the argument that attempts to move from the existence of the universe as a whole to the existence of God as the ultimate cause of or reason for it.

Counterexample: in logic, a particular case that proves that a generalization is false, or a particular argument that shows that a form of argument is not valid.

Counterfactual conditional: a conditional proposition in which the antecedent specifies a scenario that is different from how things actually are and the consequent specifies how things would have been different as a result.

Creationism: the view that the biblical account of the creation of the world is literally true.

Cultural transmission: the process whereby ideas are passed along through social mechanisms such as children's stories, myths, artworks, and education.

Deductive: applied to arguments, it means that the premises are put forth as guaranteeing that the conclusion is true.

Deontological conception of epistemic justification: the idea in epistemology that the justification of a belief is a matter of the believer fulfilling various intellectual obligations.

Dependent being: a being that cannot exist without some other being existing.

Design argument: the argument from the seemingly designed aspects of the universe and/or its parts to the existence of a designer (God); it is also known as the teleological argument.

Divine command theory: the theory in ethics that what makes wrong acts wrong is that God forbids them and that what makes right acts right is that God commands them.

Dualistic religion: a religion in which there are two fundamental spiritual beings in conflict with one another.

Empirical: said of a proposition, it means that it concerns observation and experience rather than pure theory.

Entailment: the relationship between two propositions A and B such that if A is true B must also be true.

Epistemology: the branch of philosophy concerning belief, justification, rationality, and knowledge.

Eschatology: the part of religious doctrine that concerns the ultimate goal or fate of humans, including the purpose of the universe and what happens in the afterlife.

Eternal: either existing in time but at all times (see sempiternal) or existing outside of time (see atemporal).

Ethics: the branch of philosophy concerning moral right and wrong, as well as value judgments generally.

Evidential problem of evil: the argument that the existence, nature, and distribution of the evil in the world is powerful but not conclusive evidence against the existence of God.

Evidentialism: the view in epistemology that, for a belief to be held reasonably or permissibly, it must be backed up by evidence, so that believing anything solely on faith is unreasonable or impermissible.

Evolutionary psychology: the approach to psychology according to which human thought – both conscious and unconscious – is best explained as the product of selective pressures shaping the human mind over millions of years of evolutionary history.

Ex nihilo: Latin for "out of nothing," it is often applied to God's creation of the world.

Exclusivism: the belief that only one religion's core doctrines are true and that the failure of the adherents of the other religions to hold the right set of core beliefs excludes them from salvation.

Expected value: a concept from the mathematical theory of probability, it is the average return in the long run on a given wager or expenditure.

Fideism: the idea that belief in God is purely a matter of faith, with reason playing little to no role in proper belief in God.

Fine-tuning argument: the version of the design argument that appeals to the near-perfect fitness of the cosmic parameters for the eventual existence of life in the universe.

Foreknowledge: knowledge of some future contingent proposition.

Future contingent proposition: a proposition about the future that could be true and that could be false, for example, "You will eat a banana for breakfast 500 days from now."

Genuine options: cases of belief in which the act of believing is momentous (of great importance), forced (unavoidable), and live (a real possibility for the believer).

Hard fact: a fact about the past that is solely about a past time, without any relationship to any future time built into its description.

Heuristics: in psychology, unconscious decision-making shortcuts that work much of the time but that fail in specific, identifiable circumstances (e.g. making hasty generalizations).

Hyperactive agency detection device: in psychology, it is an unconscious mental module that is biased toward attributing agency to natural objects and events so as to guard against dangers (e.g. predators) and to detect opportunities for rewards (e.g. large game).

Hyperactive explanation: the inbuilt human tendency to seek explanations for as many facts and occurrences as possible.

Identification problem: the problem facing the cosmological argument and the design argument of showing that the first cause or the designer of the universe just is the God of traditional theism.

Ideology: a set of ideas that works to impose social control at an unconscious level, for example, the idea that kings rule by divine right.

Immutable: unchanging; perfectly constant.

Impassible: incapable of suffering or pain.

Impossibility: a proposition that has to be false just on the basis of its logical character (e.g. "All dogs are cute and not all dogs are cute").

Inclusivism: the belief that only one religion's core doctrines are true but that adherents of other religions can achieve salvation nonetheless.

Incompatibilism: the idea that acting freely requires that, at the time a person makes a choice, they have more than one option open to them.

Inconsistency: the relationships between a set of propositions where it is not possible that all of them are true.

Independent being: a being that exists without needing any other being to exist.

Inductive: applied to arguments, it means that the premises are put forth not as guaranteeing that the conclusion is true, but only as making the conclusion probably true.

Invalid: applied to a deductive argument, it means that it is possible for all of the premises to be true but for the conclusion to be false.

"Know-how" knowledge: knowledge in the sense of possessing abilities, for example, "Sam knows how to fix bikes."

"Know-that" knowledge: knowledge of propositions, for example, "Christie knows that Sam is from Maine."

Knowledge by acquaintance: familiarity with an object, person, or state of being, for example, "I have known Raul for almost thirty years."

Laws of nature: universal rules governing how physical objects behave, for example, the laws of gravity or of electromagnetism.

Limitation of perfection: a restriction on God's power arising from God's other perfections, for example, the inability to sin due to being morally perfect.

Logic: the branch of philosophy that concerns the standards of proper reasoning.

Logical consistency problem for theism: the problem of whether any being can have all at once all the properties that God is supposed to have (omniscience, omnipotence, moral perfection, and so on).

Logical problem of evil: the argument that the existence of evil in the world is not logically consistent with the existence of God.

Logically necessary existence: the property of being such that the bearer's nonexistence is inconceivable or logically impossible.

Logically possible: the property of being such as to not involve a logical contradiction; so, for example, flying to London, Beijing, and Rio de Janeiro in one hour, although technologically impossible, is logically possible.

Meme: in evolutionary psychology, a unit of culture that gets people to speak or act in certain ways and that makes other people store a replicated version of that unit.

Mental module: in evolutionary psychology, a brain subsystem devoted to a specific task (e.g. remembering people's faces).

Metaphysics: the branch of philosophy that concerns the nature of ultimate reality (e.g. whether or not the only things that exist are material, physical things).

Miracle: an event that violates one or more laws of nature in such a way as to indicate a divine purpose.

Modal proposition: a proposition about the way things could be, could not be, or must be.

Modus ponens: this form of deductive argument: "If A, then B; A; therefore, B."

Modus tollens: this form of deductive argument: "If A, then B; not-B; therefore, not-A."

Monistic religion: a religion in which there is only one fundamental being.

Moral evil: evil that results from the free actions of humans (e.g. murder).

Multiverse hypothesis: the idea in contemporary physics that there are other universes besides the one we inhabit, with the cosmic parameters varying from one universe to the next.

Natural evil: evil that results not from the free actions of humans, but from the workings of nature (e.g. earthquakes).

Natural selection: the process whereby organisms that are well suited to their environments tend to survive and reproduce more than organisms that are poorly suited to their environments.

Natural theology: the attempt to gain knowledge of God through reason and observable evidence rather than through revelation.

Naturalism: the view that only natural entities exist, so that there are no gods, no ghosts, and no immaterial minds.

Naturalistic explanation of religion: any explanation of religion that presupposes naturalism, that is, it supposes that all the phenomena of religion can be explained without supposing that there really are gods, spirits, miracles, and so on.

Necessary being: a being that could not fail to exist; its nonexistence is impossible.

Necessary condition: a condition a thing must satisfy in order to qualify as being of a certain kind; for example, taking the final exam may be a necessary condition for passing the class.

Necessitarianism: the view that every feature of reality, down to the smallest detail, is necessarily what it is and could not have been the slightest bit different.

Necessity: a proposition that has to be true; it is not possible that it be false.

Neurotheology: the field of inquiry that tries to connect modern brain science with the phenomena of religion, in particular, religious experience.

Observational selection effect: any factor that filters a subject's experience based on there being necessary conditions for the subject even having that experience (e.g. footage of attempted freerunning ends up on a parkour video only if the attempt is successful).

Omnibenevolence: perfect goodness; the complete lack of vice, evil, or moral deficiency.

Omnipotence: unlimited power; the ability to do anything.

Omniscience: unlimited knowledge; knowledge of everything.

Ontological argument: an *a priori* argument for the existence of God according to which the property of being the greatest conceivable being makes it logically necessary that God exists.

Oppression thesis: the idea that religion plays a crucial role both in keeping down the weak, vulnerable members of a society and in helping the weak, vulnerable members of that society cope with their oppression.

"Ought" implies "can": a slogan indicating that, when we say someone ought to have done something, we are implicitly saying that the person could have done that thing; if they cannot have done it, then it is wrong to say that they should have done it.

Paradox of the stone: a challenge to the idea of omnipotence, it is the question of whether God could create a stone so heavy that God could not lift it; whichever way one answers the question, it seems that there is something God cannot do, and so God cannot be omnipotent.

Pascal's wager: the argument that believing in God is the right choice even if it turns out that God does not exist because the expected value of believing in God is greater than that of not believing in God.

Philosophy of religion: the subfield of philosophy that addresses the "big questions" raised by or within religions.

Pluralism: the belief that seemingly incompatible religions can be "true" in the sense that they all seek to achieve the same ultimate goal; thus religions are not to be evaluated by their truth or falsity, but by their efficacy in achieving the goal.

Positive atheism: the kind of belief that God does not exist that is held by people who understand what God is supposed to be.

Premise: in an argument, it is a proposition that supports the conclusion.

Principle of sufficient reason: for every truth there is a sufficient reason for why it is true, and for every being there is a sufficient reason for why it exists rather than not; that is, there are no brute facts.

Problem of evil: the problem of reconciling the existence of God – a being that is supposed to be omnipotent, omniscient, and morally perfect – with the existence of so much evil and suffering in the world.

Problem of foreknowledge and human freedom: the problem of reconciling the existence of God – an omniscient, infallible, and eternal being – with the existence of human freedom.

Problem of impassibility: the problem of how God, a being who by nature is incapable of suffering, can relate emotionally to (e.g. love) beings who do suffer.

Problem of religious diversity: the objection to theism from the existence of multiple, seemingly incompatible religions.

Projection: the psychological phenomenon of attributing to someone else one's own thoughts and feelings.

Proposition: in logic, something that is either true or false; it asserts either that something is the case or that something is not the case.

Purposive explanation: an explanation that involves goals, intentions, and purposes such as desire, need, jealousy, or love.

Reductio ad absurdum: the strategy in logic of assuming the opposite of what you are trying to prove, then showing that this assumption leads to a contradiction.

Reflection thesis: the idea that the religion of a society is just a reflection of the underlying social dynamics of that society.

Regression: in adults, the psychological phenomenon of responding to some form of mental strain by returning to an earlier, age-inappropriate psychological stage.

Religious diversity: the fact that there are many, varied religions in the world.

Religious experience: an experience where it appears to the subject that they are directly aware of some sort of divine or religiously significant reality.

Revealed theology: the attempt to gain knowledge of God by studying the information God revealed to humans, either directly or through prophets.

Secularization: the societal trend away from religious belief and toward nonbelief.

Secularization thesis: the idea that, once universal social equality and justice is fully achieved, religion will disappear.

Sempiternal: existing within time but at all times past, present, and future (as opposed to atemporal, which means existing outside of time).

Sensus divinitatis: the innate knowledge humans have of God as a result of God having built that knowledge into us when we were created.

Sociobiology: the biological theory according to which animal and human social behaviors are best explained as the result of evolutionary forces.

Sociological thesis: the idea that religious beliefs and practices are fundamentally just further aspects of human societies.

Soft fact: a fact about the past that is not genuinely and solely about a past time, but has a relationship to some future time built into its description.

Sound: applied to a <u>valid</u> <u>argument</u>, it means that all of the <u>premises</u> are, in fact, true.

Sufficient condition: a condition that is enough for a thing to qualify as being of a certain kind (e.g. being a professional volleyball player is a sufficient condition for being an athlete).

Theism: the belief that God exists.

Theistic evolutionism: the view that God created the universe sufficiently long ago that there would be enough time for a slow evolutionary process to produce intelligent life eventually.

Theodicy: a justification of God having created a world with evil in it.

Thought experiment: an imagined scenario that brings out the thoughts and presuppositions underlying our judgments.

Valid: applied to a <u>deductive</u> <u>argument</u>, it means that if the <u>premises</u> are true, then the <u>conclusion</u> must be true; it is impossible that all of the premises are true but that the conclusion is false.

Voluntarism: the idea that nothing whatsoever – not even morality, mathematics, truth, or logic – is beyond the will of God.

Wish fulfillment: the psychological phenomenon of reducing mental strain by presenting as probable or actual states of affairs that in reality are very unlikely to occur.

INDEX